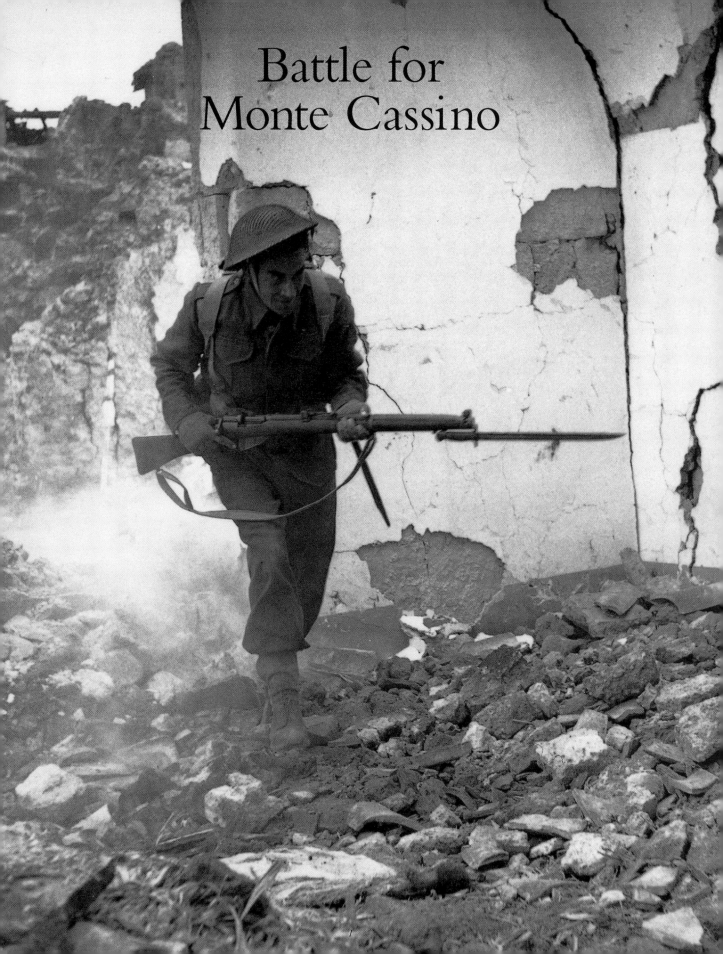

Battle for
Monte Cassino

Battle for
Monte Cassino

George Forty

Ian Allan
PUBLISHING

Half title page:
Whatever sophisticated weapons were used, the fighting usually ended up in hand-to-hand combat between infantrymen, using the rifle and bayonet and other hand-held weapons. *(IWM NA 13285)*

Title page:
German paratroopers — such as these machine gunners, with their MG 42 — clung tenaciously onto the monastery ruins, using the rubble to fortify their positions. One of the best machine guns of the war, the MG 42's high rate of fire produced a sound like tearing linoleum. *(Bundesarchiv 101/577/1923/37)*

Above:
A New Zealand infantryman, armed with a Thompson sub-machine gun, takes cover amid the ruins on Castle Hill. The Thompson Model 1928 was modified into a simpler weapon and the cumbersome 50-round drum magazine replaced by a 20- or 30-round box magazine. *(IWM NA 13373)*

Opposite:
On the lookout for mines. This sapper has sensibly dug under this tempting doll in the ruins and found it was attached to the pull-igniter of a Teller mine, which he disconnected, 21 August 1944. *(IWM NA 18009)*

First published 2004

ISBN 0 7110 3024 3

Published by Ian Allan Publishing

an imprint of Ian Allan Publishing Ltd, Hersham, Surrey KT12 4RG.
Printed in England by Ian Allan Printing Ltd, Hersham, Surrey KT12 4RG.

Code: 0411/B1

Contents

Introduction 6

Acknowledgements 7

Chronology 8

1. Background History 10

2. The Attackers — Allied Organisation
   and Equipment 27

3. The Defenders — German Organisation
   and Equipment 48

4. The First Battle (The Prelude Battle):
   12 January–12 February 1944 62

5. The Second Battle: 15–18 February 1944 80

6. The Third Battle: 15–26 March 1944 100

7. Operation 'Diadem', The Fourth
   and Final Battle: 11–18 May 1944 120

8. Return to Cassino 148

Bibliography 157

Index 158

Introduction

Why Cassino?

'It is pointless to consider any battle critically without relating it to the precise circumstances and conditions prevailing at the time and place. This may be a truism, but military critics more often than not ignore it. Recollecting in the tranquillity of their studies an engagement at which they were not present, they will murmur placidly that "more divisions should have been thrown in" or "more boldness might have been shown".' Those words, quoted from the late Fred Majdalany's masterly study *Cassino — Portrait of a Battle*, ring just as true today as they did when he wrote them nearly 50 years ago. And if anyone should know how and why such a statement can be made about many of the studies published over the years on this bloody series of battles, then it is he, having served there in the Lancashire Fusiliers. These battles were spread over a six-month period from December 1943 to May 1944, and took place deep in the inhospitable Italian mountains during ghastly winter weather and under conditions more reminiscent of those experienced on the Somme and Passchendaele battlefields during the Great War. However, before getting down to the battles themselves, we need to trace the strategic background to the Italian campaign in general and the battles on the Gustav Line/Monte Cassino position in particular.

After three years of see-sawing fortunes, 1943 had at last seen the successful culmination of Allied operations in North Africa and their first tentative step towards Europe. Rommel and his 'Africans' had finally been beaten and the whole of North Africa was now safely in Allied hands, as was the important island of Sicily, just a few miles from the Italian mainland. This latter operation had been decided upon at the Casablanca Conference of January 1943 as the logical step to follow on from victory in North Africa, rather than a first step in the main Allied assault on Europe. This would come logically from the UK onto North-West Europe, probably in the early summer of 1944. However, at the Trident Conference, held in Washington in May 1943, the Supreme Commander in the Mediterranean Theatre (General Dwight D. Eisenhower) was ordered to plan to exploit any success on Sicily by landing in southern Italy, with the twofold aim of eliminating Italy from the war and at the same time containing the maximum number of German divisions which might otherwise be able to reinforce their garrisons along the Atlantic Wall protecting *Festung Europa* from invasion from the UK.

Subsequently, successful landings had been made on mainland Italy by the US Fifth and British Eighth Armies, following which steady progress had been made towards its capital, the Eternal City of Rome, this progress being co-ordinated between the two armies by General Alexander's 15th Army Group headquarters. By the end of 1943, the Allied armies had closed up on the German Gustav Line that ran across the breadth of the country from one coast to the other without a break. Here the soldiers of the Fifth and Eighth Armies would spend nearly six months trying to break through the German defences of the formidable Gustav Line. This then is the story of those unforgettable six months when the 'D-Day Dodgers', as they came to be called, fought a series of bloody battles around a massive Benedictine monastery which cast its glowering shadow over the battlefield, even when it had been reduced to rubble. Here, at the beginning of January 1944, the American and British soldiers of the US Fifth Army won their first toehold over the Garigliano River. Heroic attacks by Allied forces then met an equally heroic German defence during three more bloody battles, until the Allied troops, led on this occasion by the Poles, eventually managed to enter the ruined monastery buildings.

Since the war the ruined town of Cassino and the monastery above it have been rebuilt, the former to a completely new plan, the latter substantially on the lines of its predecessor, whilst the battles have been the subject of many books. So what makes this one different from all the rest?

To begin with, it follows the usual Ian Allan 'At War' pattern, so it contains a wide selection of photographs from varying sources, plus numerous battle accounts, which I hope will give readers a graphic idea of what it was like to be fighting in these inhospitable mountains during the bitter winter weather. Linking these accounts is the outline of the four battles, together with information about other important events — such as the bombing of the monastery, as well as a fair amount of detail on the organisations and equipment of the opposing forces. I hope, therefore, that the resulting mix will form a valuable addition to studies of this fascinating subject.

Left:
The monastery at Monte Cassino. A ruined chapel where the monks used to pray, 18 May 1944. *(IWM NA 15153)*

Above: Cassino and its surroundings were a 'no-go' area for a long time after the fighting was over, with uncleared minefields being a particular hazard. This sign was actually near the Garigliano River in February 1944. *(IWM NA 11852)*

Acknowledgements

First and foremost I must thank my old friend Colonel Tom Huggan OBE, late Royal Tank Regiment and now at the British Embassy in Rome, for his considerable help, especially when ill-health prevented me from visiting Cassino myself. He has been a tower of strength, providing not only a CD on the history of the Abbey and a number of photographs, but also writing much of the last chapter for me. His generous assistance has been much appreciated. Similarly I must thank historian Richard Doherty of County Londonderry for generously supplying me with some fascinating copies of some of his interview notes and other materials from his study of veterans of the Irish Brigade who served at Cassino. Next I must thank the Royal Signals Museum at Blandford for allowing me to quote from a most interesting study of the battles at Monte Cassino held in its archives (*see Bibliography*). My thanks go similarly to Mr John Clarke, Hon Secretary of the Monte Cassino Veterans Association; Mr A. Suchcitz of the Polish Institute and Sikorski Museum; the curators and staffs of the Gurkha Museum; the Royal Hampshire Regiment Museum; the Fusilier Museum Lancashire; The Imperial War Museum Department of Photographs; the Imperial War Museum Sound Archive; Mrs Lola Chizmar of Real War Photos; the Indian Armed Forces Film & Photo Division, New Delhi; the Alexander Turnbull Library of New Zealand; the Commonwealth War Graves Commission; the Royal Engineers Library; the Queen's Own Royal West Kent Regimental Museum; plus any others whose names I may have inadvertently omitted who have also kindly allowed me to quote from their reminiscences. I must also thank the following individuals: Brigadier John Chapman, late Royal Tank Regiment, for kindly allowing me to use his excellent photographs of modern-day Cassino; Mrs Denise Elsby, whose father was a member of the *Fallschirmjäger* and defended the monastery; Mr Jim Furness MBE, MC, late RNZAC; Major Les Pye, late RNZAC; Major George Knight MC; Mr Ken Thatcher, late 16th/5th Lancers; Mr Bill Hawkins, late 4th Essex; Mr Leonard Griffiths, late 17th/21st Lancers; Mrs Betty Yates (re her late husband Neal Hopkins) and not forgetting my son Adam, Business Manager at the Royal Signals Museum, all of whom have helped me immeasurably.

Finally I must as always thank the Ministry of Defence Library for its continued helpful forbearance in allowing me to keep books out for far too long — at long last those gaping holes in your bookshelves are once again full!

George Forty,
Bryantspuddle,
May 2004

Chronology

1943

12 May	End of campaign in Tunisia.
10 July	Operation 'Husky', the invasion of Sicily, begins.
22 July	Palermo captured.
25 July	Mussolini resigns.
18 August	All German resistance on Sicily ceases.
3 September	Operation 'Baytown' XIII (British) Corps of Eighth Army crosses Straits of Messina and lands on the Calabrian coast of Italy.
8 September	Italy surrenders and signs Armistice.
9 September	Operation 'Slapstick' 1st (British) Airborne Division, Eighth Army, captures Taranto.
	Operation 'Avalanche' Fifth Army lands at Salerno.
13 September	German Tenth Army launches counter-attack against Salerno beachhead.
16 September	Allied bridgeheads link up.
23 September	Allies begin general advance northwards from Salerno.
1 October	Naples reached by armoured cars of X (British) Corps (Fifth Army).
	XIII (British) Corps (Eighth Army) pushes on towards the line Vinchiaturo–Termoli, 78th Division on coast and 1st Canadian Division inland across the mountains.
2 October	While 3rd Division (US VI Corps) on the left of the line makes for the Volturno, 34th and 45th Divisions move by separate routes towards Benevento. Allied commandos land near Termoli, seize harbour and town, then 78th Division links up with them, advancing along the coast to stabilise a bridgehead over the Biferno.
3 October	133rd Infantry Regiment (34th Division of VI Corps) takes Benevento and establishes a bridgehead over the Calore. A fierce battle begins in the Termoli sector, as 16th Panzer Division attempts to drive the British back across the Biferno. A brigade of 78th Division crosses into the bridgehead, whilst in the Canadian sector 1st Canadian Division is held up some 12 miles from Vinchiaturo.
5 October	Fifth Army reaches the south bank of the Volturno, 10th (British) Division takes Capua.
12 October	Fifth Army begins assault over the Volturno on a 40-mile front, continuing its attack that night, but torrential rain and stiff German resistance make for slow progress.
13 October	Italy declares war on Germany.
14 October	*Oberstleutnant* Julius Schlegel visits the monastery to try to persuade the abbot that the monastery treasures are vulnerable.
14 October	Progress is made over the Volturno, US V Corps advancing astride the river towards the Venafro–Isernia area, taking the Volturno valley, whilst in the XIII (British) Corps sector 1st Canadian Division takes Campobasso.
15 October	56th (British) Division crosses the Volturno and joins other Fifth Army units securing the crossing and aiming at the ridge that separates them from the rivers Rapido and Garigliano. The Germans have established and manned three defensive lines: Barbara, Reinhard and Gustav, behind which are their main forces.
	Having crossed the Volturno US 3rd Division takes Cisterna, whilst in the north, 1st Canadian Division takes Vinchiaturo.
October & November	Germans move treasures from the monastery by lorry to Rome.
2 November	Garigliano River reached by Fifth Army whilst Eighth Army crosses the Trigno.
5 November	First battle for Camino by Fifth Army.
6 November	First assault on Monte Lungo fails.
8 November	Eighth Army reaches Sangro River.
15 November	First battle for Camino ends and next day preparations start for the attack on the Reinhard Line.
19 November	Eighth Army start preliminary operations to cross the Sangro; however, the following day torrential rain stops everything for the next eight days.
21 November	Field Marshal Kesselring confirmed as German C-in-C South-West.
	Eighth Army again begin operations to cross the Sangro.
30 November	Eighth Army begins assault on Winter Line.
1 December	Rocca captured.
2–10 December	Operation 'Raincoat' (second battle for Camino).
6 December	Monte Camino captured.
4–7 December	First battle for Orsogna (Eighth Army), followed by second battle on 18th and third on 23rd which is finally successful.
9 December	Rocca d'Evandro and Monte Maggiore captured.
16 December	Monte Lungo captured by 142nd Regiment, US 36th Division.

17 December	Monte Samoucro taken by Fifth Army.
20–28 December	Battle for Ortona (1st Canadian Division, Eighth Army).
30 December	Montgomery hands over Eighth Army to General Oliver Leese and departs for UK.

1944

8 January	General Wilson takes over as C-in-C Allied Forces in the Mediterranean from General Eisenhower, who returns to UK to become SAC Europe.
9 January	US VI Corps (Fifth Army) withdrawn from line to prepare for Anzio landings.

FIRST BATTLE OF CASSINO

12 January	French Expeditionary Corps attacks towards Atina.
15 January	Fifth Army troops reach Gustav Line positions opposite Cassino.
	Monte Trocchio captured and Sant'Elia evacuated by Germans.
17 January	X (British) Corps successfully cross the lower Garigliano.
20 January	Abortive attack over the Rapido by 36th US Division at Sant'Angelo, after crossing the Gari.
22 January	Operation 'Shingle' — Allied landings at Anzio.
24 January	Hitler orders destruction of Anzio beachhead, German Fourteenth Army and LXXVI Panzer Corps move on Anzio beachhead.
24 January– 11 February	II US Corps fights the First Battle of Cassino.
25 January	34th US Division attacks across the Rapido.
3 and 7 February	Preliminary German attacks at Anzio
16–19 February & 28 February–3 March	Main counter-attacks at Anzio.
11 February	II New Zealand Corps (4th Indian Infantry Division) takes over in the hills north of Cassino.

SECOND BATTLE OF CASSINO

15 February	Bombing of monastery.
15–18 February	2nd New Zealand and 4th Indian Divisions fight the Second Battle of Cassino.
15–16 February	1st Royal Sussex attacks from Snakeshead Ridge.

17–18 February	4th Indian Division attacks the monastery.
17 February	New Zealand attack on station via railway track.
18 February	Both attacks fail.
24 February	New Zealand Corps again ready to attack at Cassino once weather improves.

THIRD BATTLE OF CASSINO

15 March	Bombing of town of Cassino.
15–25 March	Third Battle of Cassino.
15 March	New Zealand attack on Cassino town.
	5th Indian Brigade moved onto Monastery Hill.
16 March	1st/9th Gurkhas reach Hangman's Hill.
17 March	New Zealand troops reach station via town.
19 March	Tank attack up Cavendish Road.
	German counter-attack.
25 March	Troops withdraw from Hangman's Hill.
26 March	XIII (British) Corps relieves New Zealand Corps at Cassino.
	78th (British) Infantry Division takes over from 4th Indian Division in the positions north of Cassino.
All April	Preparation and rest before spring offensive.

FOURTH BATTLE OF CASSINO

11 May	Attacks by US II Corps, French Corps and Polish Corps on Gustav Line.
12 May	First Polish attacks on Points 593, 575 and Albaneta Farm.
13 May	Monte Maio taken.
17 May	Second attack on Points 593, 575 and Albaneta Farm.
18 May	Polish II Corps takes the monastery which is occupied by 12th Podolski Lancers.
23 May	The breakout from Anzio begins.
	Canadian Corps breaches Hitler Line at Pontecorvo.
25 May	Link up between US II Corps and VI Corps.
4 June	Rome falls.

1945

2 May	Final surrender of German forces in Italy.
8 May	VE Day.

Chapter 1

Background History

The End in Africa

On 12–13 May 1943, two very different signals were sent by the opposing armies in North Africa. The German one, which emanated from the headquarters of the *Deutsches Afrika Korps* (German Africa Corps) was sent to the *Oberkommando des Heeres* (Armed Forces High Command) in Berlin and read:

> 'Ammunition shot off. Arms and Equipment destroyed. In accordance with orders received the Afrikakorps has fought itself into the condition where it can fight no more. The Deutsches Afrikakorps must rise again. *Heia Safari!* *'Cramer'*, General Commanding.'

The Allied one was sent by General Harold Alexander to Prime Minister Winston Churchill at 10 Downing Street and it read:

> 'Sir,
> It is my duty to report that the Tunisian Campaign is over. All enemy resistance has ceased. We are masters of the North African shores.'

This exchange of signals marked the end of two years and nine months of warfare in North Africa, which had started with the first Italian attack into Egypt in September 1940. The glittering prizes within Egypt — Cairo and Alexandria for example, and above all

the Suez Canal — had tempted the Italians into action, but their half-hearted endeavours had been thwarted by a tiny British and Commonwealth force under the brilliant leadership of Generals Wavell and O'Connor, which had not only driven back the invaders, but also virtually annihilated the entire Italian Tenth Army. By early 1941 the Western Desert Force had advanced 500 miles, driven the Italians back into Tripolitania and, when coupled with similar successes in East Africa, appeared to have ended the threat to Egypt and the Suez Canal. The 'Desert Rats' as they soon became called, were riding high.[1]

However, in mid-February 1941, German forces began to land at Tripoli harbour, under the command of the charismatic General Erwin Rommel, soon to become a living legend to both armies as the 'Desert Fox'. Even before the whole of his specially formed *Deutsches Afrika Korps* had landed he was already on the attack, pushing back the British and Commonwealth forces, much depleted because many had been sent to fight an abortive campaign in Greece and then Crete, which ended in total disaster. Rommel had reached the Egyptian frontier by 15 April, having cleared the British out of Libya — apart from a stubborn British–Australian garrison in Tobruk, which refused to surrender. Under pressure from Churchill, Wavell launched an ill-prepared counter-attack

Below:
Map showing the Mediterranean theatre, November 1942–September 1943.

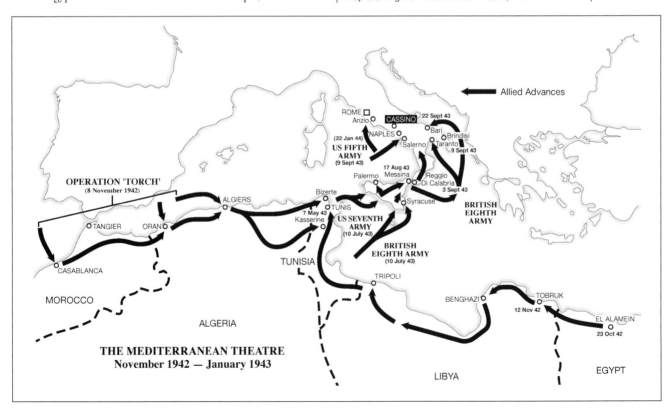

THE MEDITERRANEAN THEATRE
November 1942 — January 1943

(Operation 'Battleaxe') against Sollum and the Halfaya Pass, to relieve Tobruk; this foundered after heavy fighting.

This was the first of a series of 'see-saw' campaigns in which first one side then the other held the initiative, but was never able to prevent the other side from disengaging, regrouping and building up its strength for yet another push across the inhospitable and virtually empty deserts of North Africa. The need for constant re-supply of ammunition, weapons, food and, most importantly, water, was the Achilles' heel of most of these bitterly fought campaigns. By June 1942, Rommel and his 'Afrikans' were once again in the ascendancy; the British were falling back to the Alam Halfa ridge and there was panic in Cairo. However, a new, confident commander — Lieutenant-General Bernard Law Montgomery — was shortly to arrive to take over the Eighth Army and he managed to hold the Germans and Italians at Alam Halfa, soon forcing Rommel back onto the defensive. Now it was the Allied turn to take the offensive.

Montgomery attacked on the night of 23/24 October 1942, the ensuing battle of El Alamein lasting for more than a week, until the Axis forces broke and began to withdraw. This was the definitive turning point in the war in North Africa. There followed a long, hard-fought pursuit across Cyrenaica all the way to the Mareth Line which was reached in mid-February 1943. In the meantime, Operation 'Torch', the Anglo-American landings in French North Africa at Algiers, Casablanca and Oran had taken place. After some resistance the Vichy French forces capitulated, leaving Algeria and Morocco in Allied hands. These landings threatened Tunisia and Rommel's rear. German forces were rushed in by Field Marshal Albrecht Kesselring who, as Commander-in-Chief South, had

responsibility for the German land and air forces in North Africa. The stage was set for the battle for Tunisia which would end with the virtual annihilation or capture of all the German and Italian forces in North Africa and the end of this phase of the war in the Mediterranean theatre.

The Invasion of Sicily — Operation 'Husky'

At the Casablanca Conference in January 1943 Allied leaders decided to invade Sicily as the next logical step in the freeing of the Mediterranean sea lanes for Allied shipping. One essential prerequisite to such an invasion was the need to deal with the Italian island fortress of Pantelleria, which was only some 70 miles south-west of Sicily and had been heavily fortified. However, unlike the similar British fortress island of Malta GC, Pantelleria did not hold out for years of air and sea bombardment, but instead surrendered on 15 June 1943, after only five days, leaving the way clear for the successful amphibious invasion of Sicily to begin less than a month later, on 10 July 1943. Detailed planning had been carried out by General George Patton's I Armored Corps (Reinforced) which was made up of what remained of the Western Task Force Headquarters after it had provided officers and men for the newly created US Fifth Army.[2] To prevent confusion this planning HQ was known as 'Force 343' and then on D-Day became HQ US Seventh Army. In brief, the forces allocated to Operation 'Husky' comprised two Task

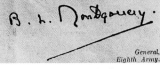

EIGHTH ARMY

PERSONAL MESSAGE FROM THE ARMY COMMANDER

To be read out to all Troops

1. The time has now come to carry the war into Italy, and into the Continent of Europe. The Italian Overseas Empire has been exterminated; we will now deal with the home country.

2. To the Eighth Army has been given the great honour of representing the British Empire in the Allied Force which is now to carry out this task. On our left will be our American allies. Together we will set about the Italians in their own country in no uncertain way; they came into this war to suit themselves and they must now take the consequences; they asked for it, and they will now get it.

3. On behalf of us all I want to give a very hearty welcome to the Canadian troops that are now joining the Eighth Army. I know well the fighting men of Canada; they are magnificent soldiers, and the long and careful training they have received in England will now be put to very good use—to the great benefit of the Eighth Army.

4. The task in front of us is not easy. But it is not so difficult as many we have had in the past, and have overcome successfully. In all our operations we have always had the close and intimate support of the Royal Navy and the R.A.F., and because of that support we have always succeeded. In this operation the combined effort of the three fighting services is being applied in tremendous strength, and nothing will be able to stand against it. The three of us together—Navy, Army and Air Force—will see the thing through. I want all of you, my soldiers, to know that I have complete confidence in the successful outcome of this operation.

5. Therefore, with faith in God and with enthusiasm for our cause and for the day of battle, let us all enter into this contest with stout hearts and with determination to conquer.

The eyes of our families, and in fact of the whole Empire, will be on us once the battle starts; we will see that they get good news and plenty of it.

6. To each one of you, whatever may be your rank or employment, I would say:

GOOD LUCK AND GOOD HUNTING IN THE HOME COUNTRY OF ITALY

B. L. Montgomery.

General,
Eighth Army.

July, 1943.

Above: This personal message from Monty to his troops says it all.
(Author's collection)

Forces — the Western Task Force, being the US Seventh Army under Lieutenant General Patton, the Eastern Task Force, being the British Eighth Army under Lieutenant-General Montgomery. General Dwight D. Eisenhower would be in overall command, with General Alexander as his principal deputy, charged with the detailed planning and execution of all ground operations. Patton had been made to accept a number of major changes to the original plan, which were intended to let the more experienced Eighth Army do most of the fighting, while the Americans merely protected their left flank. However, it was clear from the outset that Patton objected to this secondary role and was determined to show what he and his troops could do should the opportunity present itself — and this is exactly what happened. D-Day had been chosen as 10 July 1943, with H-Hour fixed for 0245 hours, when there would be no moonlight to illuminate the seaborne landings. Airborne forces would capture certain strategic targets, beginning at 0600 hours. Taking a number of airfields was an essential part of the plan, so that air support could be switched from North Africa as soon as possible. There were over 30 operational airfields on Sicily at the time of the assault, the key group being on the Catania plain around Gerbini.

The Landings

Unfortunately the weather deteriorated as H-Hour approached and a Force 7 gale blew up. Most soldiers were soaked to the skin by the time they reached the beaches, but managed to land successfully, and without much opposition. However, the unfortunate airborne troops were badly affected by the weather and were scattered across the countryside, well away from their scheduled drop zones. Although they did manage to regroup and did a good job of continually harassing the Germans behind their front lines, they did not achieve their proper missions. The overall plan had been for Montgomery to drive up from the south-east, direct for Messina in the north-east corner of the island, whilst Patton cleared the west of the island and protected his left flank. However, the British were held up by fierce German resistance at Catania, only half-way to Messina. Patton was meanwhile sweeping triumphantly through western Sicily and took Palermo on 22 July. He then began advancing eastwards, along the northern coast road, closing the jaws of the trap around Messina. His advance was materially assisted by a number of small-scale amphibious operations, but hindered by the fact that Montgomery was apparently able to get priority for everything. Events reached boiling point when Patton decided to broaden his advance by creating a Provisional Corps HQ under General Keyes and bringing it up parallel with General Bradley's II Corps, thus making continuous re-supply even more vital. To his chagrin, Patton discovered that Alexander had given the British priority over the central route, which had already been allocated to the Americans. This was the last straw and Patton flew back to see Alexander, protesting violently that he must be allowed to operate more freely. Alexander fortunately at last realised the strength of American anger, retracted and from then on almost took a back seat, whilst letting the two prima donnas slug it out.

The Allies were faced in Sicily by Axis forces ostensibly under the Italian commander General Alfredo Guzzoni, who had as his German advisor General Frido von Senger und Etterlin, a cavalryman and a first-class soldier, who had already fought with great success in Russia as a corps commander. The other senior German commander was General Hans-Valentin Hube, commander of XIV Panzer Corps, who had two of his divisions on Sicily (15th Panzer Grenadier Division and 1st Luftwaffe Panzer Division *Hermann Göring*). Hube was sent from mainland Italy on 13 July to command all German troops on the island and would carry out a masterly withdrawal, the highspots of which were the defence of the Etna Line and the final withdrawal across the Straits of Messina, which has been described by some historians as a 'tactical masterpiece'. Undoubtedly, had the Allies been able to cut off this evacuation and capture or neutralise the German forces involved, then the subsequent campaign on mainland Italy would have been much less costly.

Eventually, however, it became a race between Patton and Montgomery to see who could reach Messina first, whilst opposition was fast disintegrating on both fronts. The remaining Italian forces on Sicily, left to their own devices by their erstwhile Allies, were now either surrendering or hastily crossing the Straits of Messina to temporary safety in mainland Italy. By 17 August it was all over and both Allied Army commanders emerged with glory. Now it was time to prepare for the invasion of the mainland, whilst Italy sought to surrender to someone.

A New Strategic Step

While the invasion of Sicily had been the logical sequel to the cessation of hostilities in North Africa, in that it was vital in order to secure unrestricted passage within the Mediterranean for Allied shipping, the invasion of mainland Italy that followed was undoubtedly a whole new ball game, heralding as it did, the next major step in Allied strategy that would culminate in the long-awaited opening of the 'Second Front', namely the Allied invasion of North-West Europe. The break between the two is made all the more clear when one compares the two all-important Combined Chiefs of Staff directives, issued during the first half of 1943. The

Above: Commander-in-Chief 15th Army Group, General Sir Harold Alexander (later Field Marshal 1st Earl Alexander of Tunis), is photographed here at his HQ, standing in front of the map of Italy, 4 May 1944. Alex was in command of all Allied troops in Italy. *(IWM NA 14516)*

first one was issued after the Casablanca Conference in January 1943 and dealt with the proposed invasion of Sicily as the next logical step to follow on from victory in North Africa and does not look any farther ahead. However, the directive that was issued after the Trident Conference, held in Washington in May 1943, took a much wider view, the Chiefs of Staff explaining to Commander-in-Chief Mediterranean that the major assault on 'Fortress Europe' would be launched from the UK, probably in the early summer of 1944, and that his main tasks were therefore to plan operations following on from the capture of Sicily as would be best calculated, firstly, to eliminate Italy from the war and, secondly, to contain the maximum number of German troops in the Mediterranean theatre. They were careful not to include any restrictive geographical objectives in these tasks; in other words, conquest of terrain was not a requirement.

Thus, all the subsequent Allied operations in Italy must be considered against this requirement, namely the tying down of the largest possible Axis forces which would otherwise have been available to be used against the 'Second Front'. Eliminating Italy as a belligerent meant the immediate loss to the Axis of some 59 active divisions — roughly two million fighting men. And whilst they could not all be considered as first-class front-line troops, they were still extremely useful for garrison duties both at home and in occupied territory. It was estimated, for example, that there were seven Italian divisions in southern France in the summer of 1943,

Above: Monty with his troops. The Commander-in-Chief of the Eighth Army when they entered Italy was General Bernard Montgomery. He made a point of talking to his troops before battles to ensure that they were, as far as possible, put in the picture. Here in fact he is addressing New Zealand officers (plus some British tank commanders) in Tunisia, towards the end of the campaign there. *(IWM BNA 1683)*

and probably up to another 32 in the Balkans, together with coastal defence and anti-aircraft units in both regions. If Germany had to replace even a proportion of these troops, then it would represent a considerable additional manpower commitment. Additionally, there was the need to send German troops to replace Italians in the front line in Italy, not to mention the additional forces needed to fight against those Italian troops who had decided to change sides or, even worse from the German point of view, to become anti-German partisans. From 26 July, German forces from southern France, the Tyrol and Styria poured over the Alps and on into Tuscany, occupying all the main lines of communication, defiles and bridges, so as to retain their grip on the country. Details of the rise in numbers of German divisions in Italy between summer 1943 and spring 1945 are given in the table below.

German Strength in Italy: July 1943–April 1945

DATE	NO OF DIVISIONS
July 1943	6
August 1943	16
September 1943	18
October 1943	25
November 1943	25
January 1944	22
May 1944	23
June 1944	25
August 1944	26
September 1944	28
April 1945	21

(Source: British Troops Malta Study of 1968)

Whilst an invasion of mainland Italy was clearly the best way of achieving both of the Combined Chiefs of Staff's requirements, other possible scenarios had also first to be studied, analysed, discussed and ruled upon. These included, for example, operations against the Balkans; against the 'outer Greek islands' (especially Crete and Rhodes); and against Corsica and Sardinia. The first of these was almost immediately ruled out by the Americans, as they had always been most reluctant to engage in operations in the Balkans and had made little secret of their distrust of Churchill's motives in that area — what he referred to as being 'the soft underbelly of Europe'. They were undoubtedly worried about the number of casualties which might result from operations in such an area, citing the Great War disasters in the Dardanelles and Gallipoli of 1915/16, which had come about when Churchill was First Lord of the Admiralty. Besides, the terrain was even worse than in mainland Italy and the Allies lacked suitably trained mountain troops. Assaulting the 'outer islands' would have involved numerous smaller operations that would quickly tie down considerable numbers of troops and, even more importantly, scarce amphibious craft, yet not necessarily involve large numbers of Germans, so that was also ruled out as a non-starter. The same applied to taking out Corsica and Sardinia. Granted, their capture would eliminate various Axis airfields and perhaps the islands could be used as stepping stones for any invasion of Southern France, but the arguments against such operations were as for those against going for the 'outer islands'. Besides, they could be left until later without affecting the issue. Thus it was soon clear that the invasion of

mainland Italy was the only sensible choice. However, it would undoubtedly be a difficult operation.

It had been Napoleon who, likening the map of Italy to the shape of a boot, had recommended that it only be entered 'from its open top'. This was clearly impossible for the Allies, but the quickest way to subdue the whole country would still be to land as far north as possible. Unfortunately, there was a vital need for air cover to protect such a major amphibious undertaking, and this clearly limited the location of any potential landing area. Carrier-based aircraft would be a bonus, but land-based fighters were essential in order to provide the all-round protection necessary. Even taking the use of long-range fuel tanks into consideration, the planners were limited to an area of operations within a radius of some 180 miles, centred around the north-eastern corner of Sicily where suitable airstrips were located. This limited the possible amphibious landing area to an arc stretching from the island of Capri, just short of Naples in the west, to some 15 miles short of the Italian naval base of Taranto in the east. Both these prime targets (Naples and Taranto that is) were thus just out of range and would probably require a major assault to take them once the successful landing had been achieved.

Following a radio announcement broadcast by 'Radio Roma' on 25 July that Mussolini had resigned,[3] General Eisenhower, Supreme Commander Mediterranean, called a conference at Carthage which was attended by Admiral Cunningham, Air Marshal Tedder and General Alexander, at which it was agreed that the Gulf of Salerno would be the landing site for the assault on Naples. This was in addition to the site already chosen directly across the Straits of Messina at Reggio di Calabria and for which planning was already well advanced. This decision was not taken lightly and there was considerable argument against entering the Gulf of Salerno — for example, there were known to be extensive sea minefields and net barrages there, not to mention the 40-plus heavy coastal guns and other permanent fortifications, whilst it went without saying that the Germans would defend Naples in strength. Nevertheless, after much discussion, the Salerno beaches were chosen, as they provided the best sea approaches and had good underwater gradients that permitted ships to come close in to land. Additionally, the port facilities at Salerno and nearby Amalfi would be most useful for unloading supplies, whilst there were marginally fewer beach defences in the area than elsewhere. Finally, Montecorvino airfield, a few miles inland, would be able to hold at least four fighter squadrons which would prove to be a bonus.

German Defences

Whilst the Allies were planning their assault on Italy, the Germans were also busy planning their defences; indeed, the defence of *Festung Europa* now became central to their overall strategy. In addition to the hundreds of miles of fortifications built along the Atlantic and Channel coasts, certain areas in southern France, Italy and the Balkans were also well defended, especially around the important sea ports and naval bases. As the German divisional table above shows, one of the immediate German reactions to their defeat in North Africa had been quickly to reinforce their troops in Italy and the Balkans. By early September 1943, there were, for example, 16 German divisions in Italy and a further one and a half (90th Panzer Grenadier Division and an SS brigade) in Corsica and Sardinia. In the German Tenth Army area in southern Italy each of the potential Allied landing areas was made the responsibility of a corps commander.

Reading from the south, General Herr's LXXVI Panzer Corps was responsible for the whole of Italy south of the line Salerno–Bari. His corps comprised 26th Panzer, 29th Panzer Grenadier and 1st Paratroop Divisions — all three were weak but the area in which

they would operate in the toe of Italy was considered ideal for defensive fighting. Next north of them was General Hube's XIV Panzer Corps, whose main task was the defence of Naples, although like Herr, he had a 'slice' of Italy from coast to coast to defend, with 16th Panzer Division on the Adriatic side and his two already battle-proven Sicilian divisions — 15th Panzer Grenadier and the *Hermann Göring* Division — responsible for the defence of Naples. To the north in the Rome area, was General Kurt Student's XI Paratroop Corps, with 2nd Paratroop and 3rd Panzer Grenadier Divisions responsible for defending the Eternal City, but with defence of the coastline as a secondary requirement. Whilst Student's corps came directly under Commander-in-Chief South (Kesselring), the other two were commanded by General Heinrich von Vietinghoff's Tenth Army. Thus, it can be seen that, despite all the problems that the imminent collapse of the Italians and the Allied successes in North Africa and Sicily had created, the Germans were still far from being beaten. They had already given a good account of themselves in their spirited defence of Sicily and were now ready to carry out a slow fighting withdrawal up mainland Italy.

Operations 'Baytown', 'Avalanche' and 'Slapstick'

The first of the three landings that began the Allied conquest of the mainland took place on 3 September, on the toe of Italy. Under the code-name Operation 'Baytown', troops of Montgomery's British Eighth Army (13th and 17th Infantry Brigades of 5th British Infantry Division, together with 3rd Infantry Brigade of 1st Canadian Division — the vanguard of XIII Corps) crossed the narrow Straits of Messina at Reggio di Calabria. On the same day, the first convoys bound for Salerno (Operation 'Avalanche') sailed from North Africa. The rest would follow over the next four days, all linking up off the Gulf of Salerno on the evening of the 8th. On the following day, troops of Lieutenant General Mark Clark's US Fifth Army, namely the British 46th and 56th Divisions, together with GIs of the 36th US Division, were landed on the beaches at Salerno. Simultaneously, men of the 1st British Airborne Division occupied the Italian naval base of Taranto. This last landing (Operation 'Slapstick') met no resistance whatsoever and was

perhaps the most successful of the three operations. However, the invasion force was too small to exploit the tactical opportunities of the situation fully.

In the midst of all this activity, on 8 September the Italian government — now led by Marshal Badoglio — announced Italy's surrender to the Allies. Badoglio then fled south with his staff, leaving vast numbers of Italian soldiers without any orders. Some attempted to fight against their erstwhile allies, whilst others still supported them, but within 24 hours the Italian Army had all but disintegrated. Most had been swiftly disarmed by the Germans and over 650,000 of these would subsequently be deported to Germany to be used virtually as slave labour. From now on, the Italians were no longer active members of the Axis and Italy became merely a battleground where the Allied army group under General Alexander fought an increasingly bitter campaign against the Germans under Field Marshal Kesselring.

As already explained, the US Fifth Army's landing site at Salerno had been deliberately chosen so that air cover would be immediately available from the recently captured air bases in Sicily. However, this meant that tactical surprise was quickly lost, and heavy fighting ensued during the initial landings and in the week that followed, as the invading forces endeavoured to push forward against continual German counter-attacks which threatened to drive them back into the sea. At one stage — between 12 and 14 September — the Allied line was pushed back to within a thousand yards of the beaches, but managed to hold. Additional support was eventually forthcoming, from the US 82nd Airborne Division and much heavy naval gunfire from the Allied battle fleet operating just off the coast. Eventually the German counter-attacks were beaten off and General Clark's forces were able to advance and link up with the Eighth Army spearheads from the other two landings. As well as suffering casualties from conventional weapons, the naval force had also

taken losses from German Fritz-X, or FX 1400, radio-guided bombs which had been perfected in 1942. These 3,900lb armour-piercing bombs hit and damaged several Allied warships, including the battleship HMS *Warspite*. Nevertheless, by 27 September, the Eighth Army had taken one of its main objectives, the airfields at Foggia, and by 1 October Fifth Army had reached Naples. The two armies then pressed on northwards, Fifth Army on the west coast and Eighth Army in the east, whilst the Germans, under Kesselring (now Commander-in-Chief Italy), fought a masterly defensive campaign as they withdrew slowly northwards.

Senior Officer and Other Personnel Losses

Alexander's 15th Army Group was soon to be severely weakened by the loss of several battle-hardened formations — such as the original 'Desert Rats' (7th Armoured Division) — which were sent back to the UK to prepare for D-Day. Those senior officers leaving Italy included the charismatic commander of the British Eighth Army himself, General Bernard Montgomery, who had been chosen to command 21st Army Group, the major Allied formation created for the invasion of Normandy in June 1944. His departure from the theatre undoubtedly had its effect, despite the fact that his successor Lieutenant-General Sir Oliver Leese was a commander of no mean ability and experience. However, it was just another blow that adversely affected the Italian theatre, and inevitably led to the morale-sapping experience of becoming a 'Forgotten Army'. This would happen yet again when more troops were taken away for the 'Anvil' landings in southern France in August 1944, whilst most of the headlines that might have followed successes earlier that summer had already predictably been 'stolen' by the D-Day landings on 6 June. I will return to this topic again, but clearly the 'D-Day Dodgers', as they would call themselves, inevitably felt angry and forgotten.

Additionally there had been a change at the very top. On 10 December 1943 General Eisenhower was informed of his new appointment as Supreme Commander, Allied Expeditionary Force, and told that he would hand over to General (later Field Marshal Lord) Sir Henry Maitland 'Jumbo' Wilson on 8 January 1944.

Wilson would thereafter command 'Allied Forces HQ, Mediterranean'. From Alexander's point of view this meant that to a large extent this senior HQ would be mainly concerned with political and logistical matters, leaving him responsible for the conduct of the campaign in Italy. Indeed, the title of his HQ was soon changed from HQ Fifteenth Army Group to HQ Allied Armies in Italy (also known for a short time as Allied Central Mediterranean Forces). At the same time Alexander was relieved of his duties as Deputy Allied Commander-in-Chief, being succeeded in this appointment by Lieutenant General J. L. Devers, US Army.

A Lack of Amphibious Vessels

At the same time, the Mediterranean theatre also had to face the loss of a large number of its amphibious vessels — 80% of its tank landing ships and 66% of the smaller tank landing craft for example — all of which were due to return to the UK by mid-December 1943, so that they could be repaired and refitted before being used in the forthcoming Normandy landings. The D-Day plans also had a considerable effect upon the availability of general shipping in the theatre, which directly and adversely influenced the way in which General Alexander could fight his battles. No longer would the Allied forces have the landing craft available to make amphibious 'hooks' around behind any of the known series of strong defensive positions that faced them as they fought their way up Italy; instead they would have to take these positions head on. There followed a series of high-level meetings to discuss this knotty subject, which fortunately led to a readjustment in the proposed programme for the refitting and repair of landing craft in the UK, making it possible to allow such craft to remain in the Mediterranean until late January 1944, so that they would be available for use in the landings at Anzio. However, these landings had to take place during January 1944 as sufficient shipping would definitely not be available any longer than the end of that month.

Climate and Terrain

As well as having to face a brave, determined, well-equipped and skilful enemy that was master of the slow withdrawal, the Allied troops also had to face other major handicaps. The first was the climatic conditions under which they had to fight for much of the year, namely, the rain, mud, ice and snow that they experienced during the terrible winter weather, especially in the high mountains. As one soldier wrote:

> 'These things constitute war and battle: rain and mud, cold and discomfort . . . of digging and of sleepless nights and tiring days, of being afraid and of being hungry, of repairing roads and of building bridges, of being lonely . . . and of an endless number of little things.'[4]

Heading northwards through the autumn rains and mud, they cleared Naples in early October, then reached the Volturno River some 25 miles to the north, where they were held up by the first of Kesselring's many defensive lines, with which he would try — most successfully — to control the progress of the Allied advance up Italy. Next they would face the Winter Line, some 25 miles further north. Swollen rivers such as the Sangro on the Eighth Army front and the Garigliano on the Fifth Army front, also slowed Allied progress — 'Enemy resistance is not nearly so great as that of Mother Nature' wrote one American general in his diary, as his troops struggled to make some progress against the elements. Although these strong German positions were not nearly as sophisticated as the Gustav Line, which was yet to come, the Winter Line was still a formidable obstacle, particularly as there was no single key position which

presented the attackers with the opportunity to break the line with one bold stroke. Instead each successive defensive position had to be taken, in appalling battlefield conditions — 'foxhole-engulfing mud' is how they were described. And to make matters worse, winter kit had yet to be issued to combat the weather: 'Trucks bogged down in the soupy ground, machine-gun barrels froze solid, shoes wore out in a single day on the sharp rocks, whilst howitzer trails just wouldn't stay dug in — one round and the guns buried themselves.'[5]

But Why Cassino?

By the end of December 1943 the Allied armies had advanced about one-third of the way up Italy, but were now faced by the most difficult obstacle yet encountered, namely the Gustav Line. It would take them a further six months to break through this defensive barrier — thus nearly a third of the entire Italian campaign would be spent trying to penetrate this line without success. The Gustav Line stretched right across Italy from the Tyrrhenian Sea to the Adriatic, but the focal point has inevitably always been seen as being the little town and monastery of Cassino — but why Cassino? What was the reason why this small place should assume such importance? Clearly this dilemma continually worried Churchill, so much so that he eventually sent the following signal to Alexander:

> 'I wish you would explain to me why this passage by Cassino Monastery Hill, etc, all on a front of two or three miles, is the only place which you must keep butting at. About five or six divisions have been worn out going into its jaws. Of course I do not know the ground or the battle conditions, but looking

Above: Field Marshal Lord Wilson of Libya GCB, GBE, DSO. 'Jumbo' Wilson was appointed to take over as Commander-in-Chief Mediterranean Theatre from General Eisenhower when 'Ike' went to become Supreme Allied Commander, North-West Europe. Wilson was responsible for overall policy and strategy in the Mediterranean theatre. *(IWM E 448)*

Left:
During the long months of battle some were able to snatch a few hours of peace at rest camps, like this one run by the Eighth Army, where they had a chance to read treasured letters from their loved ones and write replies away from the stress and strain of the fighting. *(IWM NA 13688)*

Below:
The Italian front late in 1943, showing Alexander's plan for breaking the Winter Line.

Right (inset):
Tonight is bath night. I wonder if the water was as cold as it looks? *(IWM NA 122208)*

Right:
Kiwis relaxing — and naturally playing rugby. A few miles behind the line, men of 22nd Motorised Infantry Battalion play in an inter-company competition. *(IWM NA 12670)*

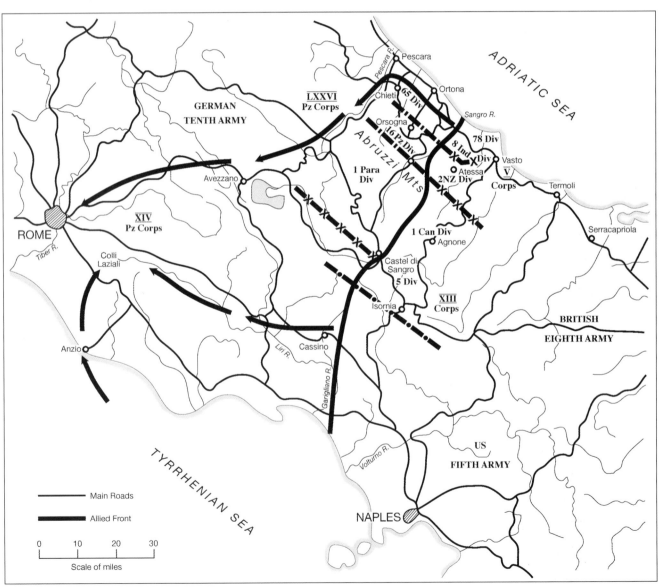

at it from afar, it is puzzling why, if the enemy can be held and dominated at this point, no attacks can be made on the flanks. It seems very hard to understand why this most strongly defended point is the only passage forward, or why, when it is saturated (in the military sense), ground cannot be gained on one side or the other. I have the greatest confidence in you and will back you up through thick and thin, but do try to explain to me why no flanking movements can be made.'[6]

Before dealing with Alexander's reply, a few words about the little town and monastery that were the subject of Churchill's puzzlement would not go amiss. The small town of Cassino (population some 31,000 in 1981) which had originated as Casinum (a town of the Volsci who were an ancient people prominent in the region in the fifth century BC), lies in the Frosinone province in the Lazio region of central Italy, near the Rapido River and at the foot of Monte Cairo. In AD 529 St Benedict of Nursia established the nucleus of the now famous monastery in nearby Monte Cassino. The story is that he was guided to the spot by three ravens. Over the centuries the monastery has had a chequered history of sieges and sackings, the most recent, prior to the Second World War, being by French troops in 1799. Despite periods when it was temporarily deserted, the monastery was refounded on its original site on every occasion, and during the Middle Ages it became an outstanding centre for the arts and learning. Nature was no kinder to the much-besieged buildings and in 1349 they suffered a severe earthquake, the church and monastery having to be almost entirely rebuilt during the centuries that followed. However, nothing would be quite so destructive as the period during the first half of 1944, when the full might of Allied firepower — both from the ground and the air — was turned against both the town and the monastery. As we shall see, the town was destroyed by some 1,400 tons of bombs being dropped by Allied aircraft in March 1944, whilst the month before, on 15 February, the monastery had itself received similar treatment, its 25ft-thick walls being reduced to rubble. Little remained recoverable, apart from the massive bronze doors — cast in Constantinople in 1066 — which were subsequently rescued and restored. The austere medieval style of its buildings (which have been fully restored since the war) and white central courtyard are in great contrast to the ornate baroque style of its church. There is also a small museum.

Moving the Monastery Treasures

During the fighting the Allies were convinced that the Germans were occupying and fortifying the monastery, whilst the Germans claimed that not only had they ordered their troops not to set foot within its precincts, but had also removed the archives, the library and some of the paintings, to safer premises in Rome. After the war this was definitely shown to be the case, numerous historians having

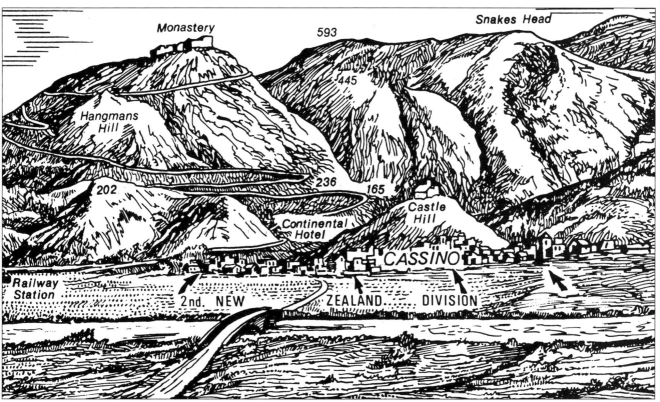

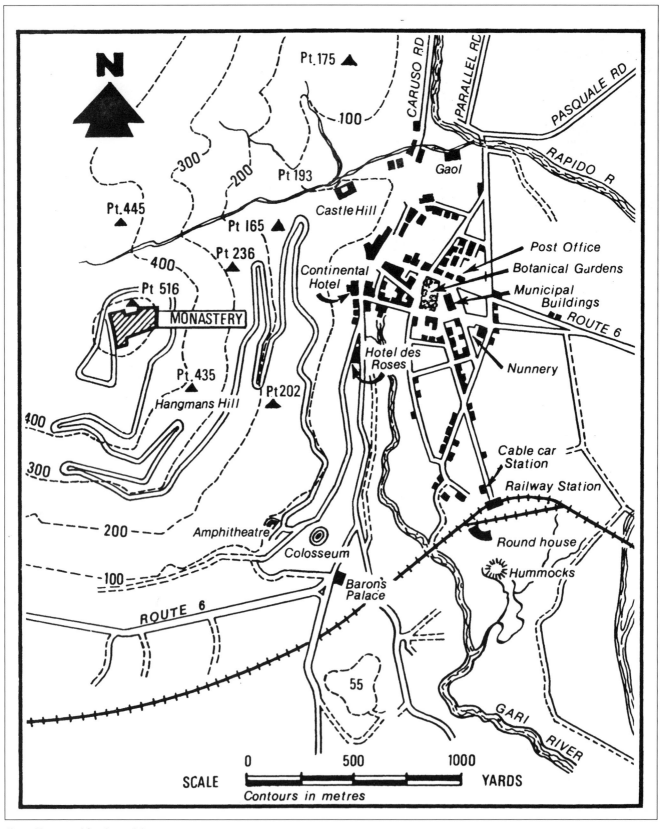

Above: The town of Cassino and the monastery.

Above: Archbishop Diamare, with hand upraised (and cross around his neck), gives his blessing to one of the convoys of artworks which was about to leave for Rome. *Oberstleutnant* Schlegel, the instigator of the rescue operations, is in the background behind the group of monks. *(Bundesarchiv 1011/729/0005/39)*

explained what happened in considerable detail. For example, Rudolf Böhmler, in a chapter entitled 'German Troops Rescue the Monastery Treasures' in his book *Monte Cassino*, explains how the initiator and organiser of the rescue mission was one *Oberstleutnant* Julius Schlegel, the commander of the divisional maintenance section of the *Hermann Göring* Division.

A lover of the arts and a keen visitor to museums and art galleries, Schlegel had been very worried about what would happen to the unique contents of the monastery during the forthcoming battles. Having wrestled with his conscience for some time, on 14 October 1943 he had gone to see the bishop and abbot of the monastery, Gregorio Diamare, 'a venerable old gentleman of 80'. Lieutenant-Colonel Schlegel did not find it easy to persuade the abbot that the monastery and its contents were in danger, but eventually he was able to do so, although it took repeated visits and much talking to convince the old cleric that this really was the true situation. Colonel Schlegel must then have been somewhat shattered to discover that it would take no fewer than 120 lorries to move just the most valuable treasures (including the mortal remains of St Benedict), let alone the monks, the nuns and the orphans who had been sheltering within the monastery walls. But, having made the monks realise that there was real danger and found a suitable refuge for everything in Rome, there was no going back. Later, Schlegel realised that the whole matter had mushroomed almost out of control, so it was necessary for him to spill the beans to higher authority as he had so far acted mostly without orders. Fortunately at divisional level his superior (*Generalleutnant* Paul Conrath) approved as did everyone else all the way up to and including Field Marshal Kesselring. Then, whilst the moving was still in progress, trouble threatened when an Allied broadcasting station suddenly announced: 'The *Hermann Göring* Panzer Division is busily engaged in looting the monastery of Monte Cassino.' Fortunately Schlegel was able to continue his work and, by early November, the moving had been completed. After an impressive Mass, attended by the remaining monks together with all the soldiers who had been involved, Schlegel was given a parchment manuscript which read (in Latin):

'In the name of our Lord, Jesus Christ, to the illustrious and beloved Tribune, Julius Schlegel, who saved the monks and the possessions of the holy monastery of Monte Cassino, these monks of Cassino give heartfelt thanks and pray to God for his future well-being.
'Monte Cassino, in the month of November 1943
'*Gregorius Diamare*
'Bishop and Abbot of Monte Cassino'

However, as we will see later, the monastery ruins were undoubtedly occupied and fortified after the bombing, so that they became one of the most pivotal and difficult to capture elements of the Gustav Line defences.

Alexander's Explanation

Naturally Alexander was quick to reply to his prime minister as it was essential to have Churchill solidly behind the Allied drive for Rome from the outset, especially because operations were now taking place in what had inevitably become only a second-rank battlefront, since the final preparations for the landings in Normandy had begun to take centre stage. He therefore spelt out the situation clearly and succinctly, explaining how, along the entire battlefront from the Adriatic to the western coast, only the Liri valley led directly to Rome and provided suitable terrain for making maximum use of the Allied superiority in armour and artillery. He also explained how the main access road — the famous 'Route 6' — which passed close beside, and was thus dominated by, Monte Cassino was the only road (apart from cart tracks) that led through the mountains where the Allies were, across the Rapido River,

Above: Pre-war (*circa* 1927?) views of the Benedictine monastery at Cassino, which featured in so much of the fighting. *(IWM MH 11250 & MH 11251)*

thence along the Liri valley and on to the plain where the prize of the Eternal City beckoned.

Alexander noted that repeated efforts had been made to outflank Monastery Hill from the north, but all had failed — principally because of the difficulties of the terrain with its rocky escarpments, deep ravines, and knife-edge slopes. Even small, well-trained infantry units which could cope with such difficult countryside needed masses of porters (both human and animal) to maintain them even at basic scales. To the south things were no better and crossing the Rapido River had already proved highly dangerous, because such attacks had come directly under very heavy and accurate enfilade artillery fire from German positions tucked away at the foot of the mountains. The monastery position thus held the key.

Alexander then went on to describe other problems with the crossing of the Rapido River — such as it being swollen at that time of year with floodwater, causing the presence of soft, marshy ground to be added to the other bridging difficulties like the strength of the current and of the German positions on the far bank. Nevertheless, he added, if they had to call off the final assault on Cassino, at least they would hold bridges over the Rapido and would thus be in a strong position, after regrouping, to force an entrance into the Liri valley, albeit '. . . a little later, when the snow goes off the mountains, the rivers drop and the ground hardens', when he was confident that '. . . movement will be possible over terrain which at present is impassable'. Churchill thanked General Alexander for this detailed explanation, saying that he hoped they would not have to 'call it off' after they had gone so far. He concluded his signal with the words 'The war weighs very heavy on us all just now.'

'A Strong Thrust Towards Cassino'

On 2 January 1944, General Alexander gave orders to General Clark of US Fifth Army to:

'. . . make as strong a thrust as possible towards Cassino and Frosinone shortly before the assault landing to draw in enemy reserves which might be employed against the landing forces and then create a breach in his front through which every opportunity will be taken to link up rapidly with the seaborne operation.'[8]

The 'assault landing' to which he refers was of course the planned landing at Anzio, scheduled for 22 January 1944, when the US VI Corps would land behind the Gustav Line, thus outflanking its positions and, it was hoped, revitalising a campaign which had become almost stationary, the exhausted troops having to stop, lick their wounds and reorganise after, to quote one report, 'weeks of nothing but mud and mountains'. It was therefore essential that Clark's thrust be as strong as possible, so he intended to use all three

of the corps that made up his army. The French Expeditionary Corps (2nd Moroccan and 3rd Algerian Divisions) was to begin the attack on 12 January, through the mountains north of Cassino, then wheel first west and then south towards the Liri valley and Route 6. Five days later, on 17 January, British X Corps (5th, 46th and 56th Infantry Divisions, together with 23rd Armoured Brigade) was to force a crossing over the Garigliano, open up the Ausente River valley and threaten the German positions in the Liri valley from the rear. Finally, US II Corps (34th and 36th US Infantry Divisions), after capturing Monte Trocchio and then closing up on the Rapido and Gari rivers, with their flanks now protected by the French on the right and the British on the left, would attack on 20 January across the rivers Rapido and Gari astride the village of Sant'Angelo, then advance towards Pignatare to form a bridgehead over which US 1st Armored Division could pass, thus outflanking Cassino and opening up the Liri valley — all this being achieved before the Anzio landings actually began.

This was the plan and we shall have to wait until a later chapter to see how this assault, which I have called 'The First Battle of Cassino', was played out. Interestingly, German accounts do not

Below:
Operation 'Shingle'. The landing at Anzio on 22 January 1944 was, initially anyway, most successful. Here US Army Shermans roll ashore, watched by the crew of the *LST.77*. *(IWM NYF 24580)*

recognise this as being anything more than a preliminary phase or 'prelude', rather than a concerted attack. They could be considered as being correct in this conclusion as the first battle was undoubtedly a hurried resumption of what had become something of a weary advance that had almost battered itself to a standstill. And, to make matters even more difficult, because the amphibious assault at Anzio had already been fixed for 22 January, it was necessary to rush everything — not the ideal way of ensuring success. There were also doubts about its success at high level. For example, on Christmas Day 1943 General Clark had had a meeting at General Keyes' II Corps command post with Major General Lucian K. Truscott of 3rd US Infantry Division, whose division was one of the potential participants in the proposed Rapido/Gari crossing. General Truscott some years later recalled the meeting in his book *Command Missions* thus:

'On Christmas Day, I was called to the II Corps Command Post to confer with General Clark and General Keyes. The next step would be the breakthrough into the Liri valley and the advance on Rome. General Clark proposed . . . to force the Rapido crossing and General Keyes' staff had prepared outline plans for the operation. In conjunction with the attack of II and VI Corps to take Cassino and the surrounding heights, the 3rd Infantry Division was to establish a bridgehead over the Rapido River, near the village of Sant'Angelo below Cassino through which 1st Armored Division would drive up the Liri valley.

'Although the Rapido was swollen from recent rains, the problems looked much easier than our Volturno crossing. Leaving the staff to begin their studies and plans, I set off for the 15th Infantry Command Post on Monte Lungo.

'The heights above Cassino and the mountain masses opposite the junction of the Liri and the Garigliano Rivers dominated the bridging sites from both flanks and were within easy artillery range. From past experience there was no reason to believe that the few regiments available to II Corps would be able to storm the Cassino heights even if they were able to take the town. There was no plan for attacking the heights on the western flank. In these rough areas, German artillery could be concealed from our observation and find relative safety from our own artillery and aircraft. At such ranges, German 88s could destroy our bridges faster than we could build them. Without bridges, we could not cross armour, artillery and anti-tank guns to support the infantry battalions, nor could we supply them adequately. My fine infantry battalions would be eventually whittled away by German armour, artillery and infantry. And 1st Armored Division would still be south of the Rapido.

'Viewed this way, the plan was unsound, so the following day I informed General Clark of these conclusions, to which he agreed, and the plan was abandoned.

'On December 28th, General Clark asked . . . "Would you be willing to undertake the Rapido crossing if these heights on either flank were under attack although not actually in our possession?" After some deliberation I replied "Yes, but these attacks should be so powerful that every German gun would be required to oppose them, for only two or three concealed 88s would be able to destroy our bridges. I doubt our capability for making any such attacks."'[9]

There was thus considered criticism of the proposed plan at an early stage; in addition, the importance of the Monte Cassino position is once again emphasised throughout. Clearly its very presence cast a long shadow on Allied plans. It would have to go.

Above: Lieutenant General Mark W. Clark at his HQ. *(IWM NA 14721)*

Notes

1. The nickname came from the arm badge of the 7th Armoured Division, one of the original formations in the Western Desert Force. The arm badge was the brainchild of Major-General Michael O'More Creagh, the first operational commander of the division and portrayed a 'Desert Rat' — the Greater Egyptian jerboa (*jaculus orientalis*) to be more accurate — in bright scarlet which became their vehicle sign. The nickname 'Desert Rat' was later adopted by all who fought in the Eighth Army.
2. We will be dealing with the detailed composition of the US Fifth Army in a later chapter. However, it was activated at Oudijda, French Morocco, on 5 January 1943 and at that time comprised: I Armored Corps, II Corps and XII Air Support Command. Its first commanding general was Lieutenant General Mark Wayne Clark. It would be used for the invasion of Italy at Salerno.
3. Arrested as he was leaving the palace, *Il Duce* was taken to a series of guarded hiding places — the last one being in the highest mountains of the Apennines (Gran Sasso d'Italia) from where he was rescued by Otto Skorzeny, self-styled 'Chief of German Special Forces', who was personally chosen by Hitler for the rescue mission. Mussolini was flown first to Rome, then to see Hitler. Later, he would be discovered in another hiding place by Italian partisans and shot, together with his mistress, on 28 April 1945.
4. Historical Division of the US War Department, *The Winter Line*, as quoted in *British Troops Malta Study in Italy, 1968*.
5. George Forty, *Fifth Army at War*.
6. 20 March 1944. Prime Minister to General Alexander; quoted in Winston Churchill, *The Second World War*, Volume 5, *Closing the Ring*.
7. Rudolf Böhmler, *Monte Cassino*.
8. Quoted in *British Troops Malta Study in Italy, 1968*.
9. *Command Missions*, Lucian K. Truscott, Dutton, New York, 1954.

Chapter 2

The Attackers — Allied Organisation and Equipment

In this chapter we will consider the commanders, basic organisation, weapons and equipment of the Allied forces which were directly concerned with the battles for Monte Cassino. Details of the make-up of the armies, corps and divisions that comprised the Allied (and axis) formations for each of the four battles are shown in the appropriate chapters (4,5,6 and7). We will therefore be mainly concerned here with the Allied armies in Italy, namely, 15th Army Group, but first of all a general word about the sort of battle that would be fought is appropriate.

An Infantry Battle

Whilst the all-arms team plus air was eventually responsible for the capture of Monte Cassino, the fighting was basically an infantry battle. Therefore I make no apology for quoting once again a tribute that I first included in my book *Fifth Army at War* in 1980. It was taken from a privately published history of the US 88th Infantry Division — 'The Blue Devils' — who fought in Italy as part of US Fifth Army, and in my opinion encapsulates every aspect of the fighting which took place in what was without doubt one of the hardest-fought contests of the war. And because of the nature of the ground and the weather, the fighting became a very personal affair, with the infantry soldier whatever his nationality, unit or rank, playing the major role.

'The Air Corps "pulverises" and "obliterates" targets; the artillery "blasts" enemy installations, and the tankers "smash through" stone walls of opposition. That's the way it is always done. But despite the preparatory assaults and the glowing adjectives, the infantryman in any battle is the deciding factor. To the infantryman falls the toughest job. When the bombers have finished their runs and the artillery has dumped its shells, the infantryman must rise out of his foxhole, charge the contested position, clear out the remaining opposition, take and hold the ground. He seeks out the enemy in his hiding place and with rifle, bayonet, hand grenade or bare hands wrings final surrender from the enemy soldier. In the final stages, the infantryman goes alone. He does the job by himself; succeeds or fails by his own efforts. It is a man to man, kill or be killed proposition. He moves in and takes the ground. If he fails then the Air Corps and the artillery and the tankers fail. If he succeeds, all other arms succeed and another little patch of ground, another pillbox, another hill, is added to the sum total of victory. War is never on a grand scale. It is a composite of little battles for bridges, road junctions, houses and even single machine-gun emplacements. To the men engaged in these individual struggles, these little battles are the most important of all, for their lives are at stake in the outcome. The foxhole occupied by one doughboy is the most important hole in all the world because he is in it. The successes or failures in all the little battles, added up mean victory or defeat in the final analysis. Without the infantry, all other arms and services would be useless. In back of the infantryman are all the support weapons and supplies so necessary for war. In front of him there is "nothing but the enemy".'

Infantry/Tank Co-operation

One of the most vital link-ups on the battlefield was between the infantry and the tanks supporting them. To facilitate this link there was an external telephone in an armoured box on the back of each tank — but it didn't always work. One young platoon commander wrote:

'I remember trying to communicate with the tank troop commander by using the telephone on the outside of his Sherman tank. Of course the thing would not work. But the tank commander obligingly opened his turret when I hammered on it with a rifle. I then showed him where I supposed some German fire was coming from.'

Allied Commanders

As already mentioned in the last chapter, about the same time as the Allied armies reached the Gustav Line, their Supreme Commander, General Dwight D. Eisenhower, was posted to the UK to become Supreme Allied Commander for the coming invasion of France. His place in the Mediterranean was taken by a British general — Henry Maitland 'Jumbo' Wilson, a large, affable man who had been given his nickname as a schoolboy at Eton. Born in 1881 into a military family — his ancestors included Lord Cardigan of the Crimean War, who had famously led the Charge of the Light Brigade — he was a veteran of both the Boer War and Great War and had held senior posts with the British forces in the Middle East since 1939. On 8 January 1944 he took over from Eisenhower, being promoted to field marshal about the same time. He was responsible for overall policy and strategy for Allied troops in the Mediterranean, whilst the detailed direction of the war in Italy was the task of the Commander-in-Chief 15th Army Group (Alexander). In December 1944 Wilson handed over command to Alexander and became head of the British Joint Staff Mission in Washington, being elevated to the peerage as the 1st Baron Wilson of Libya and Stowlandtoft in 1946. His last public appearance was in 1964 and he died that December, aged 83.

Above: Alexander visits his troops. The Commander-in-Chief can be seen over the gun-shield of this Indian 25-pounder field gun. *(Armed Forces Film & Photo Division, MOD New Delhi)*

Above: Here General Alexander not only visited these Italian troops (now part of his forces) but also gave them a hand repairing the roads. *(IWM NAM 110)*

General Sir Harold Alexander (later Field Marshal, 1st Earl Alexander of Tunis) was born in 1891, commissioned into the Irish Guards in 1910 and fought with distinction during the Great War. Promoted to major-general in 1937 — at the time the youngest in the British Army — he came to prominence in the early years of World War 2 when he was responsible for covering the withdrawal of the British Expeditionary Force from France in 1940. He then took command in Burma at the end of 1941 and managed to extricate the British and Indian forces to India. In the summer of 1942 he took over from Auchinleck as Commander-in-Chief Middle East and worked in harmony with the brilliant, but difficult, Montgomery. After the defeat of the Axis in North Africa 'Alex', as he was known to one and all, led 15th Army Group in the short campaign in Sicily and then the long grind up Italy. Always immaculate, charming and diplomatic, he was the ideal person to command a force containing a number of different national elements and to maintain harmony between them, although it has to be said that he did not find it easy keeping egotists like Monty and George Patton under control. Promoted to field marshal after the capture of Rome on 4 June 1944, he succeeded 'Jumbo' Wilson as Supreme Allied Commander in the Mediterranean in December 1944. At that time he was responsible not only for Italy, but also for the Balkans and Greece. General Lucian K. Truscott, Jnr, a US general who served in Italy and was an outstanding combat commander had this to say about 'Alex':

'He had all the personality and drive of Patton and Montgomery without any of their flamboyance. He had the intellect and diplomatic skill of Eisenhower; he was outstanding among the Allied leaders.'[1]

Above: General Sir Harold Alexander pinning the insignia of a Knight Commander of the British Empire on General Mark Clark's chest, 29 April 1944. *(IWM NA 14288)*

Above: After receiving his decoration General Clark presented awards to officers and men of the Allied Forces. Also present was General Alphonse Juin, commander of the French Expeditionary Corps, to the left of Alexander. *(IWM NA 14294)*

Above: General Sir Oliver Leese (*nearest camera*), Commander Eighth Army, who took over from Monty in late December 1943, is seen here with two of his senior commanders watching the effect of Allied bombing on German positions around Cassino. The officer on the far left is General Wladyslaw Anders, the Polish Corps commander. *(IWM NA 12808)*

After the war, he should have taken over as Chief of the Imperial General Staff (CIGS), but instead became governor-general of Canada, where he was extremely popular. Alexander died in 1969.

Wilson's deputy was American General Jacob Loucks Devers, who had been born in Pennsylvania in 1887 and commissioned into the field artillery in 1909. By May 1940 he was a brigadier general and the following year was appointed chief of the Armored Force at Fort Knox. Promoted lieutenant general in September 1942 (on his 55th birthday), he was initially responsible for the American build-up in Europe, but was sent to the Mediterranean by Eisenhower (according to Bradley, Ike 'sought to remove him from the scene' and thereafter their relationship was 'frosty'.) He later took command of US Sixth Army Group, which landed in southern France in Operation 'Anvil' in August 1944. He would get promotion to four-star rank, but when Eisenhower became Army Chief of Staff he was relegated to command of the Army Ground Forces. Retiring in 1949, he died 30 years later in October 1979.

Fifth US Army

General Mark Wayne Clark, commander of Fifth Army, was born in Madison Barracks, New York, in 1896, son of a serving military officer. He was commissioned from West Point in 1917, fought and was wounded in the Great War, and in June 1942 was appointed to command II Corps in England, being nicknamed 'the American Eagle' by Churchill. He came to prominence after his secret meeting with Vichy French officers in Algiers prior to Operation 'Torch', then, in January 1943, was designated to lead US Fifth Army, which he continued to command until he took over 15th Army Group from Alexander in December 1944. At the end of the war, he was appointed commander of US occupation forces in Austria, then of the United Nations forces in Korea for the last 15 months of the Korean War. He died in 1984. Here are three opinions of him, as quoted in Martin Blumenson's biography:

'I shall keep of you the image of a great leader . . . the memory of a prompt and lucid intelligence, always perceiving clearly through the smoke of battle.' *Letter to General Clark from General Alphonse Juin, 22 July 1944.*

'A cold, distinguished, conceited, selfish, clever, intellectual, resourceful officer who secures excellent results quickly. Very ambitious. Superior performance.' *General Jacob L. Devers, Chief of the Army Field Forces, rating Clark's performance.*

'Concern for personal publicity was his greatest weakness. It may have prevented him from acquiring that feel of battle.' *General Lucian Truscott.*

Eighth Army

Taking over as commander of the Eighth Army, when Montgomery left to command 21st Army Group in late December 1943, was General Sir Oliver William Hargreaves Leese, a tall (6ft 4in), good-natured Guardsman, who had been born in 1894 and served with distinction in the Great War. When Montgomery took over Eighth Army in North Africa, he had sent for Leese to replace General Lumsden in command of XXX Corps. Montgomery had a high opinion of Leese, once telling General Brooke, the CIGS, that Leese was: 'the best soldier out here'. Leese was thus in command of the Eighth Army during the Cassino battles. He later went on to become Commander-in-Chief Allied Land Forces, South-East Asia and after the war Commander-in-Chief Eastern Command. He died in 1978.

The Corps

15th Army Group initially had a total of six corps under command in its two armies, but they would be joined by a further three, so there were nine in all concerned in the Cassino battles — and what an amazing mixture of nationalities they were.

In US Fifth Army there were, for example, the American II and VI Corps, together with the British X Corps and the French Expeditionary Corps. In the British Eighth Army the British V and XIII Corps were joined by the Canadian I Corps, the New Zealand II Corps (which contained both New Zealand and Indian divisions) and the Polish II Corps. And of course the mix of nationalities did not stop there — for example, there was a South African armoured division, an Italian battle group, plus Brazilian, Greek and Jewish units, and even Japanese-American 'Nisei' battalions in the US formations. It is to their enormous credit that they managed to function so efficiently and for the most part with such good sense and friendliness.

US II Corps was commanded by Major General Geoffrey Keyes and VI Corps by Major General John P. Lucas. Keyes lacked the practical battle experience of his divisional commanders (Major General Charles W. Ryder of 34th Division and Major General Fred L. Walker of 36th Division), so tended to be taken for granted by Mark Clark. He has been described as being 'quiet, competent, neat and likeable', and clearly did not make waves. General Lucas went on to command the landing force at Anzio, where he showed far too much caution at the wrong time and had to be removed from his command and replaced by General Lucian Truscott on 22 February 1944. British corps commanders were: X — Lieutenant-General Sir Richard McCreery, V — Lieutenant-General Sir Charles W. Allfrey (until 3 August 1944, then Major-General Charles F. Keightley) and XIII — Lieutenant-General Sir Sidney C. Kirkman.

McCreery was especially noteworthy, having been a highly successful strategic planner during the North African campaign, after being sent in May 1941 by the CIGS to advise General Auchinleck on tank warfare. His somewhat vociferous opposition to Auchinleck's proposals for the reorganisation of his armour eventually lost him the job, but he was then appointed chief of staff to General Alexander. Alex described him as being 'one of those rare soldiers who are both exceptionally fine staff officers and fine commanding officers in the field'. After commanding X Corps, he was, in November 1944, appointed to command Eighth Army in succession to General Leese. Born in 1898 and commissioned into the 12th Lancers in 1915, he won a Military Cross in the Great War, commanded his regiment 1930–33, and was awarded the Distinguished Service Order as GSO1 (chief staff officer) of the 1st Division in France in 1940. After the war he was Commander-in-Chief of British Army of the Rhine and retired from the Army in 1949, by then General Sir Richard Loudon McCreery GCB, KBE, DSO, MC. He was also incidentally a fine polo player and all-round horseman, winning the Grand Military Gold Cup at Sandown Park in 1923 and again in 1928.

Lieutenant-General Sir Charles W. Allfrey KBE, CB, DSO, MC was born in 1895, educated at the RN College Dartmouth and joined the Royal Artillery in August 1914. After service in World War 1 (wounded twice, awarded MC and Bar) and after in northern Kurdistan (DSO 1932), he was commanding 43 Inf Div Home Forces at the outbreak of World War 2 and went on to command V Corps in North Africa, then Italy. In August 1943 he became GOC British Troops in Egypt, handing over the corps to General Keightley (late GOC 78 Inf Div). He retired in 1948 and died in 1964.

Finally, General Sir Sidney Chevalier Kirkman GCB, KBE, MC, was born in 1895, commissioned into the Royal Artillery, and after Italy became Commander-in-Chief, Southern Command, then Commander I Corps BTA (British Troops Austria), then Deputy CIGS and finally, Quartermaster-General, before retiring in 1950.

Whilst the British and American formations did not differ in organisation and equipment to any great degree from those found in other theatres, perhaps a word or two of explanation of some of the other less well-known fighting units and their commanders would not go amiss.

Above: Close-up of General Anders, Eighth Army Polish II Corps commander, whose troops would eventually capture Monte Cassino. *(IWM NA 13685)*

The Poles

The Polish II Corps was commanded by General Wladyslaw Anders, an immaculate, 'stern-looking' cavalryman, who had been badly wounded whilst commanding a brigade in southern Poland at the beginning of the war. Taken prisoner by the Russians, he had been imprisoned by them for refusing to join the Red Army, but was later released, so that he could raise an army of Polish prisoners of war in Russia. He had excellent results but the Russians were reluctant to provide them with arms and equipment, so Churchill proposed that Anders complete his work under British auspices in the Near East. Subsequently, Anders' elite corps of three divisions joined the Eighth Army in Italy. By the end of the war Anders had some 125,000 well-trained and well-motivated troops whom Churchill wanted to use in the British zone of occupied Germany. However, the Russians objected, seeing them as a threat, and insisted that the force be disbanded. Anders, who died in 1970, was the head of Polish exiles in the UK after the war. It would be Anders' Polish troops who would eventually capture the Cassino Monastery.

French Forces

The Free French Forces were all part of the French Expeditionary Corps (*Corps expéditionnaire français* — CEF), its commander being *Général d'Armée* Alphonse Pierre Juin, a swarthy, burly soldier born in 1888 in Algeria of old colonial stock. This future marshal of France graduated from the St Cyr military college in 1912, the top cadet in a class which included Charles de Gaulle, with whom he formed a firm friendship. As a lieutenant he was one of the first French officers to command a formation of Moroccan irregulars, the forebears of the famous *Tirailleurs Marocains*, who were skilled mountain fighters and fearsome warriors. He did well in the Great War, leading his Moroccans in many attacks, being wounded and awarded the Legion of Honour. By the time war came again, he was commanding 15th Motorised Infantry Division located around Cambrai. When fighting began in 1940 the division was moved into Belgium where it was cut off by the German advance. Taken prisoner in the Lille pocket, Juin was incarcerated with other senior officers but later paroled. In service with the Vichy French forces he was sent to North Africa and put in command of all Vichy troops in Morocco and later of all French land forces in North Africa. After the Allied 'Torch' landings and the subsequent armistice between the invaders and the French troops in Morocco, Tunisia and Algeria, he was promoted to *général d'armée* and began to plan the formation of the CEF for operations outside North Africa. Juin arrived in Naples by air on 25 November 1943 and was assigned to General Mark Clark's Fifth Army to command the CEF, even though this meant him dropping in rank. His CEF soldiers would win high recognition for their fighting ability, despite the inevitable distrust amongst some of the other Allies over their previous loyalties to Vichy France. Later, having handed over the CEF to General de Lattre de Tassigny, Juin took the top French military post under de Gaulle. After the war, he was Resident-General in Morocco 1947–51, then Commander-in-Chief Land Forces Central Europe in NATO, being made a marshal of France in 1952. He retired from active duty in 1956, but still played an important role on France's supreme defence council. His implacable opposition to Algerian independence caused his removal from the council and he was forbidden to visit Algeria ever again. He died in 1967, the last marshal of France. It is interesting to see that those who came into contact with Juin in Italy formed a very high opinion of his abilities. Major-General Francis Tuker of 4th Indian Division for example, who went to see him before the second Cassino battle, wrote in a letter after the war that he 'regarded Juin

now and even at that time as being probably the best tactical commander in Italy' — high praise indeed.

The initial organisation of the CEF is shown in chapter 4 (pages 64-5). However, it is worth remembering that the majority of its units were composed of native troops from the French North African colonies. In their colonial days they had been only lightly equipped and supplied mainly with obsolete weapons, but had been re-armed and re-equipped by the US Army before the CEF left North Africa. Unless modifications had been ordered and arranged beforehand, then the equipment provided for the French units was identical to that authorised for the US Army. It covered everything 'from uniforms and medical supplies to rifles, machine guns and tanks.'[2] Some units received this equipment from supplies held by the Allied forces in Tunisia; others would receive their equipment direct from the United States, although some units already had a proportion of British or French equipment. The stated aim was to create a French force that was capable of taking part with other Allied forces in the liberation of France and this was undoubtedly achieved, the rehabilitated French North African Army becoming a truly effective fighting force in every respect.

The French colonial troops were mainly tough mountain fighters, rather like the Gurkhas, mostly recruited from among the Berber tribesmen of the Atlas Mountains, and they fought under the command of French officers and NCOs. Individually they became known as *goumiers*, a corruption of the name of their basic sub-unit the *Goum*, which was the equivalent of an infantry company. These *Goums* (goums was also the term commonly used in English for the men themselves) were then grouped together into *Tabors* — units somewhat larger than a battalion. A Tabor normally included an HQ, a heavy weapons *Goum* and three normal infantry *Goums*, with a total strength of 65 French officers and NCOs and 859 Berber NCOs and men. They also had some 247 horses and mules, a mounted platoon being attached to the HQ. A total of three *Tabors* and an HQ made up a *Groupement*, a unit of some 3,100 men. For example, in February 1944 the Moroccan *Goums*, under the command of Brigadier-General Augustine Guillaume, were composed of 1st, 3rd and 4th Groups of *Tabors*, in all about 10,000 men. They were adept at moving over rough terrain, making maximum use of both their horses and mules, and were thus not as tied to the metalled roads as were some other more mechanised Allied forces.

Initially the CEF comprised only two divisions of these hardy colonial troops (2nd Moroccan Infantry Division and 3rd Algerian Infantry Division) which landed in Italy from November 1943 onwards. The 2nd Moroccan Infantry Division included the 4th, 5th and 8th Regiments of Moroccan Tirailleurs, plus the 3rd Moroccan Spahis and the 63rd African Artillery Regiment; the 3rd Algerian Infantry Division included 3rd and 7th Algerian Tirailleurs, the 4th Tunisian Tirailleurs, 3rd Algerian Reconnaissance Spahis and 67th African Artillery Regiment. They were shortly to be followed by the 7th Chasseurs d'Afrique and the 3rd and 4th Groups of Goums, already mentioned at the end of the previous paragraph. Two more divisions subsequently arrived from North Africa in time for the final battles of May 1944, the 4th Moroccan Mountain Division under Major-General François Sevez, together with the Gaullist 1st Motorised Infantry Division (Brigadier-General Charles Brosset), the last of these containing Foreign Legionnaires and Marines as well as colonial troops. There were also various general reserve units comprising two regiments of tank destroyers, six battalions of artillery, various services and 'Base 901'. Finally a fifth re-equipped division arrived — 9th Colonial Infantry Division of mainly West African origin (17,000 strong of whom 10,000 were Africans and the rest French). However, this formation was to be used exclusively

Above: Statue-like on their steeds, these Goum horsemen were fantastic mountain fighters, guaranteed to strike fear into any opposition. The Goumiers are dressed in their flowing burnouses, the normal dress of these rugged fighters from the Atlas Mountains of Morocco. *(IWM NA 14434)*

in storming the island of Elba, so would not be employed on the mainland. By the beginning of May 1944, Juin's corps numbered some 105,000 all ranks — a formidable force. It had grown from a two-division corps in January 1944 to an oversize corps of equivalent strength to nearly five divisions. Among the reinforcements were sufficient engineers so as to allow the release of American engineer units which had previously been attached. However, the US armour and artillery units still remained — the latter being under command of 13th US Field Artillery Brigade. All five divisions would eventually become part of First French Army for the 'Anvil' landings in the south of France.

In some notes he prepared for a lecture on the final battle of Cassino to the Military History Society of Ireland, Lieutenant-Colonel Brian Clark MC, GM who had been adjutant of 1st Royal Irish Fusiliers in 1944, included this evocative description of his first meeting with Goums during the relief of a mountain position:

'Into the hole I plunged, pushed aside the tattered blanket and saw the ante-room of Hell. At least 30 Goums were jammed in the dugout, a solitary lamp made of a 50-cigarette tin with a rag wick smoked in the middle. Thin up-curled beards, Attila moustaches and eagle beaks of noses filled the shadows, implacable eyes stared at nothing, the air reeked with saltpetre, tobacco and human excrement. I coughed, blinked and beat a hasty retreat to join Johnny outside. In Wellington's words: "I don't know if they frightened the enemy — but by God they frightened me!"'

The CEF was praised both by its allies and by the Germans. General Mark Clark, for example, said in his autobiography *Calculated Risk*: 'I shall always be a grateful admirer of General Juin and his magnificent CEF . . . A more gallant fighting organisation never existed.' On the other side of the hill Field Marshal Albert Kesselring wrote: 'The French fought with great élan and exploited each local success by concentrating immediately all available forces at the weakened point.'

New Zealanders and Indians

II New Zealand Corps had as its commander the most famous 'Kiwi' soldier ever — namely General Bernard Cyril Freyberg — whom Churchill called, alluding to his fearlessness, 'the Salamander of the British Empire' because, like that mythical animal, he 'thrived in fire'. He had been wounded six times during the Great War, mentioned in despatches five times, been awarded the Distinguished Service Order and two bars, together with the highest award of all — the Victoria Cross. As commander of the New Zealand Expeditionary Force in the Middle East he had formed and led the 2nd New Zealand Division during the disastrous British intervention in Greece, then Crete in 1941, where he had had to be ordered to leave his doomed troops rather than be captured. His re-

Above: A typical Gurkha despatch rider. *(IWM NA 11154)*

formed division would become famous in North Africa during the pursuit of the Axis forces, then, in January 1944, he would be nominated to command II New Zealand Corps, formed from his division and 4th Indian Division. Inclined to be headstrong and outspoken, Freyberg would be awarded a third bar to his DSO, raised to the peerage and later become governor-general of New Zealand (1946–52). He died in 1963. Rated by the Germans as one of the best among the Allied fighting forces, his two divisions would be heavily involved in the battles for Cassino, until objections from home (mainly about high casualties) caused them to be withdrawn and the corps broken up.

He did not see eye to eye with his army commander, Mark Clark having been given something of an inferiority complex by this exceptionally brave (and stubborn) soldier.

There is little that needs to be said about the fighting prowess of the Indian divisions — 4th Indian Division in II New Zealand Corps and 8th Indian Division in British XIII Corps. Both contained Gurkhas, together with other famed fighters such as Rajputanas, Mahrattas and Punjabis, so the fighting ability of this all-volunteer force was second to none. The same of course can be said about the Kiwis, who had already earned an enviable reputation in North Africa.

Italian Forces

In addition to the various Allied units, the British XIII Corps of the Eighth Army had an Italian battle group (*gruppo combattimento*), which was equivalent in size to a US Army brigade. However, by far the greatest contribution made by the Italians was the large number

Above: Now on the Allied side: Italian gunners swab out their 194mm railway gun near Cassino, 8 March 1944. *(US Army via Real War Photos)*

of labourers, porters and muleteers which they provided, thus freeing up Allied soldiers for more active combat duties.

'The Italian mule outfit is under two Italian lieutenants, who wear plumed Tyrolian hats and look sort of romantic,' wrote Ernie Pyle, famous war correspondent, in *The Fighting 36th*, a pictorial history of the 'T-Patchers':

> '. . . neither speaks English, but in the American Army you only have to yell twice to find a soldier who speaks Italian, so the little group has an interpreter. Everybody has to depend upon him so that he practically runs the show. He is Cpl Anthony Savino of 262 14th Avenue, Newark, NJ. His job would drive anybody crazy. The Italians are not quick and efficient like we are, and about the time Savino gets a pack train all arranged, everything collapses and chaos takes place. Then he catches it from both sides.'

A normal load for an Italian mule was some 150lb, a little more than half the load that would be normal on an American mule. This was because Italian mules were usually smaller and weaker than their American cousins, and some of them were sick from being bussed around in trucks from one place to another. On their return journey down the mountains, having delivered the water and cases of ammunition and rations, the mules carried the dead — the GIs who had been killed in action. However, the Italian muleteers did not like to walk beside the corpses which were lashed onto the backs of the mules, head hanging down on one side of the mule and legs on the other, so GIs had to lead these mules down at night, unload and lay out the bodies as reverently as possible in the difficult, dirty conditions. The unburdened mules would then be moved off to their base. Initially, some white mules were used in the pack trains, but they were clearly too visible in the moonlight so had to be stopped being used. Of course daylight pack trains were even more dangerous as the trails were heavily shelled if any signs of movement were detected.

Basic Organisations

British and American Infantry Divisions

The basic organisations of American and British infantry divisions of the period were not dissimilar, the Americans having three infantry regiments plus supporting arms, whilst the British had three infantry brigades of similar size, if slightly larger than their American equivalent, plus similar support. British brigades were commanded by brigadiers, and American regiments by full colonels. In manpower totals the British division was somewhat larger (18,347 all ranks as compared to 14,253), but otherwise not too dissimilar. Both had

Above: Making fritters in a quarry on Monastery Hill. Even in the most difficult conditions, the battalion cooks managed to produce reasonable grub. The problem was then getting it up to the forward troops in an edible condition. The rock-bound terrain is very evident in this photograph. *(IWM NA 13364)*

Above: Communications were vital, but on occasions very difficult due to the nature of the terrain. Nevertheless, the signallers soon became adept at working under unfavourable conditions. *(IWM NA 13363)*

integral artillery — field, anti-tank and anti-aircraft — but it was the massive weight of back-up artillery firepower upon which the Allied formations could call, together with their overwhelming air support, that should have made all the difference. However, as we will see, circumstances did not always allow this firepower to be used to its fullest effect. It is also worth recording that few Allied soldiers had had previous training in mountain warfare apart from the 1st Special Service Force (1st SSF) and the US 10th Mountain Division.[3] This last formation did not join Fifth Army until January 1945, however, so only the 1st SSF took part in operations against the Winter and Gustav Lines. 'The Braves' or 'The Force' as it was called, consisted of volunteers from both the USA and Canada, between the ages of 21 and 35, trained in skiing, climbing mountains and parachuting. All had been lumberjacks, backwoodsmen, forest rangers and the like and their three regiment strong force was unique within Fifth Army. Commanded by Colonel Robert Frederick (US Army), they were armed and clothed with US equipment but drilled mostly like the British, although they saluted in either British or American style.

They had a very high proportion of non-commissioned officers and were able to take on the most rugged missions that involved speed and low-level manoeuvre. 1st SSF had some drawbacks, including no integral artillery, so had to call on outside assistance to support it for a particular operation. When, for example, it was given the mission in early December 1943, of seizing Monte La Difensa, the attackers left their trucks well out of earshot of German listening posts, walked several miles across country with each man carrying about 40lb of personal equipment and then climbed half-way up the side of the mountain so as to reach the scrub growth of its upper slopes before first light. They next went on to scale the heights, withstood heavy German fire, broke through German defences and finally held out until relieved.

Left:
First aid was essential and the battalion medics performed many acts of extreme bravery. This pile of stones is a company aid post where the medics would give first aid even when under mortar and machine-gun fire. *(IWM NA 13798)*

Below:
GIs of B Company, 2nd Chemical Weapons Battalion firing their mortars near Cassino. The weapon is the 4.2in Chemical Mortar which fired a bomb of either 25.5lb or 32lb out to 4,400yd. *(US Army via Real War Photos)*

Above:
Backbone of the US Army field artillery was the 105mm Howitzer M2A1, a very sturdy and reliable weapon. It had a range of 12,500yd and fired a shell weighing 33lb. *(US Army via Real War Photos)*

Right:
Towed through the glutinous mud and brought into action over very bad country, this 5.5in medium artillery gun belonged to 99th Battery, 74th Medium Regiment, RA. With a shell weight of 100lb and a range of 16,200yd, it was both useful and popular. *(IWM NA 8787)*

Left:
New Zealand gunners firing their 6-pounder anti-tank gun. It could penetrate 2.7in of armour at 1,000yd and was brought in to replace the tiny 2-pounder, but soon needed to be replaced itself by the 17-pounder. *(IWM NA 12815)*

Right:
In action near Monastery Hill, an Ordnance QF, 17-pounder anti-tank gun could penetrate 5.1in of armour at 1,000yd and remained in service after the war. *(IWM NA 12810)*

Regimental Combat Teams

For a special task the US Army often formed a regimental combat team (RCT), typically a formation of some 200 officers and 3,800 men, under the command of the deputy division commander (a full colonel). The standard RCT comprised an infantry regiment, a light field artillery battalion, an engineer company, a medical company, signal and military police detachments.

Machine-Gun Battalions

Every British infantry division included a separate machine-gun battalion, normally containing three machine-gun companies (each three platoons of four machine guns) and one mortar company (four platoons of 3in mortars). This organisation allowed a company of machine guns to be attached to each brigade, their tripod-mounted, water-cooled Vickers .303in machine guns being able to put down accurate, sustained and highly effective fire that was most helpful in the battles that took place, as was the highly accurate and effective fire from the ubiquitous 3in mortar, one of the best weapons of its kind in service.

Left: Stock section light machine gun for the British and Commonwealth infantry was the Bren gun, seen here as a Kiwi infantryman fires through a smokescreen. The Mark I had a rate of fire of 500 rpm, was fitted with a 29-round overhead magazine and was still in service (the simplified Mk 2) in 1974. *(IWM NA 12818)*

Below: Another widely used machine gun was the Vickers .303in, belt-fed medium machine gun, seen here in position covering the ground in front of Monastery Hill. It entered service in 1912 and was still in worldwide use 65 years later. *(IWM NA 15057)*

Above: A 3in mortar crew in action. A popular weapon, it had a maximum range of 2,750yd and the bomb weight (HE or smoke) was 10lb. *(IWM NA 13365)*

Armour

This part of Italy was not a place where armour could be used to its fullest effect, although on occasions the armoured regiments of America, Britain, Canada, New Zealand, Poland and South Africa, both in divisions and in independent armoured brigades, or in Combat Commands/Task Forces, performed outstandingly well. As far as US armour was concerned, the only formation to be used in the Cassino battles was 'Combat Command Bravo' (CC B)[4] of 1st Armored Division, under the command of Colonel Frank A. Allen, Jnr, being initially located near Mignano in January 1944, whilst the rest of the division (the HQ and main body) was on the Anzio beachhead. The division did get back together, but not until May 1944. The order of battle of CC B is given at the start of Chapter 4. During the war US armoured divisions underwent no fewer than six separate reorganisations; however, only two of these were really significant. The first (March 1942) resulted in what was called the 'heavy' armoured division, whilst the second (September 1943) produced what was called the 'light' armoured division. It was all

about reducing tank strengths by replacing two regiments (each of three tank battalions) by three tank battalions. However, the new tank battalions were stronger in numbers of tanks, so the overall reduction was only about one-third. In fact it took time for this major change to be put into effect and in 1st Armored this was not completed until July 1944. French armour was organised and equipped on American lines and with US Army vehicles and equipment.

In a similar manner, the basic organisation of the British armoured division underwent numerous changes between 1939–45, in fact nine in all, the relevant ones for this period being the seventh (April 1943) and the eighth (March 1944). This led to an increase in tank numbers; however, as with the US Army, the changes no doubt took their time to be implemented. Undoubtedly one of the major changes was the replacement of the armoured car

Above:
None of the battles for
Cassino could be described
as being fought over good
tank going. Nevertheless
both sides employed tanks
or tank destroyers as will be
seen from later chapters.
Here Sherman M4 medium
tanks move up into battle,
whilst the town and
monastery are bombed
and shelled.
(IWM NA 14891 & NA 15027)

Left:
The result of trying to
negotiate the difficult going
was often this — a Sherman
overturned. One hopes the
crew were safely extracted.
(IWM NA 12917)

Above: Under these conditions, wheeled and tracked vehicles were limited in their cross-country ability, so mules and horses came into their own. In the first of these photos a long line of pack mules, with Italian muleteers, heads for the heights around Castelforte. In the second, porters of the 17th Indian Mule Company transport supplies in the mountains. *(IWM NA 11241 and NA 13282)*

regiment of the 1942 organisations by an armoured reconnaissance regiment, the former becoming corps troops. Fortunately the armoured regiments in British armoured divisions in Italy were equipped with the tried and tested American M4 Sherman tank which the units had had since North Africa, rather than the British cruiser (by then the Cromwell), which lacked protection despite its speed (which needed good going not normally found in this part of Italy) with no increase in firepower. Commonwealth armour was organised and equipped along British lines, with the Sherman once again being the main medium tank. The same applied to Polish armour which was also British-equipped.

Mountain Fighting

One of the skills needed to operate in the Cassino area, which many infantrymen had to learn quickly — and to learn on the job and under fire in most cases — was living and fighting in a mountainous, stony landscape, overlooked by the Germans and close enough to them to be prey to ever-watchful snipers. Here are two typical descriptions, the first one written by the late Major Desmond Woods MC, a company commander in 2nd London Irish Rifles. He recalled:

'. . . we then moved into a place called Monte Castellone. This was a position at the back of the monastery and our B Echelon, which supplied us, was about eight miles back. The battalion moved up at night and we took over from the French and occupied the top of this mountain and I

remember we could actually see the Germans in the monastery. Down below between us and the monastery was a very, very deep ravine and we used to take forward positions by night and then by day the men would be brought back to the reverse slope of the hill and just leave OPs up in position. Supplying us there from B Echelon was quite an administrative task; the rations were brought up by jeep and trailer — sometimes the jeeps were pulling two trailers and they had to cross what was known as "The Mad Mile". This was a place that the Germans were continually stonking and when the drivers came to this stretch they just put their foot down and went through "The Mad Mile" as quickly as possible, hoping for the best. Then when they got to the base of Monte Castellone the rations were transferred from the jeep trailers to mules and they came up to us in the mountains on the mules. Every night the colour-sergeant used to arrive with our mail and our rations and the rations were organised so that they could be sent out in what they called platoon dumpers; the food was worked out so that each platoon would get its dumper and then it would be handed out to the men.

'It was an extraordinary time up there on Monte Castellone. I suppose that we must have been there for the best part of six weeks. The battalion headquarters was down below and from time to time I went back to talk to the CO — he very often came up at night and we walked around the positions and he saw that the men were manning the forward

Above: One of the smaller British anti-tank weapons was the PIAT (Projector Infantry Anti-Tank). It fired a 3lb hollow-charge grenade some 100yd, but was heavy (32lb) and difficult to cock. *(Armed Forces Film & Photo Division, MOD New Delhi)*

positions as they should do. We couldn't dig slit-trenches up there — it was rock hard — so we lived in what we called stone-sangars — little sangars instead of slit-trenches. They gave a certain amount of protection but the problem here was that we could get splinters from them very often.

'The Germans did do a lot of shelling but we were quite all right on the top of the hill because their shells went down in the valley behind us so we weren't actually suffering from the effects of the shellfire on top of the hill although down at the HQs of the various formations they were getting it. However, we did get a certain amount of trouble from their mortars — they were able to put their mortar shells down and this mortaring could become very unpleasant and I did have a certain number of casualties in the company merely from mortar fire.

'We did our period on Monte Castellone and then it was time for us to be relieved. It was the Poles who came up to take over from us and this takeover had to be done at night, the timing had to be absolutely right so that there would be enough darkness for the Poles to get up and for us to get back in the one night because you could not move at all by daylight. All the movement back to our B Echelon position had to be done when it was dark because the Germans were occupying the monastery and they had observation and could give us a very nasty time indeed. We came out of the handover pretty well and I was very relieved really to get away from there. Sitting for six weeks in a position like that is not terribly good for morale — it gets extremely monotonous, we didn't seem to be achieving very much and it was great to get out of that position.'[5]

Now some reminiscences from Rifleman John Ledwidge, also of 2nd London Irish Rifles:

'One of the worst positions I can recall was a place called Monte Nero, which was in the foothills of the Apennines. As we reached there a blizzard started and in next to no time we were marching through three feet of snow. The snow continued all night. We were in sangars and if you left the sangar for any length of time you might lose it under the snow. We were warned about falling asleep at night because the white flakes continually falling against the black background were inclined to make you drowsy. If you fell asleep you could be buried in no time. We were still in khaki uniforms but the Germans were quick to adapt to snow and early one morning attacked us from behind. They had got behind us because they were all dressed in white, while I'm sure we stuck out like sore thumbs . . . Another bad experience was that a lot of men got snow blindness. Most of us had never seen it before and were amazed how a person's eyes became inflamed and swelled up. We took the precaution of getting soot from the bottom of the tea dixies and rubbing it under our eyes and on our noses and this helped.

'Another bad time was when the Poles came to relieve us on Monte Castellone, the positions where we were directly under the view of the Monastery and Monte Cairo and could not

Above: In March 1944 this was the most forward American observation post, high up on Monte Trocchio. *(IWM NA 12859)*

show ourselves during the day for fear of being plastered with shell and mortar fire. We were in sangars and went into them before daybreak and stayed there until darkness. If we had to go to the toilet then we had to go before going in or take a tin with us in case we needed to pass water. We also took haversack rations. When the advance party of Poles arrived they could not speak any English and we could not make them understand they were not to show themselves. How we escaped being shelled is a miracle. And when the main body arrived that night it was even worse. You would think you were at a football match with all the shouting. We got off the mountain as quick as we could that night.'[6]

'D-Day Dodgers'

In addition to having to fight in the most difficult conditions of climate and terrain, the soldiers of General Alexander's command had to face the morale-sapping experience of becoming, like General Bill Slim's Fourteenth Army in Burma, a 'Forgotten Army'. Initially, of course, they had received their fair share of publicity, but it was inevitable that once D-Day had arrived, the North-West Europe theatre of war would steal all the headlines. This situation was not helped by the early removal of senior commanders like

Eisenhower and Montgomery to take up senior command posts well in advance of D-Day, and of seasoned troops like the famous 7th Armoured Division being extracted from Italy, to give a leavening of experience to the relatively inexperienced divisions thirsting for action in the UK. Further troop reductions would also follow, when more troops, landing craft, supplies, ammunition and so on were removed for the 'Anvil' landings in southern France. The general feeling of being left out and of being forgotten and unloved by the folks back home, apart of course from their nearest and dearest, is nothing new to many servicemen — as those who served in 'peacetime' in theatres like the North-West Frontier of India in the 1930s or in the Korean War of the 1950s would also vouch for — but the situation was undoubtedly made even worse for those in Italy, by the stupid and unthinking remarks of a British politician, Nancy Astor, who referred in Parliament to those servicemen in Italy as 'Dodging D-Day'. Her remarks gave rise to a bitter parody entitled *The D-Day Dodgers*, which was sung to the tune of the haunting German song *Lili Marlene*[7] that had been adopted by both sides during the Desert War:

'We're the D-Day Dodgers, out in Italy,
Always on the vino, always on the spree,
Eighth Army skivers and the Yanks
We go to war, in ties like swanks,
We are the D-Day Dodgers, in sunny Italy.

We landed at Salerno, a holiday with pay,
Jerry brought his bands out to cheer us on our way,
Showed us all the sights and gave us tea,
We all sang songs and the beer was free.
We are the D-Day Dodgers, the lads that D-Day dodged.

Palermo and Cassino were taken in our stride,
We did not go to fight there, we just went for the ride,
Anzio and Sangro are just names,
We only went to look for dames.
We are the D-Day Dodgers, in sunny Italy.

Looking round the hillsides, through the mist and rain,
See the scattered crosses, some that bear no name.
Heartbreak and toil and suffering gone,
The boys beneath, they slumber on.
They are the D-Day Dodgers, who'll stay in Italy.'

For the record there were 189,000 casualties sustained by the Fifth Army and nearly 124,000 by the Eighth, making a total of some 313,000 for the whole campaign — so much for 'Dodging D-Day'.

Notes
1. *Command Missions*, Lucian K. Truscott, Dutton, New York, 1954.
2. *Rearming The French* by Marcel Vigneras.
3. This does not of course include the CEF, which, as already explained, had many troops well used to mountain warfare, including an entire Mountain Division.
4. It was normal practice for an American armored division to operate under two (later three) Combat Commands — CC A, CC B and later CC R. However, this did not change in Italy until July 1944.
5. From reminiscences kindly supplied by Richard Doherty, historian of County Londonderry.
6. Ibid.
7. *Lili Marlene* by Norbert Schultze became a hit with both German and British soldiers in North Africa. Originally sung by Lale Andersen, the first English version was recorded by Anne Shelton.

Above: The Cassino Monastery was the graveyard of many brave men. This hand and arm of a partly buried body are symbolic of the grim scene after the battle.
(IWM NA 15154)

Chapter 3

The Defenders — German Organisation and Equipment

Fighting the Defensive War

The Italian surrender in September 1943 put the onus for defending mainland Italy squarely onto the shoulders of the Germans, so that by the time that the *Führer* issued the last of his numbered Directives (No. 51 of 3 November 1943, which was mainly concerned with the manning of the Atlantic Wall), it must have been clear, even to him, that he had lost the overall initiative and that strategic control was slipping away. As we have seen, nowhere was this more apparent than in the Mediterranean, where surrender in North Africa had been swiftly followed by the loss of Sicily and the successful Allied invasion of the Italian mainland. The anticipated assault on North-West Europe was still awaited but, judging by the vast build-up of Allied troops in the UK, it could take place at any moment. Therefore it was essential not to weaken the strength of those who would have to meet this invasion when it came, that is, Army Group West. The Eastern Front could also not be neglected, so it followed that other areas such as Italy could not expect much in the way of reinforcements. And those that did arrive were in for a shock — as one senior officer commented: 'They had expected the sunny south with orange harvests and bathing; instead they met fierce, cold gales and snow on peaks 6,000ft high.'

There were in fact two very different German tactical proposals for defending Italy, both very much dependent upon the strongly held but opposing views of the two field marshals — one army and one air force — who were vying for overall command in Italy, namely Rommel in the north and Kesselring in the south. Rommel favoured a complete withdrawal out of most of Italy to a northern defensive position roughly astride what was called the Gothic or Green Line in the Apennines, north of the Arno valley — roughly in other words along the line: Pisa–Florence–Pisaro. Despite this tactic meaning that he would give up much of Italy to the Allies, the 'Desert Fox' still felt it was the most sensible place to defend *Festung Europa* — Italy was after all now a 'busted flush' and not worth the loss of even more German lives. Kesselring, on the other hand, advocated a much slower fighting withdrawal, making use of other defensive lines farther south — such as the Winter Line and the Gustav Line, both well to the south of Rome. Not only were these lines much shorter than the Gothic Line and so needed fewer troops to defend them but also, by holding much farther south, Allied warplanes would be limited to using air bases that much farther away from the Fatherland and its precious centres of production. And there was the added bonus of more time being gained to make the Gothic Line even stronger for later use. After some vacillation, Hitler finally decided on Kesselring's southern defence plan and took Rommel and his staff out of Italy, leaving Kesselring in sole charge. Most of the senior German commanders in Italy agreed with his tactics. After the war General Frido von Senger und Etterlin, one of Kesselring's corps commanders, wrote:

> 'I backed Kesselring's plan. For one thing I saw no other choice. Secondly, successful defence seemed a better means for re-establishing the morale of the divisions which was somewhat weakened and would be even more so by continual retreat.'[1]

The Defensive Lines — Many Names

The positions that Kesselring decided to defend were known by a variety of names, though some, unfortunately, were called by a number of different names at different times.

The Winter Line was the collective name given by the Allies to a number of defensive lines — some designed to impose tactical delay, others designated as possible covering positions, varying in strength and complexity, but all positioned in locations spread across the Italian peninsula to the south of the Gustav Line. And to make matters more complicated as we have already mentioned, some lines had more than one name during their existence. There was, for example, the Barbara Line which was a tactical delaying line behind the Volturno River positions, running along the ridge of high ground between the Volturno and the Garigliano and thence over the Apennines to the Trigno River; then there was the Bernhard Line (sometimes also called the Reinhard Line) based on the Mignano defile which had been reconnoitred by the erstwhile XIV Panzer Corps commander General Hube, before he handed over command to General von Senger und Etterlin. It was originally intended to be only lightly defended but, in October 1943, when Kesselring was ordered to consolidate on the line Gaeta–Ortona, it was considerably strengthened. Behind the Gustav Line was the Hitler Line, which the *Führer* had personally ordered to be built in November 1943, as a fall-back/switch line for the Bernhard Line and to defend the Liri valley. It ran from Terracina on the west coast to Fondi, through the Aurunci Mountains to Pontecorvo, Piedimonte San Germano and Monte Cairo. In January 1944 it was renamed as the Senger Line, when it became clear that it was being threatened and might be breached, as it was thought by the 'spin doctors' that such a catastrophe might harm the *Führer*'s invincible image.

Of course the strongest of them all was the Gustav Line, which incorporated the town of Cassino and the monastery of Monte Cassino in the west and the Sangro River, which ran into the Adriatic near Ortona, in the east. It had begun life as the rearmost and strongest part of the Bernhard Line, but was then upgraded

Above: Interior of one of the Gustav Line bunkers, just north of Cassino, now under new management. These GIs (probably medics, from the armband) were photographed on 10 February 1944. *(US Army via Real War Photos)*

when Hitler decided to hold the Allies much farther south than at first anticipated. By the close of 1943 the Allies had reached this line, where they found themselves opposed not only by determined German troops, but also by both nature and the elements, as the hills turned into rocky mountains and the winter weather worsened. Even when they had crossed the Rapido River, they were still unable to make much progress against the ever-dominating Monte Cassino lynch-pin position. They then attempted to get around the Gustav Line, by the daring seaborne landing at Nettuno, near Anzio, in January 1944. At first the beachhead position was consolidated and it looked as though the Gustav Line had been turned and that the race for Rome would commence. At this time (28 January 1944) Hitler sent the following order to Kesselring, at the same time giving him unlimited authority over all the Axis armed services in Italy, including even the SS:

'Within the next few days the "Battle for Rome" will begin. It will be decisive for the defence of Central Italy and for the fate of the Tenth Army. However, the significance of this struggle goes even beyond that, because the landings at Nettuno marked the opening of the invasion of Europe planned for 1944. The purpose of the enemy is to hold down large German forces as far away as possible from the bases in England, where the main invasion forces are standing ready, to wear down the German forces and to gain experience for future operations.

'Of the significance of the battle which 14th Army is about to fight, every one of its soldiers must be thoroughly aware.

'It is not sufficient to give clear and tactically correct orders. All officers and men of the army, the air force and the naval forces must be penetrated by a fanatical will to end this battle victoriously, and never relax until the last enemy soldier has been destroyed or thrown back into the sea. The battle must

be fought in a spirit of holy hatred for an enemy who is conducting a pitiless war of extermination against the German people, who is prepared to adopt any means to this end, and who, without any higher ethical purpose, seeks only the annihilation of Germany and, with her, of European culture.

'The fight must be hard and merciless, not only against the enemy, but against all officers and units who fail in this decisive hour.

'The enemy must be forced to recognise, as he did in the fighting in Sicily, on the Rapido River, and at Ortona, that the fighting strength of Germany is unbroken, and that the great invasion of 1944 is a hazardous enterprise which will be drowned in the blood of Anglo-Saxon soldiers.
'Adolf Hitler.'[2]

Whilst it is unclear whether the *Führer*'s stirring message ever reached down to the individual *Landser* (infantry soldier) grimly hunkering down in his foxhole along the Gustav Line, under a constant hammering from Allied artillery and air power, plus all that nature could bring against him, undoubtedly the German forces in Italy fought bravely and determinedly. The Allied landing at Anzio did not cause the western end of the Gustav Line to be turned and Hitler even sent some reinforcements into central Italy. In mid-February he ordered a major counter-attack at Anzio, which, whilst preventing a break-out, did not drive the Allies into the sea as had been its intention.

To close on this description of the Gustav Line, here is what one British officer, the late Major Desmond Woods MC, who was commanding H Company, 2nd London Irish Rifles, had to say:

Above:
One of the strongest parts of the
defensive lines was the Hitler
Line, into which had been
incorporated a number of
Panther tank turrets, embedded
into concrete with room for the
gun crew, ammunition and so
on underneath.
(Author's collection)

Right:
German troops' sleeping
quarters underground near the
monastery were snug and
shellproof. Photograph taken on
18 May 1944.
(IWM NA 15136)

'I'd like to say something about the Gustav Line. The Germans had been preparing this for the past year. They had used forced Italian labour. It was sited in considerable depth. In front of the line lay the River Rapido. It was both an infantry and an anti-tank obstacle — fairly deep and the line was in depth back from there. There were a number of Italian farmhouses — they had all been fortified and a system of trenches were dug around the gardens in the bases of these farmhouses. The Germans could live in these houses comparatively easily but once the battle started all they had to do was man their trenches. They were also of course down in the cellars of these houses. They had a preponderance of 88mm guns. These were absolutely lethal against our tanks — some were cemented into pillboxes, others were on tracks and could be moved about as the Germans required. Of course the whole position was dominated by Monte Cairo and below it Monte Cassino. As long as the Germans held their positions they had complete observation in daylight of the Liri valley and they could therefore bring their artillery to bear with great accuracy as we were to find out in the forthcoming battles. They had every type of weapon available. They had learned to perfect their artillery, bringing down defensive fire when we were moving behind barrages and they would bring it down to catch us on our side of the barrage. They had six-barrelled Nebelwerfers or mortars which were lethal, MG 42 and MG 44 machine guns, mortars, tanks and they even used to fire airbursts. They had every type of conceivable weapon that you could think of. So we were up against a very formidable position and I don't think any of us had the slightest doubt about what lay ahead.'[3]

'Battle Strengths' and 'Paper Strengths'

Before examining in some detail the organisation and equipment of the German troops who were involved in the Cassino/Gustav Line operations, it is essential to put the numbers who had to fight into perspective. In January 1944 there were 22 German divisions in Italy compared with 21 Allied; by May the figures were 23 German as opposed to 28 Allied — but of course German divisions were normally smaller than Allied ones. Most importantly, it must also be appreciated that few German units were up to their establishment strength when the battles commenced. Many units had suffered heavy casualties either holding the Winter Line or their defensive positions as they withdrew. For example, 15th Panzer Grenadier Division, which had been in action almost continually since Sicily, had fewer than 400 men in each battalion by January 1944 (about 50% normal strength). In fact, between mid-1943 and mid-1944, the German Army as a whole underwent considerable organisational changes due to manpower shortages. One of the major results was an across-the-board reduction in the number of regiments in infantry divisions from three to two, although these reductions did not all come into effect in Italy immediately. On the plus side, however, in order to endeavour to offset these reductions in manpower, more automatic weapons (both machine pistols and extra machine guns), also hand-held anti-tank weapons (*Panzerfaust* and *Panzerschreck*) and with heavier support weapons had been introduced. These last included, in corps artillery units, 21cm Mörser 18s, (heavy howitzers) and the 15cm and 21cm *Nebelwerfer* rocket projectors.[4] The lack of numbers was also somewhat made up for by the excellent defensive positions they occupied.

The Commanders and their Units

Let us now look in more detail at the German forces which the Fifth and Eighth Armies would be fighting against, starting with a brief résumé of the careers of some of their senior commanders who would be most concerned with the battles for Cassino.

Commander in Chief

At the top of the German hierarchy in Italy at the time of the Cassino battles was *Generalfeldmarschall* Albert Kesselring, an exceptionally able, affable and astute commander, who was given the nickname 'Smiling Albert' by the Allies. The tall, genial Bavarian, who was born in Marktsheft on 30 November 1885, had undertaken his initial military training at the Munich Officer Candidate School in 1905–06, receiving his commission in 1906, with seniority as a lieutenant antedated to 1904. After a number of appointments with artillery units and on the General Staff during the Great War, he was appointed to become Administrative Chief of the Reich Air Ministry on 1 October 1933, then Chief of the Luftwaffe General Staff in 1937. The same year he was promoted to *Generalleutnant* and appointed Commanding General of Airforce Service Area III (Dresden) and later promoted to *General der Flieger*. In 1938 he assumed command of the First Air Fleet, which he led in the Polish campaign. He was promoted to *Generalfeldmarschall* in 1940 and transferred to the Second Air Fleet in the West. In November 1941, he was appointed as Commander-in-Chief Mediterranean, his HQ being designated in full *Oberbefehlshaber Südwest, Wehrmachtbefehlshaber Mittelmeer-Italien* (Command-in-Chief South-West, Armed Forces Command, Mediterranean and Italy). A lifelong friendship with Luftwaffe chief Hermann Göring undoubtedly helped his career, during which he was awarded the Knight's Cross, with both Oakleaves and Swords. He was seriously injured on 25 October 1944 in a road accident — his staff car collided with an artillery gun coming out of a side road — and he was in hospital for three months.

Just before the end of the war he was transferred to become Commander-in-Chief West, with his HQ at Nauheim and later was Commander-in-Chief South, with HQ at Saalfelden, where he was finally taken prisoner on 8 May 1945. The only field marshal whom Hitler did not relieve at some point in the war, he was charged with war crimes, including the inhumane treatment of Italian civilians, by a British military tribunal in Venice. He was condemned to death on 6 May 1947, but the sentence was later commuted to life imprisonment. He was released in October 1952 on health grounds and died in July 1960 at Bad Nauheim. Judging him on his performance in Italy, Kesselring showed himself to be a master of defensive operations and adept at the tactics of the slow, controlled withdrawal. He was undoubtedly one of the best German generals of World War 2 and arguably the best general on either side in Italy.

Tenth Army

The commander of the German Tenth Army was *Generaloberst* Scheel Heinrich Gottfried von Vietinghoff. Born at Mainz in December 1887, he entered the army in 1906. He was appointed commander of 5th Panzer Division in 1938 and by 1940 he was a *General der Panzertruppe*. After further promotion to *Generaloberst*, he commanded first XII, then XXXXVI Corps under Guderian in Second Panzer Group. He then commanded Ninth Army, then Fifteenth Army in occupied France, before taking over Tenth Army in Italy in August 1943. He showed considerable initiative in opposing the US Fifth Army landings at Salerno and then conducted an almost textbook withdrawal from the Volturno River to the Gustav Line. As we will see, his army then held fast through the Winter Line campaign (mid-November 1943 — mid-January 1944). Later, after Mackensen's Fourteenth Army was formed to deal with the Anzio landings, the Tenth Army operated on the eastern flank. Von Vietinghoff was on leave to receive his Knight's

Above: Commander of the German Tenth Army was *Generaloberst* Heinrich von Vietinghoff, whose troops held the Gustav Line for three long months. (Bundesarchiv 101/313/1019/14a)

Corps Commanders

Commander of XIV Panzer Corps was *General der Panzertruppe* Fridolin von Senger und Etterlin. Von Senger, whose corps would be responsible for holding the line around Cassino, was born in Waldshut, Baden-Württemberg, in September 1891. Holder of the German Cross in Gold and the Knight's Cross with Oakleaves, von Senger was probably one of the most underestimated of all German generals, perhaps because of his anti-Nazi sympathies. A Rhodes scholar and Anglophile (he went to Eton and St John's College, Oxford), he was both an intellectual and sophisticate, who in his youth had trained as a monk (he was a lay member of the Benedictine Order, hence his great personal interest in safeguarding the monastery at Cassino). A keen horseman, he became a world-class equestrian between the wars, then commanded the 3rd Cavalry Regiment in Poland and a motorised brigade in France. His direction of the battles for Cassino would show his considerable skill and ability. He died in 1963.

Commander of LI Mountain Corps was *General der Gebirgstruppen* Valentin Feurstein, holder of the Knight's Cross. He was born in Bregenz in 1895, joined the army in 1906, then was a member of the Austrian *Bundesheer* after World War 1 and had reached the rank of major-general by 1935. His first appointment in World War 2 was as the commander of 2nd Mountain Division, and his last as inspector of mountain training. Clearly an officer with the best interests of his men at heart, he fell out with von Vietinghoff over Hitler's orders to hold the Melfa River Line for several days, which would, he considered, mean heavy casualties.

Divisional Commanders

Commander of 90th Panzer Grenadier Division, was *Generalmajor* Ernst-Günther Baade, who had been born in Falkenhagen in August 1897. A close friend of von Senger, he was one of the most colourful characters to reach the senior ranks of the German Army during World War 2. Son of a Brandenburg landowner, he farmed his own estate in Holstein, where he bred horses. He disliked pomp and probably had more in common with British officers in the Western Desert, where he was famous for leading night patrols wearing a kilt — he is reputed to have signalled the end of one night patrol by radioing the British (over their own radio network): 'Stop firing. On my way back, Baade.' Richard Brett-Smith in his *Hitler's Generals* tells of a rumour circulating in December 1943, when Baade was defending Cassino, that he had accepted an invitation to dine with the British at Christmas. The OKW (*Oberkommando des Wehrmacht* — Armed Forces High Command, Hitler's main military headquarters) got so agitated about this rumour that von Senger had to deny it personally (he did not tell them that Baade had sent the Allied forces a New Year greeting in English). Baade was undoubtedly a brilliant commander and gave the US 34th Infantry Division a tough time in February 1944, whilst his defence of Cassino town earned him special praise from von Vietinghoff, who put him and General Heidrich (*see below*) into a class by themselves. Promoted to command LXXXI Panzer Corps in 1945, this holder of the German Cross in Gold and Knight's Cross, with both Oakleaves and Swords, was to die of wounds received in an air raid on the very last day of the war.

Commander of 1st Paratroop Division was *Generalleutnant* Richard Heidrich, who was another brilliant and highly decorated officer. He was born in Lewalde, Saxony, in July 1896. He had volunteered for military service in World War 1, was commissioned and won the Iron Cross both 2nd and 1st Class. After the war Heidrich served in a number of posts in the infantry, but in 1938 was appointed, as an infantry major, to form and command a parachute battalion. He and his unit were taken into the Luftwaffe

---

Cross from Adolf Hitler on 11 May 1944 when the final assault on Cassino and the Gustav Line began. Returning immediately, he was involved in the action and the subsequent German withdrawals through Rome. Taking over from Kesselring after Smiling Albert was badly injured, he later succeeded him to become Commander-in-Chief Italy. He would sign the surrender documents that ended hostilities on 2 May 1945 and be imprisoned by the Allies. Released from captivity in 1946, he died six years later at Pfronten.

Fourteenth Army

Generaloberst Eberhard von Mackensen was a cavalry general of the 'old school'. Born at Bromberg in 1889, he joined the army in 1908 and became a *Leutnant* in the 1st Hussar Regiment two years later. By the beginning of World War 2 he was a general, becoming chief of staff of Fourteenth Army in September 1939. In 1941 he commanded III Corps for the invasion of Russia, in which his troops did extremely well, and he was promoted *General der Kavallerie*. He rose to the rank of *Generaloberst* in July 1943, whilst commanding First Panzer Army, then took over command of Fourteenth Army in Italy on 5 November 1943. He was less successful in Italy, failing to liquidate the Anzio beachhead, then failing to prevent the break-out. It is said that he and Kesselring did not get on and 'Smiling Albert' rebuked him on at least one occasion for not obeying orders. A holder of the Knight's Cross with Oakleaves, he came of a most distinguished military family, his father being Field Marshal August von Mackensen. After the war he was accused of the massacre in the Ardeatine Caves and sentenced to death on 30 November 1945. However, like Kesselring, his sentence was later commuted to life imprisonment.

on 1 January 1939. He left the Luftwaffe at the start of the war to command 514th Infantry Regiment in France, but the next year he was persuaded to transfer back into the Luftwaffe. Whilst commanding 3rd Paratroop Regiment in June 1941 on Crete, he was awarded the Knight's Cross. This would be followed by the award of both Oakleaves, then Swords, whilst commanding 1st Paratroop Division in three of the battles for Cassino. His last appointment was as commander of XI Paratroop Corps as a *General der Fallschirmtruppe*, in which role he would oversee his corps' withdrawal from Italy and be awarded the German Cross in Gold. Captured by the Americans on 2 May 1945 he was later handed over to the British, but died in hospital in Hamburg-Bergedorf on 23 December 1947.

Commander of 5th Mountain Division was *Generalleutnant* Julius Ringel, who was affectionately known as 'Papa', and who had formed the division in the autumn of 1940, from 100th Mountain Infantry Regiment of 1st Mountain Division, together with elements of the 85th Infantry Regiment of 10th Infantry Division. Like Ringel, who was an Austrian Nazi before the *Anschluss*, the men of the division were recruited from hardy Bavarian and Austrian mountain stock. After fighting in the Balkans and Greece, the formation had come to prominence when supporting 7th Airborne Division in the taking of Crete, Ringel becoming commander of the island for a while afterwards. After spending some time in 1941–42 on occupation duties in Norway, 5th

Above: Standing talking to a seated *Generalfeldmarschall* Albert Kesselring, is *Generalleutnant* Richard Heidrich, brilliant and highly decorated commander of the tough 1st Paratroop Division during the final three battles for the monastery. *(Bundesarchiv 146/1971/017/12)*

Mountain Division was sent to Russia, where it was engaged in heavy fighting (including in the siege of Leningrad), before being sent to Italy in December 1943. It relieved 305th Infantry Division just before the first battle of Cassino. As we will see, its subsequent battles with General Juin's French Expeditionary Force came as a considerable shock in the bitter winter weather of the high Italian mountains.

The 29th Panzer Grenadier Division was commanded by *Generalmajor* Walter Fries, whom Kesselring described as being one of his most able divisional commanders. The division had an outstanding record in Russia, where for example, on 12 January 1943, even when it was surrounded and almost destroyed, it repulsed some 10 Soviet divisions and knocked out 100 tanks in a single day. The re-formed 29th Panzer Grenadier Division fought first in Sicily and took part in all the major campaigns in Italy.

The 94th Infantry Division was commanded by *Generalmajor* Bernhard Steinmetz from early January 1944. It was listed initially by Tenth Army as being inexperienced and poorly trained; nevertheless, it fought through all the major campaigns in Italy and was taken out of the line only once, briefly, in the summer of 1944, when it had to give up many of its personnel to 305th Infantry Division and simultaneously received a large number of replacements from Infantry Division *Schlesien*. It survived almost to the bitter end in Italy, being down to under 2,600 all ranks by early 1945 when it was overrun by Fifth Army's spring offensive.

The 44th Infantry Division was the second 44th to be formed, the original having been cut off in Stalingrad with Paulus' army. Recruited in Austria in 1943, the second 44th was given the honorary title *Hoch und Deutschmeister* ('High and Mighty'), having been built around 134th *Hoch und Deutschmeister* Regiment, the successor regiment of one of the elite units of the old Austro-Hungarian Army. Its commander was *Generalleutnant* Dr Fritz Franek, who had, according to one source quoted by John Ellis in

Above: The first senior German commander responsible for the defence of Cassino and the monastery was *Generalmajor* Ernst Baade, one of von Vietinghoff's most trusted subordinates, who commanded 90th Panzer Grenadier Division. *(Bundesarchiv 101/1315/1110/14)*

Above: German Luftwaffe infantrymen improving their positions. They wear the Model 1935 or 1942 steel helmets rather than the older 1917 model. Note the Luftwaffe national emblem on the left side of the nearest man's helmet; a shield containing the German national colours was on the right. *(IWM MH 6366)*

his brilliant *Cassino, the Hollow Victory*, '. . . not been fortunate in his choice of regimental commanders . . . The division was also woefully under strength, built around a reserve of young battalion commanders who led their units, each of which was only 100 men strong, more or less like combined-arms combat patrols.'

The 71st Infantry Division, commanded throughout its existence by *Generalleutnant* Wilhelm Raapke was another second division, the original one having been destroyed in the Stalingrad pocket. Re-formed in Denmark in 1943, it crossed to Italy during the autumn of that year. After fighting for much of the Italian campaign it was transferred to the southern sector of the Eastern Front.

The Paratroop Panzer Division *Hermann Göring*, which was actually part of the Luftwaffe, was an all-volunteer force (foreigners and *Volksdeutsch* — ethnic Germans brought back to the Third Reich from various Balkan countries — were not accepted) and yet another re-formed division. Elements of the original had been sent to Tunisia, where they were destroyed or lost when *Panzer Armee Afrika* surrendered. The rest were sent to Sicily, then reconstituted in Italy under *Generalleutnant* Paul Conrath, under whose leadership the division was responsible for safeguarding the treasures from the monastery on Monte Cassino. They were rushed to counter-attack the Anzio landings and succeeded in slowing up the Allied advance on Rome.

The 15th Panzer Grenadier Division was commanded by *Generalleutnant* Eberhard Rodt. (General Baade who later commanded 90th Panzer Grenadier Division was in command temporarily in Sicily). It was formed in Sicily from the remnants of 15th Panzer Division which had escaped from Tunisia. It fought well and again at Salerno, earning high praise from the corps

commander, and in the main Italian battles from October 1943 until March 1944, when it was placed in reserve. A special company of the division was deployed to man several Panther tank turrets embedded in concrete emplacements near Aquino.

The Defences

'In contrast to all other German theatres of war, full use of the construction of positions was made by the military command in Italy; it was fully supported by Hitler and the OKW.

'The construction of positions was carried out by command agencies, engineers and labour organisations with a great feeling for the situation and with a hardly surpassable zest. The eventual condition of the improvements is best proof of this.

'It is to be regretted that the defensive installations in depth of the entire area were not made use of tactically in a manner corresponding to the idea at the back of the whole system. It is inconceivable why Hitler did not permit the employment of delaying tactics after having helped, in a model manner, to create the necessary preconditions.

'Kesselring
'8 August 1948'

Above: German troops in one of the ruined buildings on Monte Cassino. Note in particular the opened box of hand grenades — stick grenades — Stielhandgranate 24 — each of which weighed just over 1.3lb and had a 4.5-second delay fuse. *(Bundesarchiv 101/578/1926/3a)*

This statement formed the concluding remarks to a paper written by Kesselring entitled 'The Construction of Positions in the Italian Theatre of War, After the Withdrawal of Royalist Italy from the Axis Alliance'. In it Kesselring commented that although German military traditions had given due weight to the construction of fortifications, under the aegis of Adolf Hitler no rear positions were built either in the East or West, presumably because the *Führer* was afraid that they would have a detrimental influence upon his principle of fighting for every inch of ground, which he preached and ordered continuously. He did not have the same attitude towards coastal defences — *vide* the great amount of effort put in on the Atlantic Wall.[5] No amount of work done in this connection was sufficient to satisfy him, although even then he stressed the linear nature of the construction and entirely disregarded any improvements in depth: '. . . clear evidence,' comments Kesselring, 'of the basically wrong idea of obstinately sticking to every inch of ground'.

Despite this critical comment, he went on to say that after the Allied landings at Salerno, when he decided to go over from delaying actions along a narrow sector to defence of the Apennine peninsula between Naples and Rome and had given the necessary orders to this effect, he was met with '. . . the most far reaching moral support from both Hitler and the OKW'. This was the main reason why he was able to build up the Reinhard Line and the Gustav Line of which the Cassino positions were the lynch-pin, together with the necessary advanced positions already described. The support from the OKW consisted mainly of the speedy transfer of engineering staffs and troops, together with work battalions, construction machinery and building materials. We will go into

more detail on the Gustav Line as far as it affected Cassino later, but it is worth while first to continue to examine Kesselring's treatise:

'In spite of the good improvements and natural strength of the Cassino front, and the already proven power of resistance of this position, I considered it of the utmost importance that it be extended in depth by building switch lines and rear positions and, in addition to the work begun on the "Senger Switch Line" etc., I requested additional resources in personnel and supplies. In authorising my request Adolf Hitler even exceeded the size of my demands, which were by no means modest and ordered that fortified improvements be constructed along the Senger Switch Line and the adjacent positions. In addition to labour, concrete, etc., a large number of tank turrets (mainly Panther tank turrets) for shelters and anti-tank guns were assigned. The latter, being emplaced flush with the ground and disappearing into the terrain entirely, were meant to close off the natural depression completely to prevent a breakthrough to Rome via Frosinone. The position actually possessed extraordinary strength; in this connection, the weak points of the valley position and those of the adjacent slopes and forest positions must not be forgotten.

'Soon after that I ordered the reconnoitring of a position south of Rome, extending up to the Adriatic, which was improved as the "C Position" . . .

'This position was the second point of concentration for construction work assigned to the armies; for carrying out this work special engineer staffs and Italian and Czech labour

detachments, as well as a sufficient number of civilians, were at their disposal. After the landing of Allied forces at Anzio, completion of this work was speeded up; once or twice I also inspected it.'

After mentioning the parallel construction of coastal defences and the protection of such facilities as naval bases, Kesselring explained that all of this required the involvement of considerable numbers of personnel from the *Organisation Todt* (OT) labour service. The OT then employed Italian construction units, firms and workers. After then outlining the difficulties which the Apennine mountains presented for the establishment of a connected line and improvement of the position, as well as the problems of procuring qualified labour and the bringing of materials up to the building sites in the mountains, he summed up by saying that:

'All forces which could be made available in the vicinity of the front and in the depth of the combat zone as well as in the endangered coastal areas, were strained to the utmost and everything possible was done in order to render combat conditions favourable, to provide sufficient flank security and to prepare covering positions which would serve as barriers in case of an unavoidable withdrawal . . . In spite of reconnoitring the positions and supervising their improvement by special, selected reconnaissance parties made up of experienced officers from all arms of the service, the course taken by the line did not always correspond to the desires of the troops. I therefore came to the conclusion that even the best-selected line never corresponds to the wishes of the occupying troops in all respects; hence, it is advisable to give the troops an opportunity to give it the finishing touches.'

Kesselring went on to list the following advantages and disadvantages which undoubtedly applied to the positions in and around Cassino:

'a. Advantages
'(i) It was by no means easy for the enemy to locate from the air the positions actually occupied; the enemy always had to be prepared for surprises. As a consequence, the slow feeling forward of the enemy offered the German troops a saving of time which in many cases was of very great value.
'(ii) Whenever our troops arrived, they found a prepared position that they only had to alter slightly to suit their own tastes. On account of this fact, many of the disadvantages listed below, could be compensated for to a certain extent.
'(iii) The troops were not compelled to accept a decisive battle in a less favourable position, but could move on without any great risk, to where combat conditions were more favourable.

'b. Disadvantages
'(i) Such large-scale construction operations demanded much personnel and supplies; there was always a great risk that, on account of doing so many things, the means would be spent uneconomically and as a result no perfect work would be done anywhere.
'(ii) The positions needed constant supervision; this was most suitably done by having them occupied by a security detachment, even if it had to be a weak one. Only thus was

Above: Yet another machine-gun nest within the ruins. The paratroopers made the fullest use of the bombed buildings to deny the area to the Allies. The man with the MG 42 wears a pair of mountain boots with heavy-duty leather soles that were hobbed and had cleats around their edge. *(IWM MH 6352)*

there any guarantee that the installations would remain fit for defence, could be turned over to the occupying troops complete in every respect and adequately supplied and could be secured against enemy surprise raids. A lack of troops and deficiencies in organisation prevented the complete execution of these measures.'

He also listed the following principles as being of decisive importance to such positions:

- Camouflage and a field of fire from flanking installations as far as possible.
- Natural anti-tank obstacles, supplemented by artificial obstacles (anti-tank ditches, steep walls, swamping, etc.) throughout the depth of the fortified zone.
- Building separated protected shelters and firing positions.
- Camouflaged and if possible covered communication trenches (approach trenches) from the rear to the advanced and lateral positions.

With typical German efficiency not only was the organisation of defensive lines standardised in principle and then adapted to fit the particular situation, but also the various types of individual field works were standardised, making their construction considerably easier as the quantities of basic commodities (concrete, rod steel, sheet steel, timber, sandbags and much more) had already been calculated, whilst construction plans for most types of fortifications had already been produced.[4]

The Gustav Line

The main line of resistance was undoubtedly the Gustav Line. This stretched from the Gulf of Gaeta in the west, along the Garigliano, Gari and Rapido rivers to Cassino, and thence from the Monte Cassino promontory, over the Apennines to the Adriatic Sea in the east. Work had begun on this line on 10 November 1943 and five days later, General Westphal (Kesselring's chief of staff) had attended a meeting arranged by the *Führer* that was also attended by Generals Jodl and Warlimont of the OKW. At the meeting all three had stressed the need to hold the Winter Line for as long as possible so as to allow more time to complete the Gustav Line positions.

In the event the Gustav Line would be strong enough to hold up the Allies for nearly six months, a staggering one-third of the entire Italian campaign. As one historian later wrote:

'Here the Germans had blasted and dug weapon pits, built concrete bunkers and steel-turreted machine-gun emplacements, strung bands of barbed wire and planted minefields — making lavish use of the box mine, which was difficult to detect because it had almost no metallic parts — to block the few natural avenues of advance. They had sited mortars on reverse slopes and placed automatic weapons to cover the forward slopes. In the town of Cassino they had strengthened the walls of the stone buildings with sandbags to protect weapons crews.'[6]

Kesselring appointed one *Oberst* von Corvin as town commandant of Cassino during the third week of November and promised him a

Above: A squad of paratroopers manhandles a 3.7cm Pak 35/36 L/45 anti-tank gun to a new position. It was the most widely encountered German anti-tank gun of the war. *(Bundesarchiv 101/579/1968/18)*

Right: In position near Cassino was this 2cm Flak 30 light anti-aircraft gun. Presumably the notation on the gun-shield signifies five kills — which sounds like very good shooting for such a small calibre weapon. Taken in March 1944. *(IWM MH 6355)*

workforce of some 45,000 OT workers. Von Corvin evacuated the entire civilian population of Cassino, moved the Todt workers in and worked them around the clock. Various buildings were selected as key strongpoints — such as the railway station and the Continental Hotel — the buildings in their vicinity being demolished so that the defenders would have a clear field of fire in all directions. Steel emplacements for tanks were installed on the ground floors, whilst the cellar walls were heavily strengthened and a series of steel pillboxes built around the outskirts of the town. In addition, both in the town and along the Gustav Line positions, there were countless snipers' posts and a considerable number of well-protected mortar emplacements, the latter located in deep gullies or behind rock shelves, well camouflaged and protected with logs and sandbags.

The peaks above Cassino town gave the defenders almost perfect observation of the advancing Allied forces, in particular, the one on which perched the Benedictine Abbey of Monte Cassino dominated everything for miles around. American historian Martin Blumenson in his official history described it as looking southwards with a:

'. . . hypnotic gaze, all seeing, like the eyes in a painting that follow the spectator wherever he moves. To the Allied soldiers on the plain below, the glistening white abbey on the peak watched them with German eyes from which there was no concealment.'[7]

Initially of course this was not in fact strictly true because, as we shall see, the German authorities placed the abbey 'off limits' and made certain that this ban was strictly observed. This would alter after the bombing; however, from the outset, the rest of the hillsides were fair game, so the defenders pulled down all the outlying buildings in order to open up fields of fire and view for observation posts and crew-served weapons. They also established at least one ammunition dump in a cave very close to the monastery outer wall.

The German defensive positions were thus based on a series of locations within the rocky mountains of the Apennines, organised in defended localities and strongpoints. In the Cassino area there were three 'defensive bastions': Monte Cassino, surmounted by the Monastery; Hill 593; and Colle Sant'Angelo. Dominating them all was Monte Cairo (over 1,600m/5,350ft high). This is how Colonel H. Piatkowski of II Polish Corps described the reasons for the success of these German positions, in an article in the *Army Quarterly* of October 1945:

'The real strength of these mountain positions lies in the protection which the gun crews are afforded in these shelters on the reverse slopes of sharp, rocky walls. Caves are used for this purpose or else shelters are dug into the rocks. Concealed in these shelters, the gun crews are immune from artillery or mortar fire. Shells either hit the rocky wall, in which case a thickness of several feet protects the crew against even the heaviest calibres, or they go over the top of the wall and fall over the precipice far to the rear of the defenders. As soon as the artillery ceases, because either the attacking infantry is approaching for the assault or the security margin does not allow firing to continue, the enemy detachments need only to come out of their hideouts, occupy positions in bunkers or simply behind rocks, and they are ready for action.
Unhindered by artillery fire and supported by their own weapons of defence, they can open fire at point blank range on the exhausted assault troops.'

Undoubtedly in such conditions, the advantages were clearly with the defence and made the attacking of such positions an extremely difficult and hazardous undertaking, especially in the atrocious weather conditions experienced in the winter in the Apennines.

Overall Defensive Aim

The main aim of the German defenders in Italy was to fight a slow withdrawal action in which they could use their resources as economically as possible, whilst inflicting maximum delay and casualties on the Allies. Hence they made use of static defensive lines, which was not a normal German tactic, although they were always prepared to employ defensive works so as to enable a relatively smaller force to defend a position than would otherwise be required. Troops were taught that fortifications existed principally not for their personal safety but rather to enable them to fight more effectively. Between the defensive lines their tactics were characterised by strong rearguard actions, with routes forward being barred by well-placed and tactically laid demolitions, invariably covered by long range machine-gun and artillery fire. Such

Below: A 7.5cm Sturmgeschütz 40 Ausf F assault gun moves into position near Cassino. (IWM MH 6376)

Above: Swollen streams did not make the movement of larger weapons any the easier for either side. This soldier is attempting the impossible if he is trying to move this massive 8.8cm AA/anti-tank gun all by himself. *(IWM MH 1904)*

Above: Some of the 150 Germans taken prisoner by the New Zealand tanks and infantry in Cassino on 19 March 1944. *(IWM NA 13089)*

Above: Wounded German soldiers being assisted out of the battle area by British medics, 18 May 1944. Both sides helped each other's wounded on many occasions. *(IWM NA 14986)*

rearguards would hold on to ground tenaciously, but then slip away when faced by superior forces. As we shall see, this was achieved even at Cassino: despite everything the attackers did to close with the Germans, many of the paratroopers who had defended the monastery so bravely were able to escape and thus live to fight another day.

From the Other Side of the Hill

One of the commanders in the Allied armies who had most experience of hill fighting was General Tuker of 4th Indian Division. He had this to say about the German defences:

'German accounts crack up their own troops enormously for their defence in Italy and they exaggerate the difficulties of the defence and minimise its advantages, while exaggerating the advantage in the equipment of the attacker and minimising his difficulties. In the mountains the business of the defender is to curb the mobility of the attacker so that he cannot penetrate by the flank and cut off the defending fortresses or positions. In [Tuker's book] *Approach to Battle* I put mobility before the use of fire in all theatres of operation. It is especially so in the mountains because shellfire is very ineffectual in the rocks and bursts are very localised. Because of the ineffectual shell, no doubt we had to go to the bomb which came in from a steep angle. However, it is really an administrative matter, this mountain fighting . . . To hold mountain areas one constructs fortresses with all-round defence. For weeks the Todt organisation was working expertly on the buildings of the Gustav Line and

certainly round Cassino it was a fully fledged fortress by the time the Fifth Army met it. In all those weeks of construction the Germans were able to ferry up, day by day and night by night, such useful stores as hand grenades, mines and wire in quantity and any amount of small arms ammunition and mortar shells. They could place ammunition in protective caves and dugouts, ready to hand for battle. A typical example of the result is when the Royal Sussex attacked Point 593 [*see Chapter 5*], took it and probably lost it because they ran out of hand grenades. The 4th Indian Division had only at most two or three days to prepare itself for any fight up there on the hill, so it is hardly to be wondered at that the German infantry defenders should keep their hand grenades going steadily and in ample supply from the nearby dugouts while our Sussex men should run out of theirs, when every grenade had to be brought up by hand with the pack mule or the porter under observation and under fire from the Monte Cassino area right from the bottom of the valley up to the point of delivery of the grenade. What wonder that the German bombs lasted out and ours fell short? This was the case all along the line because the time allotted for preparation for battle was far too short and because, instead of being permitted in a fairly peaceful area and period as had been the case with the building and preparation of the German defences, everything had been done against time and in the open. Furthermore, it has to be remembered that the attacker usually needs somewhere about five to one at the point of attack in the way of both men and material. Both the superiority of men and material has to be brought up to the site where it is to be used and has to be maintained there up to the time of the battle and right through the battle. The Germans had all these advantages and, while I admire the manner in which the paratroopers, say, in Cassino town stood up to the intense and prolonged bombing, and while I admire the tenacity of the German defence, I insist that pretty nearly every advantage was on their side and, in particular, the advantage of being able to get to ready-made cover, ready-dug caves and dugouts for shelter in that bitter climate, gave them a very marked advantage.'[8]

Notes
1. Rudolf Böhmler, *Monte Cassino*.
2. Teleprint dated 28 January 1944 to CinC SW (FM Kesselring) as quoted from *Hitler's War Directives*.
3. From reminiscences kindly supplied by Richard Doherty, historian of County Londonderry.
4. The 15cm Nebelwerfer 41 was a simple six-barrelled field artillery rocket launcher which went into widespread usage in 1942. The 21cm Nebelwerfer 42, which entered service a year later, had only five barrels, but the whole equipment was virtually the same as the 15cm (same carriage, towing vehicle, sights and four-man crew). Both were known as 'Moaning Minnies' because of their distinctive droning sound in flight. Maximum range of the 21cm rocket was 9,150m.
5. See George Forty, *Fortress Europe, Hitler's Atlantic Wall*, published by Ian Allan in 2002.
6. See Chapter 5, 'The Types of Defensive Structures', in *Fortress Europe, Hitler's Atlantic Wall* for further details.
7. Martin Blumenson, *US Army in World War II, The Mediterranean Theater of Operations, Salerno to Cassino*.
8. Extract from General Sir Francis Tuker's, '4th Indian Division at Cassino', held by the Gurkha Museum.

The First Battle (The Prelude Battle):
12 January–12 February 1944

'Stalemate, then, on the Eighth Army front, the Fifth Army poised for action and Rome only 80 miles away. A mountain barrier bristling with every type of offensive weapon, swollen rivers to cross, glutinous mud to bog down men and machines, sullen grey skies pouring down torrents of cold, saturating, demoralizing rain. Such was the background against which the opening moves of the battle for Cassino were made.'[1]

Below: Map showing 5th Army front, 6 February 1944.

Allied and German Orders of Battle for the First Battle

At the end of the opening chapter I outlined Alexander's orders and Mark Clark's resulting plan of attack for the opening onslaught against the Gustav Line. Within the area concerned, the Allies had some seven divisions now operational — (two US, three British and two French), with two more about to embark for the amphibious landing at Anzio. On the German side there were five divisions defending their formidable Gustav Line positions. Before dealing with the first battle, here is the Allied Order of Battle, then the German one.

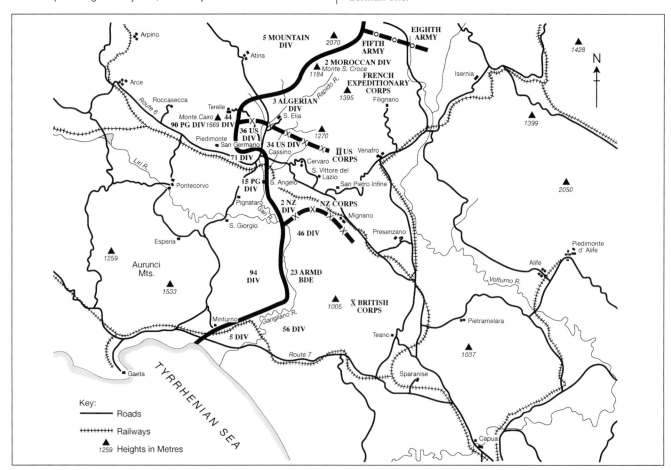

Allied Orders of Battle

15th Army Group *General Sir Harold Alexander*

US Fifth Army *Lieutenant General Mark Clark*[1]

US II Corps *Major General G. Keyes*

Corps Troops
  1108th Combat Engineer Group
  235th Combat Engineer Battalion

34th US Infantry Division *Major General C. W. Ryder*
Asst Comd: Brigadier General F. Butler

  Divisional Troops
    734th Ordnance Light Maintenance Company
    34th Quartermaster Company
    34th Signal Company
    34th Cavalry Reconnaissance Troop, Mechanized
    109th Engineer Battalion
    109th Medical Battalion

  34th Division Artillery
    185th Field Artillery Battalion (155mm howitzer)
    125th, 151st & 175th Field Artillery Battalions
    (all 105mm howitzer)

  133rd Infantry Regiment
    1st, 3rd & 100th Battalions

  135th Infantry Regiment
    1st, 2nd & 3rd Battalions

  168th Infantry Regiment
    1st, 2nd & 3rd Battalions

36th (Texas) US Infantry Division *Major General F. L. Walker*
Asst Comd: Brigadier General W. Wilbur

  Divisional Troops
    736th Ordnance Light Maintenance Company
    36th Quartermaster Company
    36th Signal Company
    2nd Chemical Battalion
    36th Cavalry Reconnaissance Troop, Mechanized
    111th Engineer Battalion, plus two companies
    16th Armored Engineer Battalion
    111th Medical Battalion

  36th Division Artillery
    155th Field Artillery Battalion (155mm howitzer)
    131st, 132nd & 133rd Field Artillery Battalions
    (all 105mm howitzer)

  141st Infantry Regiment
    1st, 2nd & 3rd Battalions

  142nd Infantry Regiment
    1st, 2nd & 3rd Battalions

  143rd Infantry Regiment
    1st, 2nd & 3rd Battalions

In Support of 34th and 36th Infantry Divisions

Combat Command B, 1st US Armored Division[2]
Brigadier General F. Allen, Jnr.

  Task Force A
    13th Armored Regiment
    636th Tank Destroyer Battalion
    16th Engineer Battalion
    6617th Engineer Mine Clearing Co

  Task Force 'B'
    1st Tank Group
    (753rd Tank Battalion, part of 760th Tank Battalion,
    and 776th Tank Destroyer Battalion)
    one company of 48th Engineer Battalion
    one troop of 91st Reconnaissance Squadron

X British Corps *Lieutenant-General Sir Richard McCreery*

Corps Troops
    King's Dragoon Guards
    57th Anti-tank Regiment, RA
    571st, 572nd, 573rd, 228th Field Companies, RE
    570th Field Park Company, RE
    22nd Mechanical Equipment Section, RE

5th British Infantry Division[3]
Major-General G. Bucknall to 22 January 1944
Major-General P. G. S. Gregson-Ellis

  Divisional Troops
    7th Battalion, Cheshire Regiment (machine-gun battalion)
    91st, 92nd & 156th Field Regiments, RA
    (each 24 x 25-pounder)
    52nd Anti-Tank Regiment, RA (12 x 17-pounder
    & 36 x 6-pounder)
    5th Reconnaissance Regiment
    245th, 252nd & 38th Field Companies, RE
    254th Field Park Company, RE

  13th Infantry Brigade
    2nd Battalion, Wiltshire Regiment
    2nd Battalion, Cameronians
    2nd Battalion, Royal Inniskilling Fusiliers

  15th Infantry Brigade
    1st Battalion, King's Own Yorkshire Light Infantry
    1st Battalion, Green Howards
    1st Battalion, York and Lancaster Regiment

  17th Infantry Brigade
    6th Battalion, Seaforth Highlanders
    2nd Battalion, Northamptonshire Regiment
    2nd Battalion, Royal Scots Fusiliers

56th British (London) Infantry Division
Major-General G. Templer

Divisional Troops
6th Battalion, Cheshire Regiment (machine-gun battalion)

64th, 65th & 113th Field Regiments, RA
(each 24 x 25-pounder)

67th Anti-Tank Regiment, RA (12 x 17-pounder
& 36 x 6-pounder)

100th Light Anti-Aircraft Regiment, RA (54 x 40mm)

44th Reconnaissance Regiment

167th Infantry Brigade
8th Battalion, Royal Fusiliers

9th Battalion, Royal Fusiliers

7th Battalion, Oxfordshire & Buckinghamshire Light Infantry

168th Infantry Brigade
10th Battalion, Royal Berkshire Regiment

1st Battalion, London Scottish

1st Battalion, London Irish Rifles

169th Infantry (Queen's) Brigade
2nd/5th Battalion, Queen's Royal Regiment

2nd/6th Battalion, Queen's Royal Regiment

2nd/7th Battalion, Queen's Royal Regiment

46th British Infantry Division *Major-General J. Hawkesworth*

Divisional Troops
2nd Battalion, Royal Northumberland Fusiliers
(machine-gun battalion)

70th, 71st & 172nd Field Regiments, RA
(each 24 x 25-pounder)

58th Anti-Tank Regiment, RA (12 x 17-pounder
& 36 x 6-pounder)

115th Light Anti-Aircraft Regiment, RA (54 x 40mm)

46th Reconnaissance Regiment

270th & 271st Field Companies, RE

272nd Field Park Company, RE

128th (Hampshire) Infantry Brigade
1st/4th Battalion, Hampshire Regiment

2nd Battalion, Hampshire Regiment

5th Battalion, Hampshire Regiment

138th Infantry Brigade
6th Battalion, Lincolnshire Regiment

2nd/4th Battalion, King's Own Yorkshire Light Infantry

6th Battalion, York and Lancaster Regiment

139th Infantry Brigade
2nd/5th Battalion, Leicestershire Regiment

2nd/5th Battalion, Sherwood Foresters
(Nottinghamshire and Derbyshire Regiment)

16th Battalion, Durham Light Infantry

Attached to X Corps for First Battle

201st Guards Infantry Brigade
6th Battalion, Grenadier Guards

3rd Battalion, Coldstream Guards

2nd Battalion, Scots Guards

Attached to 46th Infantry Division from 6 February 1944

1st Guards Infantry Brigade (from 6th Armoured Division)
3rd Battalion, Grenadier Guards

2nd Battalion, Coldstream Guards

3rd Battalion, Welsh Guards

French Expeditionary Corps *General A. Juin*

Corps Troops
Tank Group
7th & 8th Tank Destroyer Battalions

Engineer Group
201st & 202nd Pioneer Regiments and 180th Engineer
Battalion

Field Artillery
Levant Colonial Artillery Regiment (155mm gun)

64th Algerian Artillery Regiment (3 battalions x 105mm
howitzer & 1 naval battery 155-mm gun)

Anti-Aircraft Artillery
32nd, 34th & 40 Anti-Aircraft Weapons Battalions

Medical
401st, 405th & 415th Evacuation Hospitals

422nd & 425th Field Hospitals

1st, 2nd & 3rd Mobile Surgical Teams

531st Ambulance Company
541st & 542nd Veterinary Ambulance Companies

2nd Moroccan Infantry Division *Brigadier General A. Dody*

Divisional Troops
3rd Spahi (Moroccan) Reconnaissance Battalion

41st Anti-Aircraft Automatic Weapons Battalion

87th Engineer Battalion

63rd Algerian Artillery Regiment (3 battalions 105-mm
howitzer, 1 battalion 155-mm howitzer)

Regimental Groups
4th Moroccan Tirailleur Regiment

5th Moroccan Tirailleur Regiment

8th Moroccan Tirailleur Regiment

4th Moroccan Tabor Group (attached)

3rd Algerian Infantry Division *Major General Monsabert*

Divisional Troops
3rd Spahi (Algerian) Reconnaissance Battalion

37th Anti-Aircraft Automatic Weapons Battalion

83rd Engineer Battalion

67th Algerian Artillery Regiment (3 battalions 105-mm
howitzer, 1 battalion 155-mm howitzer)

Regimental Groups

3rd Algerian Tirailleur Regiment

4th Tunisian Tirailleur Regiment

7th Algerian Tirailleur Regiment

3rd Moroccan Tabor Group (attached)

Notes

1. VI US Corps which comprised 3rd US Infantry Division, 45th US Infantry Division, 1st British Infantry Division and 1st Special Service Force, was also part of US Fifth Army, but was used at Anzio, rather than taking part in operations against the Gustav Line.
2. The rest of 1st US Armored Division (basically CCA) was used at Anzio.
3. Principal reinforcements to Anzio up to April 1944 were 5th (British) Infantry Division and 56th (British) Infantry Division, then later in May: 34th US Infantry Division, 36th US Infantry Division and CC B, 1st US Armored Division.

German Forces

Tenth Army *Generaloberst Heinrich von Vietinghoff*

XIV Panzer Corps
General der Panzertruppe Fridolin von Senger und Etterlin

5th Mountain Division *Generalleutnant Julius Ringel*

85th Mountain Regiment

100th Mountain Regiment

95th Mountain Artillery Regiment

95th Anti-Tank Battalion

95th Reconnaissance Battalion

95th Engineer Battalion

44th Infantry Division *Generalleutnant Fritz Franek*
(Reichsgrenadier Division Hoch und Deutschmeister)

131st Grenadier Regiment

132nd Grenadier Regiment

134th Grenadier Regiment

44th Reconnaissance Battalion

96th Artillery Regiment

46th Anti-Tank Battalion

80th Engineer Battalion

64th Signals Battalion

15th Panzer Grenadier Division
Generalleutnant Eberhard Rodt

104th Panzer Grenadier Regiment

115th Panzer Grenadier Regiment

129th Panzer Grenadier Regiment

115th Panzer Battalion (assault gun)

33rd Artillery Regiment

115th Anti-Tank Battalion

115th Engineer Battalion

115th Signals Battalion

94th Infantry Division *Generalleutnant Bernhard Steinmetz*

267th Grenadier Regiment

274th Grenadier Regiment

276th Grenadier Regiment

194th Artillery Regiment

194th Anti-Tank Battalion

194th Reconnaissance Battalion

71st Infantry Division *Generalleutnant Wilhelm Raapke*

191st Grenadier Regiment

194th Grenadier Regiment

211th Grenadier Regiment

171st Reconnaissance Battalion

171st Artillery Regiment

171st Anti-Tank Battalion

171st Engineer Battalion

171st Signals Battalion

In Reserve

29th Panzer Grenadier Division *Generalleutnant Walter Fries*

15th Panzer Grenadier Regiment

71st Panzer Grenadier Regiment

129th Panzer Battalion (assault gun)

29th Artillery Regiment

129th Reconnaissance Battalion

29th Anti-Tank Battalion

29th Engineer Battalion

29th Signals Battalion

90th Panzer Grenadier Division
Generalleutnant Ernst-Günther Baade

155th Panzer Grenadier Regiment

200th Panzer Grenadier Regiment

361st Panzer Grenadier Regiment

190th Panzer Battalion (assault gun)

190th Artillery Regiment

190th Anti-Tank Battalion

190th Engineer Battalion

190th Signals Battalion

Hermann Göring Paratroop Panzer Division (part)
Generalleutnant Paul Conrath

Schultz Battle Group

1st Paratroop Regiment

3rd Battalion of 3rd Paratroop Regiment

1st Paratroop machine-gun battalion

(This last formation was nicknamed the: 'Feuerwehr' ('Fire Brigade') but was not used until the Second Battle – see next chapter)

Above: Their striped burnouses and sandals gave this Goum patrol a slightly comical appearance — but there was nothing comical about the way these rugged men from the Atlas Mountains fought. They already had a fearsome reputation that they justified immediately, despite being up against crack German mountain troops. *(IWM NA 13758)*

The French Attack

Generalleutnant Julius 'Papa' Ringel's 5th Mountain Division formed the left flank of the German force opposing the new Allied attack. Despite its high reputation, it had suffered considerable casualties in Russia, so many of Ringel's troops now serving in Italy were young and relatively inexperienced replacements who, like so many others on both sides, were too swift to discount General Juin's virtually untried CEF which was now opposite them on the right flank of the Fifth Army front. The CEF, on the other hand, quickly proved its expertise in mountain warfare, leading off the assault on 12 January, along a wide axis of advance, with the Moroccans in the north and the Algerians in the south, roughly between San Blagio in the north and Sant'Elia in the south, with the aim of seizing Atina and the high ground to the north and north-west of Cassino. The Moroccans were facing the 85th Mountain Regiment, supported by 115th Panzer Grenadier Regiment of 15th Panzer Grenadier Division, whilst facing the Algerians was 100th Mountain Regiment.

The 85th Mountain Regiment did not make a particularly good start against the French colonial troops and was to suffer both sharp reverses and heavy casualties. As Rudolf Böhmler wrote in his book *Monte Cassino*:

'The French Corps was ideally suited for the conditions in the Italian theatre of war. The tough, North African hillmen were always a thorn in the flesh of the German divisions and frequently caused Field Marshal Kesselring very grave anxiety.'

General von Senger also remembered Juin as being a formidable enemy and said that the direction of his initial offensive could have pierced through the Gustav Line and not met any other defensive lines. Indeed, 'If he reached the Atina Basin he might march unhindered to Rome, thereby unhinging our whole defensive system.'

'If you can get to the Rapido by the 20th of January, then you will have rendered me a great service.'
Message from Clark to Juin.

Fifth Army's attack began on schedule at 0630 hours on 12 January 1944, with General Dody's 2nd Moroccan Division crossing the start line without any preparatory artillery barrage, thus achieving a considerable degree of surprise that assisted it in the capture of its objective, Monte Casale. The other French division — General de Monsabert's 3rd Algerian — however, was 'less sure of itself' and

Above: Having brought up the rations, ammunition and other items to the front line troops, the mules of the French Expeditionary Corps were used to carry wounded soldiers on the return journey. *(IWM NA 13884)*

Above: The battle area. On the left is the forward slope of Monte Trocchio (taken by the GIs of 168th Infantry Regiment on 15 January 1944) and below it the Liri valley. In the foreground is the Rapido River.
(US Army via Real War Photos)

preferred to precede its initial attack on the commanding peak which dominated the way to its initial southern objective, the village of Sant'Elia, with a short artillery barrage. The German reaction to both these attacks was violent and immediate, both divisions quickly finding themselves engaged in hand-to-hand combat, with the principal weapons used being the bayonet and the hand grenade. Nevertheless, the CEF managed to beat off all the German counter-attacks and to press steadily forward so that, by last light on the 15th, it had made some four miles of hard-fought gains. The Moroccans were now moving up the slopes of Monte Santa Croce to the upper reaches of the Rapido River. They were thus close to some of the main defences of the Gustav Line and had almost achieved their army commander's request. They had also proved their ability to fight in such conditions and that they were prepared to take risks. One of their officers described the reasons for their success:

'The Moroccan loves the night and the mountains. Rocks, thickets and sheer crevasses, all obscured in the treacherous darkness, are his best allies and over a thousand years his eyes have become accustomed to not losing their way in the gloom. He knows when to creep forward and when to wait. He knows also that there is no more fearsome weapon than that ancestral dagger which his forefathers have plunged into sentries' backs since time immemorial. Why, therefore, wake the Germans before the striking of the hour of Baroud? The Germans are brave, but a brave man asleep is like a woman.'[2]

Despite their success, however, the four-day battle had completely exhausted the troops of both these tough divisions and they had, in addition, suffered heavy casualties, including numerous cases of severe frostbite and trench foot, so Juin was forced to call a halt. However, the Germans were equally hard hit. Casualties in the mountain battalions had been extremely heavy, the average battalion now having a fighting strength of under 200; indeed casualties in some units were as high as 80%. It could be said that Juin had gone a long way to securing the right flank for the coming II Corps crossing of the Rapido. He received a congratulatory telegram from Mark Clark, but, as his biographer wryly comments, he would probably have preferred, instead of praise, an extra division to use for the taking of Atina, his main objective, still some way safely behind the Gustav Line positions.

Monte Trocchio

South of the French, on a direct line opposite Cassino and the Liri valley, the II US Corps was mounting a strong attack against Monte Trocchio, last German strongpoint before the Rapido River and only a mile and a half in front of Cassino. This important feature was taken by men of 168th Infantry Regiment of 34th US Infantry Division on 15 January. To the surprise of the assaulting troops, they found that the Germans had withdrawn from their positions, the only defenders left being dead ones — some seemingly frozen alive. The American attack had been made in the face of a heavy concentration of artillery, the Germans having fortified their positions on Monte Trocchio with concrete gun emplacements and numerous strongpoints. Having taken the hill, the GIs advanced and took up positions just to the north of Cassino town. They crossed the river, but made no contact until they were some 300yd beyond the other bank. Heavy defences were then met. Clearly the Germans now occupied their well-prepared Gustav Line defensive positions and from now on progress would be extremely difficult.

X Corps Sector

In the British sector the 46th Infantry Division's task was to cross the Garigliano River near Sant'Ambrogio, just below the confluence of the Gari, Garigliano and Liri rivers, one of the aims being for the division to provide left flank protection for US II Corps' future attack across the Rapido River near Sant'Angelo. The remainder of X Corps — 5th and 56th Divisions — would attack further south, across the nine miles of low-lying marshy ground which lay between Monte Castellucio and the sea. General Bernhard Steinmetz's 94th

Above: This American light tank (an M5 Stuart) named *Deadeye Dick* has apparently met someone even more dead-eyed and has had its turret blown off. *(US Army via Real War Photos)*

Infantry Division was holding the whole of the Garigliano sector, Steinmetz having only recently taken command of this inexperienced division, which would nevertheless fight well in the ensuing action.

The following description gives an excellent impression of the terrain difficulties alone that faced X Corps:

> 'From the mountain valley at Monte Castellucio, the River Garigliano winds and twists across the flat alluvial plain. In winter it ran in places as wide as 30 to 40yd and was everywhere too deep for fording. Its banks in some places were about 15ft high. The flat land on either side was cut by numerous streams and ditches which restricted mechanised movement to a few tracks, whose exits on the enemy side had all been mined. The road bridge at Minturno and the two railway bridges across the river had been demolished. The plain between the river and the hills on the north side was not more than two miles wide and the main German defences were on the hills on either side of Ausente.'[3]

The 94th Division's 194th Reconnaissance Battalion had observation posts on the plain, so close German observation of the entire length of the river was good. It was therefore essential to gain early control over high ground near Minturno and the village of Castelforte, so that support weapons and vehicles could cross the river unimpeded.

It was also essential for any preparatory work to be done without the Germans finding out, so bridging equipment, rafts and assault boats were assembled under cover of darkness, as were supporting artillery batteries and their ammunition dumps. 5th Division would make a silent crossing, with the attached 201st Guards Brigade then exploiting if the crossings were successful. 56th Division had as its objective the hills around Castelforte, with 167th Brigade on the left initially advancing towards Colle Salvatite, whilst 169th Brigade on the right crossed the river in order to gain a bridgehead between Monte Castellucio and Suio.

During the evening of 17 January, X Corps artillery opened concentrated fire on selected targets along the 56th Division front,

then put down a barrage to cover the forward moves of the two brigades. The Germans replied with heavy fire, especially from their mortars, and many of the flimsy assault boats were sunk. However, by the morning all three of the Queen's Regiment battalions of 169th Brigade were across the river, plus some anti-tank guns. By the early evening they had enlarged their bridgehead onto the lower slopes of Monte Valle Martina. The intended ferry site was, however, still under observed fire and amphibious jeeps and assault boats were still the only means of resupply. On the left, 8th Royal Fusiliers of 167th Brigade had crossed near Maiano di Sotto and by first light had reached the slopes of Colle Salvatite. The first supporting tanks got over just before midday, being followed by 7th Oxford and Bucks Light Infantry who advanced to the outskirts of Ventosa. Further down the river, however, near the demolished railway bridge, 9th Royal Fusiliers could make little progress.

Meanwhile, on the 5th Division front, 2nd Wiltshires of 13th Brigade had silently crossed the Garigliano by night, some two miles above the Minturno bridge, then, after a short sharp firefight, managed to reach the village of Tufo. Higher up the river, however, 2nd Inniskillings had lost a number of its assault boats, so was switched to the Wiltshires' crossing area, crossed, and reached the shoulder of the hill east of Tufo. Mines prevented the engineers from bridging the river and the infantry had to withdraw slightly after strong German counter-attacks.

To the left of 13th Brigade, the 6th Seaforth Highlanders and 2nd Northamptonshires of 17th Brigade had also crossed the river successfully, then lost a number of men from mines on the far bank, between the Via Appia (Route 7) and the sea. More minefields — one over a mile in depth — prevented further progress. Nevertheless, by the morning of 18 January, 17th Brigade held a small bridgehead astride Route 7. On the brigade's left flank, part of a 2nd Royal Scots Fusiliers battle group (some infantry, sappers and some anti-tank guns) had tried to land from the sea near Monte

Above: Basutoland troops carrying mortar bombs up to the 2nd/6th Queen's of 56th Infantry Division, 24 January 1944. *(IWM NA 11342)*

d'Argento and was now unfortunately beached south of the river. The rest of the battalion tried to attack Monte d'Argento but was soon bogged down in yet another large minefield, bereft of engineers and 'somewhat disorganised'. Nevertheless Monte d'Argento was taken that night and by the 18th the Fusiliers had reached the railway south of Minturno. General Bucknall of 5th Division then decided that 15th Brigade should follow 13th Brigade and clear the hills around Minturno.

Kesselring had always been worried about the possibility of Allied amphibious landings, along both coastlines, but especially near Rome. He had therefore secured OKW agreement for reinforcements to be sent from France, the Balkans and Germany if this should happen. However, because it would take time for such reinforcements to arrive, he had also kept two divisions (29th and 90th Panzer Grenadier Divisions) under his direct control in the Rome area. Additionally, he also had the *Hermann Göring* Division and a spare corps HQ which he could call upon, as well as being able to demand yet another division from Tenth Army as it was now safely ensconced in the Gustav Line. Finally, *in extremis*, he could extract further divisions from Fourteenth Army in northern Italy. These forces should, he felt, be enough to deal with any Allied seaborne attack. However, X Corps' crossing of the Garigliano on 17 January had somewhat upset his calculations. If the bridgehead were sufficiently enlarged and a breakthrough made into the Liri valley behind Cassino, then the Gustav Line was in grave danger of being outflanked. Von Vietinghoff made no bones about the situation, confirming that if he were to be able to hold the current increased Fifth Army pressure all along the Gustav Line, then he could not be expected to stop the new X Corps advance without more troops. He told Kesselring that he needed at least two more divisions and what about the two divisions that 'Smiling Albert' was holding near Rome? The discussions lasted for some days, but it was soon clear that an Allied breakthrough into the Liri valley would cause irreparable damage, so Kesselring was forced to agree with the Tenth Army commander. Accordingly, he released both the 29th Panzer Grenadiers and the *Hermann Göring* Division, together with I Paratroop Corps HQ. The arrival of these troops on the 19th and 20th undoubtedly prevented X Corps from expanding its Garigliano bridgehead. The downside for the Germans was, of course, that Rome was now left virtually unguarded, whilst this necessary action tied up most of Kesselring's reserves.

During the early hours of 19 January, the first bridge built across the river above Route 7 was damaged by a mine under its ramp, exploding as the first vehicle crossed. It was repaired before first light and the bridge opened to traffic, but it was closed a few hours later by German fire. Nevertheless, despite this setback and the large minefields that seemed to be everywhere, 15th Brigade succeeded in crossing and capturing both Tufo and Minturno. The next day, its reserve battalion (1st York and Lancaster) took Monte Natale.

However, opposite 56th Division, the 94th Division had been reinforced by a battalion from the *Hermann Göring* Division and

Above: Moving forward into action. GIs on their feet and Jeeps are about all that can manage this heavily rutted dirt road. *(US Army via Real War Photos)*

Above: Here an 81mm mortar team is in action near Cassino town. Note the 'acquired' MG 42, presumably for local protection. *(IWM IA 16503)*

Above: Men of Company B, 2nd Chemical Weapons Battalion, moving up some rugged terrain with their 4.2in mortars. Note that the mortar is carried in a small handcart, together with bombs (either HE or smoke). *(US Army via Real War Photos)*

was thus able to prevent all three of the British infantry brigades from making any further progress; indeed they could do little more then hold the ground they had taken. Nearer the coast, 13th and 15th Brigades of 5th Infantry Division were ensconced on the Minturno ridge, but 17th Brigade was fully committed trying to clear the swathes of minefields that covered the coastal plain. This left General McCreery of X Corps with just 201st Guards Brigade to maintain the offensive and exploit his limited successes.

Meanwhile, there were continuing problems on the 46th Division front, as its attack across the Garigliano at Sant'Ambrogio had failed, thick fog and the swift current playing havoc with the assault boats, so that only one company out of the two battalions of 128th Brigade (2nd and 1st/4th Hants) managed to reach the enemy bank. General Clark ordered this intended crossing site to be abandoned, with just 2nd/5th Leicesters of 139th Brigade left to protect the left flank of neighbouring US II Corps. 138th Brigade was then switched from 46th Division to 56th Division to relieve 169th Queen's Brigade and to continue the attack north-west towards Monte Fuga. On the night of 20/21 January, a Bailey bridge was opened to carry Route 7 over the Garigliano, but it could only be used in the dark, whilst the smaller bridge some two miles higher up was still impeded by mines. Other would-be forward movement was also being held up; for example, some of 201st Guards Brigade's supporting artillery was unable to get over onto the German side of the river.

Whilst all this action was taking place, the Germans began a very strong counter-offensive with their two new divisions, plus part of a third division, on 21 January. They launched three heavy attacks: towards Suio, down the road from Castelforte; from the Ausente valley towards SS Cosina e Damiano; and towards Monte Natale. By the following night they had recaptured Natale and some of the hills north of Tufo and Minturno. Stubborn fighting continued all the following day, though no more ground was lost by the Allied

forces and in fact some was retaken. Then, suddenly, the German counter-offensive stopped, the situation having changed drastically, because 60 miles away the Anzio landings were taking place. Kesselring ordered the Tenth Army to transfer all the combat troops that could be spared from the Cassino line together with a corps headquarters. Von Vietinghoff selected the recently arrived HQ I Paratroop Corps, together with 29th Panzer Grenadier Division (less one regiment), 71st Infantry Division and elements of the *Hermann Göring* Division. 90th Panzer Grenadier Division was then moved from the X Corps front to join 44th Infantry Division in the mountains around Cassino.

General McCreery of X Corps was now faced with a dilemma, namely how best to use the initiative that had been suddenly offered to him. Granted, he had to bear in mind that his entire corps was very tired and battle-weary, whilst its casualties had been considerable and it had very few uncommitted reserves. Nevertheless, despite all of this, he was determined to maintain pressure all the way along the corps' nine-mile front. Initially, the right flank was even further denuded and, on 26 January, 46th Division took command of the Suio sector. Then, having established a firm base on the Suio ridge, it mounted an assault with 138th Brigade reinforced by 16th Durham Light Infantry of 139th Brigade, to clear the whole of the Suio valley. The attack was supported by the entire corps artillery and began most successfully, clearing the Suio valley by first light on the 28th. Then, however, the advance began to meet determined opposition and could make little further progress. To the south 56th Division suffered many casualties, yet made no progress against the strong enemy positions between Colle Siola and SS Cosina e Damiano. On 56th Division's southern flank, 5th Division's 17th Brigade recaptured Natale and to their left 201st Guards Brigade took the western slopes of the Trimensuoli ridge, repelling several German counter-attacks.

At this point, on 30 January, X Corps was ordered to provide reinforcements for the Anzio beachhead and accordingly 56th Division's 168th Brigade was despatched. However, General Clark insisted that X Corps should maintain its pressure in order to assist the Anzio forces further. On 6 February, 1st Guards Brigade (from 6th Armoured Division), arrived on loan from Eighth Army and was placed under command of 46th Division, which it was proposed should attack the dominating heights of Monte Maio. However, the news from Anzio worsened, so HQ 56th Division and its two remaining brigades (167th and 169th) were all withdrawn and sent to the beachhead. This further reduction of its strength brought the X Corps offensive to an abrupt end. It also meant that some reallocation of frontage was necessary. 5th Division spread to its right and took over 56th Division's sector, whilst 1st Guards Brigade took over from 138th Brigade in the mountains. From then on until nearly the end of March, the X Corps 'Garigliano Bridgehead' would remain substantially unchanged.

Whilst the X Corps operations had perhaps not been crowned with all the success that had been hoped for, they had still laid the foundations for the coming May operations which would result in the ultimate breaking of the Gustav Line. They had also indirectly helped with the Anzio landings, by keeping German divisions engaged. Indeed General von Senger would write after the war that 'one must in truth concede to the commander of the US Fifth Army that it was the attack by the British X Corps that made it possible to land at Anzio.'

36th Division Crosses the Rapido

At 2000 hours on 20 January, the day on which X Corps had penetrated over the Garigliano as far as Monte Natale, 36th US Infantry Division began its attempt to cross the Rapido in the vicinity of Sant'Angelo. The II Corps plan was for 36th Division to establish a bridgehead from which the tanks of CC B, 1st Armored Division, could sweep into the Liri valley towards Aquino and Piedimonte. 36th Division was to hold one of its regimental combat teams in readiness to accompany CC B in the Liri valley. Meanwhile, 34th Division would 'demonstrate' on the right of the corps area in order to tie down the German forces in the vicinity of Cassino. The Rapido crossing was to be supported by all the organic artillery of the two divisions, plus the fire of all their tanks and tank destroyers, together with the 12 firing battalions of the II Corps artillery. In addition there would be bombing and strafing from XII Air Support Command.

> 'In the zone of the 36th Division — south of Highway 6 — the Rapido River, even at flood stage, was small and unimpressive. Yet it flowed swiftly between nearly vertical banks 3 and 6ft high and anywhere from 25 to 50ft apart. The depth of the water in the river bed varied between 9 and 12ft.'[4]

This then was the water obstacle that faced them, but although it was not as formidable as the Garigliano, it was backed by some very strong enemy positions. The now somewhat battle-scarred village of Sant'Angelo was located at the top of 40ft cliffs, which gave the defenders very good observation over the river, whilst the shattered houses gave cover both from view and from fire for their machine-gun detachments and mortars. And of course the village was just one strongpoint in a systematically prepared defensive system, which now took in an almost continuous belt of slit-trenches, dugouts, machine-gun nests and concrete bunkers. All were protected with liberally sown mines, booby-traps and barbed wire fences, whilst the river banks to their front were also sown with mines on both sides. The assault was an unenviable prospect, especially because of the good German observation positions, in particular from the area of the monastery. Sant'Angelo could perhaps be smoked off but there was little that could be done about the 'all-seeing eyes' on Monte Cassino. Undoubtedly, the troops down in the valley floor of the Rapido felt intimidated psychologically and wished the monastery could be bombed to oblivion. However, General Keyes enjoined all his troops, especially his artillery, to refrain from firing at its sacred walls.

There was undoubtedly a feeling of foreboding among the senior officers responsible for the coming attack. General Walker wrote in his diary on 20 January 1944:

> 'Tonight the 36th Division will attempt to cross the Rapido River opposite Sant'Angelo. Everything has been done that can be done to insure success. We might succeed but I do not see how we can. The mission assigned is poorly timed. The crossing is dominated by heights on both sides of the valley where German artillery observers are ready to bring down heavy artillery concentrations on our men. The river is the principal obstacle of the German main line of resistance. I do not know of a single case in military history where an attempt to cross a river that is incorporated into the main line of resistance has succeeded. So I am prepared for defeat. The mission should never have been assigned to any troops with flanks exposed. Clark sent me his best wishes; said he has worried about our success. I think he is worried over the fact that he made an unwise decision when he gave us the job of crossing the river under such adverse tactical conditions. However, if we get some breaks we may succeed.'[5]

Clearly the only way to have any chance was to make a night crossing, with the Texas Division's 141st and 143rd RCTs attacking to the north and south of Sant'Angelo respectively. On the night of 20/21 January, therefore, and based upon information gained by previous reconnaissance patrols, engineers and infantry struggled through the dark and cold to their crossing sites. All the infantrymen carried at least one extra bandolier of ammunition, so they were weighed down even more than normal before they reached the boat dumps. They were also hindered by a heavy fog that came with the darkness. The engineers cleared the chosen lanes of German mines — which were in some cases quickly re-laid by the alert troops of 15th Panzer Grenadier Division who were manning the defences,[6] so clearing had to be repeated again and again, and even newly marked safe lanes were no guarantee of a trouble-free passage.

XII Air Support Command had flown 188 bombing sorties in the immediate area of the crossing on the 20th with P-40 Kittyhawks and A-20 Havocs striking suspected enemy positions, movements and gun placements. The crossings were also preceded by heavy artillery preparations as already explained. Nevertheless, the attackers were met by tremendous fire both during the crossing and once they had crossed, both regimental combat teams sustaining heavy casualties. One report comments especially on the German use of 'nefarious Nebelwerfer shells, a silent rocket, thrown from multiple mounts, which fell on assembly areas as well as on crossing troops.' As the German fire fell amongst them, the troops scattered for cover, inevitably getting into the minefields which caused even more casualties. Units soon became disorganised, some men being isolated on the far bank. The first attempt at crossing the river had to be abandoned and by the morning of the 21st the remnants of the regimental combat teams were back in their original positions on the home bank. They tried again that morning, but once again

the murderous German fire and the minefields took their toll and there were heavy casualties. Boats[7] and bridges were destroyed; troops were once again isolated on the enemy bank. Finally, no American fire could be heard. Later that night just 40 GIs returned to the east side of the river. The second attack had also failed. A third attempt was proposed, then cancelled at corps level.

In total the 36th Division had paid a terrible price — 1,681 casualties, comprising 143 dead, 663 wounded and 875 missing, and as the division's history sombrely records, 'How many of the missing 875 survived was not to be known for months ahead, if ever.' General Fred Walker, 36th Division's commander, was beside himself with grief: 'My fine division is wrecked,' he wrote in his diary. In his highly critical book about the handling of the Italian campaign *Circles of Hell*, historian Eric Morris gave an even more telling summary:

'Their sacrifice was made all the more poignant when it emerged that the Germans were unaware there had been a major attempt to cross the Rapido. Von Senger paid little heed to the action at the time because it caused no particular anxiety. The American assault was contained and the defenders did not even call for reserves from their own division. It was only after the war and the Congressional Committee of Enquiry that the Germans became aware of the extent of the attack, and the damage they had inflicted.'

Harold L. Bond joined the 36th that night and in his gripping autobiography of that period, *Return to Cassino*, tells how he was

Above and opposite: Men of the 132nd Field Artillery Regiment, 36th US Infantry Division, unpack and stack 105mm shells near Cassino, 17 February 1944. *(US Army via Real War Photos)*

able to piece together over the next day or two what had happened to his regiment during the 'two-night disaster':

'We had plenty of time to talk, for our orders now were simply to stay where we were and hold. As I got to know some of the men they willingly told me everything they could remember . . . The men seemed eager to recount their experiences, as if they were made better by being talked about, as if their dead friends seemed less dead when they lived in their stories. There was, also, the horrible fascination with how this man or that stepped on a mine, or how badly another was wounded, and what finally happened to their lieutenant or their sergeant. The entire attack seemed to have been conceived in haste and improperly planned . . . The men had barely a day to prepare for the assault. All the complicated operations of the division were rushed forward without enough time for anyone to do their job properly. The engineers got mixed up about their orders and left some of the assault boats in the wrong places. The company and battalion assembly areas were in some cases so far back from the river that the men could not help attracting attention as they laboriously carried their heavy equipment and boats through open fields and sparsely wooded forests.'

The list of mistakes went on and on, finally culminating in the accusation that:

> '. . . the Fifth Army had thrown the division headlong into one of the strongest defensive positions the Germans were ever to have in Italy.'

And it could have been even worse, of course, had the third attempt to cross gone ahead, as Walker wrote in his diary:

> 'Yesterday two regiments of this Division were wrecked on the west bank of the Rapido. Thank the Lord, General Keyes finally changed his mind and authorised me to call off the attack of the 142d Infantry which he had directed me to make at 2.30 this morning. I had advised against the 142d making such an attack at the same place where the 141st Infantry had failed and had suffered so many losses. But he insisted that the attack go on. Later, after thinking it over, he called on the phone and authorised me to cancel the attack which I did in a hurry. Thus many lives and a regiment were saved.'[8]

In his diary, General Clark wrote:

> 'In deciding upon that attack some time ago, I knew it would be costly but was impelled to go ahead with the attack in order that I could draw to this front all possible German reserves in order to clear the way for SHINGLE [the Anzio landings]. This was accomplished in a magnificent manner. Some blood had to be spilled on either the land or the SHINGLE front, and I greatly preferred that it be on the Rapido, where we were secure, rather than at Anzio with the sea at our back.'[9]

Having set down his explanation for the tragic events, General Clark makes no further mention of the failed attack, clearly being of the opinion that it could not have been avoided, the need to help the Anzio landings being paramount. The disaster naturally affected Walker more deeply than anyone else, but he eventually convinced himself that those above him were just as responsible — if not more responsible — for what had happened. He commented later:

> 'The great losses of fine young men during the attempts to cross the Rapido to no purpose and in violation of good infantry tactics are very depressing. All chargeable to the stupidity of the higher command.'

What he did not know was that, at the time, several officers from Texas who had met in secret, had come to much the same conclusion and decided that, after the war, they would request the holding of a Congressional investigation of the battle and of General Clark's leadership. This did indeed take place, but Clark was exonerated. As to the GIs who had had to carry out the action, a few days later they asked the Germans for a truce so that they could collect their dead and look for any wounded who might still be alive. This was agreed, and the Germans, anxious to help but not wanting to disclose their positions to close scrutiny, carried the bodies down to the river bank and maintained an amicable atmosphere throughout the desperate hours that followed as the Americans moved the corpses and body parts of their slain across the river for burial.

Success at Anzio?

Whilst 36th Division licked its wounds public attention shifted dramatically from the Garigliano–Rapido front to the coast, where, on 22 January, in the spotlight of massive publicity, British and American troops landed at Anzio and Nettuno, some 60 miles behind the Gustav Line. One leader column trumpeted its excitement:

> 'Thousands of troops stormed ashore at Anzio just 30 miles south of Rome today and are thrusting swiftly eastwards to cut the supply lines of the 100,000 German troops on the Garigliano front. The invading force met hardly any opposition, having achieved complete surprise. Reinforcements in men and material continue to pour ashore as an armada of landing craft, with powerful naval and air cover, shuttle to and from the beachhead. The sea is calm and a majestic fleet of warships and transports rides at anchor, protected by an umbrella of fighters. Occasionally the big guns of the battleships fire at targets miles inland as the Germans react to the invasion. Forward patrols, who have already achieved their first day's objectives, are beginning to meet German patrols and increased artillery opposition, but so far there is no sign of a counter-attack.'

34th Division Crosses the Rapido

With Operation 'Shingle' safely under way, General Clark visited his three corps commanders on the Fifth Army land front to impress upon them the continuing need to secure a bridgehead so as to allow American armour to break into the Liri valley and link up with the landings. Since the direct approach across the Rapido had failed could something be done on the flanks? For example, was the British X Corps able to expand its bridgehead over the Garigliano northwards into the Liri valley, or could the CEF turn south-west in a wide sweep towards the Liri valley and the elusive road to Rome? Either or both would thus help to break through the Gustav Line and get the advance moving again. Unfortunately in the south, General McCreery's bridgehead was barely holding its own against German counter-attacks and, although these eased when the defenders had to withdraw troops for transfer to the Anzio area, X Corps was far too close to sheer exhaustion to be able to go onto the offensive. In the north, things were a little better, Juin's troops having had some days to recover from their initial onslaught. Although time would be needed to move troops to the southern part of his front, Juin considered that they would be ready to mount an attack on or about the morning of 25 January, his objective being Monte Belvedere, some five miles to the north of Cassino.

Meanwhile, it would be up to US II Corps itself to initiate some pressure, and this would be done by the 34th Infantry Division crossing the Rapido to the north of Cassino, where the river was fordable. The assault would be in two prongs — one towards Cassino town, the other across the jumble of mountain peaks that contained Monte Cassino, and which jutted out over the river valleys of the Rapido and the Liri. To support this manoeuvre, 36th Division was to feint another crossing at the same sites where it had just failed on the Rapido, whilst keeping 142nd Infantry RCT (which had not been committed in the previous bloodbath) ready to force another crossing to the north of Sant'Angelo.

As the 34th's history, *The Story of the Famous 34th Infantry Division*, recounts:

> 'The mission of the 34th was to cross the Rapido, penetrate the hills, then strike south, with one column to advance down the road and enter Cassino, while other elements were to gain the heights above and to the rear of the city, finally debouching to the enemy's rear in the vicinity of Piedimonte. It was a prodigious and ambitious assignment.'

Facing the 34th was the 44th Infantry Division which had a high reputation as an excellent fighting formation. They were deployed from the village of Cairo in the north to the Liri valley in the south. In reserve were elements of 29th Panzer Grenadier and the *Hermann Göring* Divisions.

The Story of the Famous 34th Infantry Division goes on:

'The enemy was ready. Before the troops lay the deep, icy cold, swift-flowing waters of the Rapido, with all strategic crossings heavily laid with mines. Higher up the river the enemy had blown a dam, diverting the stream so as to render the valley an area of quagmire. Incessant rains fell, often turning to sleet. Beyond loomed the great wall of mountains into which the Germans, with their famous Todt Organisation, had dug entrenched positions. Before those hills lay endless fields of mines, tripwires, booby traps and merciless enfilade fire. Again, as with the 36th, surprise was impossible. On January 23rd, orders for the attack were issued. That night, Colonel Carley L. Marshall moved the 133rd forward to its assembly area, prepared to strike across the Rapido in the vicinity of Monte Villa, about one half mile north of Cassino. The massed artillery laid down heavy concentrations on targets beyond the river, causing the enemy to throw up colored flares, announcing to his troops that an attack by the 34th was imminent.

'At 2200 hours on January 24th, the 133rd commenced its attack, the 1st and 3rd Battalions striking on schedule, the 100th Battalion being delayed 30 minutes by enemy fire. The crossing of all troops, however, was held up by minefields cleverly laid by the Germans along the east bank in anticipation of the attack. Tanks of the 756th Battalion then attempted to clear the lanes before the 1st Battalion [of the

133rd], but failed because of inability to ford the high stream. Despite this initial setback, the resolute General Ryder on the 25th ordered the 100th and 3rd Battalions to cross, with the 1st Battalion to remain on the east bank of the river. By noon of that day, against terrific enemy opposition, all three battalions had reached the west bank, there to encounter minefields and wire. But the troops hung on, meanwhile, effecting reorganisation.

'Later on the 25th of January, General Ryder issued new orders. The 133rd was to resume its drive to capture Hills 56 and 213, and the Italian barracks which lay some 2000yd north of Cassino. The going was tough for the 133rd. Through the balance of the 25th and throughout the 26th, the regiment made gains towards its objectives, but by nightfall the troops were driven back to the river bank where they stood in determined, defensive positions. In the early morning of January 27th, Company "C" of the 135th Infantry effected a crossing of the Rapido slightly north of Cassino, striking immediately towards, and reaching, the very edges of the city before being repelled by enemy wire, mines and flooded ditches. Here the struggling 100th and Company "C" of the 135th waited in vain for armored support, but the 756th was unable to move its tanks across until the engineers had improved the way. The troops withdrew to the west bank.

'While the Division's assault had thus far failed to achieve its objectives, enough information had been gained to plan a renewed attack on the Gustav Line. By noon the three battalions of the 133rd had established precarious bridgeheads

Above: This Sherman M4 medium tank is well and truly bogged down in the marshland around Cassino, as the winter snows melt and the low-lying ground becomes a sea of mud. *(US Army via Real War Photos)*

on the opposite shore. The crossing so far had been costly, the 133rd having sustained over 300 casualties. But the dauntless 34th was not to be denied.

'Orders came to renew the attack on the 27th, the immediate objective again being Hill 213. The plan called for the 168th to pass through the 133rd preceded by elements of the 756th Tank Battalion, without whose assistance little progress could be expected. The attack was preceded by one hour of heavy artillery preparation. At 0130, elements of the 1st and 3rd Battalions of the 168th, led by tanks of the 756th, commenced the crossing half a mile south of Cairo, advancing behind a rolling barrage. By 1300 hours, four tanks had crossed the river, all soon being immobilised: two by direct enemy hits, one by mines and the fourth becoming helplessly bogged down in the infernal mud. But the efforts of the tanks were not in vain: four companies of the 1st and 3rd Battalions of the 168th crossed the Rapido over the bank cleared by the tanks. Joined in the night by Company "C", the troops reached the base of Hills 56 and 213, elements of Company "C" even reaching the summit of the latter hill. The losses being heavy and the positions of our troops appearing untenable, Company "C" withdrew across the river, but Companies "A" and "B" were held at the west bank. Companies "I" and "K" of the 3rd Battalion recrossed to the east side of the river but that night again crossed to the enemy side some 500yd north of the tank lane, two platoons advancing to dig in just short of the village of Cairo. Our bridgehead showed signs of being made secure.

'On the 29th of January, General Ryder organised a special Combat Team that was now to be thrown into the breach. Preceded by tanks of the 760th Battalion, the 1st and 2nd Battalions of the 168th, with the latter serving as a spearhead,

were to capture the saddle between Hills 56 and 213. Other units assigned to the team were the 175th Artillery and all II Corps Engineers. The engineers, working as always under the most adverse conditions created by the rushing stream and constant fire from the enemy, had laid out three additional crossings. Tanks and troops moved over, encountering resistance which immobilised five of the seven vitally needed monsters which had gained the other shore. Once across, however, the infantry struck rapidly towards their goal: all three battalions of the 168th reaching the base of the coveted Hills 56 and 213. Before dawn the 2nd and 3rd Battalions had fought their way to the top of Hill 213, while the 1st Battalion drove the enemy from Hill 56. Troops mopped up the area and dug in to repel determined counter-attacks. By noon that day, Company "K" assisted by the tanks of the 760th Battalion, had assaulted and captured the village of Cairo. The bloody days of the Rapido took on a brighter outlook; the first defense positions of the Gustav Line had been cracked, though the ultimate breaking of that line still lay many bloody months ahead.'

Success for the French

To the north of the American crossings, General Juin's forces were also having their own successes. On 25–26 January, Monte Marrone was taken by the Moroccans, whilst the Tunisians took the Belvedere and Abate Hills and the Algerians drove the Germans out of Propaia. However, this left their flank exposed, so General Clark ordered 142nd RCT, under the command of Brigadier General

Frederick Butler, to be attached to 34th Division so as to help the French. Despite the weather worsening with snow and cold rain falling, 142nd RCT captured Manna Farm and pushed further south towards Monte Castellone, whilst 3rd Algerian Division retook Colle Abate. This cleared a more direct approach on Cassino. However, realising the new threat, the Germans brought in fresh reserves, namely 211th Grenadier Regiment of 71st Infantry Division.

Just before their attack on Colle Belvedere, Juin had addressed his troops: 'In the days ahead,' he told them, 'both France, who fights and suffers, and our Allies, will have their eyes fixed on the small French Army in Italy and its first actions.' And they had not let him down. Monsabert's 3rd Algerian Division had begun its assault on Belvedere on the morning of 25 January, the 4th Tunisian Tirailleurs beginning the attack and passing through the deep valley of the Rapido, picking off the German outposts, then climbing a 500ft cliff to reach a plateau on which stood the casemates of the Gustav Line. Here the 4th Tunisians attacked and broke through, turning the line at its most northerly point. Then for the next eight hours the regiment clung on to Belvedere, resisting every counter-attack despite all the German reserves in the region being thrust desperately against it. Different peaks changed hands several times in the course of the fighting; Hill 356 was twice retaken, then resisted 12 German counter-attacks. When this regiment was relieved, the true cost of its action was revealed — the CO and 14 officers killed, 19 officers wounded, along with half the unit killed, wounded or missing in action. Juin, who recognised this outstanding bravery, later wrote in his memoirs:

'I do not know if in the annals of the French Army, in the course of its entire history, there has ever been a feat more striking, nor actions more heroic than those accomplished by the 4th Tunisians at Belvedere.'

In dense fog in the early hours of 1 February, 135th RCT began its attack. From Cairo, its 3rd Battalion captured Monte Castellone (Point 771) within three hours. Despite meeting heavy German artillery fire, the 2nd Battalion, helped by the fog, took Monte Maiola (Point 481). Though there were heavy losses, the advance continued yard by yard until, by last light on 3 February, the 2nd Battalion, plus the 3rd Battalion of 168th RCT, were only a mile and a half to the north of Route 6. However, at the critical moment, more German reinforcements arrived in the shape of Battle Group *Schultz* and Point 593, the highest peak in the immediate neighbourhood, was held by 3rd Battalion, 3rd Paratroop Regiment, commanded by the redoubtable *Major* Rudolf Kratzert. An Austrian, ex-member of the old Imperial Army, he was no longer young, but would nevertheless ensure that his battalion continued to hold its bare slopes, no matter who was attacking, for weeks to come. Meanwhile, the 133rd, having 'cleaned out' the Italian barracks, sent its 3rd Battalion towards Cassino, following behind tanks of the 756th. This force reached the outskirts of the town, but lost five tanks and was compelled to withdraw. A second attack, on 3 February, was also repelled, but a third was successful and scaled the heights of Point 175, overlooking the town. The divisional history recalled the events:

'In three days of terrific fighting the 34th had made momentous gains. Not only had we won a great area to the rear of Cassino, but also troops were now entrenched in the northern part of the city itself. On February 4th and 5th, the 135th fought desperately to force its way across Highway 6, but its advance was repelled. Never were fresh reserve troops

more greatly needed, but none came. Indeed, thus far in the Italian Campaign, reserves were almost an unknown quantity. One fresh battalion at this juncture might well have cut Highway 6 and forced a general withdrawal of the enemy. Men wondered then and wonder now, how planners of the campaign failed to have sufficient reserves at all times to meet such situations which would obviously arise.'

Perhaps the 34th Division historian who wrote those words was somewhat in ignorance of what reserves were or were not available to the Italian theatre at that time. The 'Forgotten Army/D-Day Dodgers' syndrome was already making itself felt, so it was more a question of General Alexander robbing Peter to pay Paul than being able to request additional troops from outside Italy. At the end of January, he had in fact ordered the transfer of 2nd New Zealand and 4th Indian Divisions, which formed the New Zealand Corps, from the Eighth Army to the Fifth Army. 2nd New Zealand Division would relieve US II Corps on the river line south of Cassino and 36th Division would be moved into the mountains to attack towards Piedimonte on the right of the 34th Division. The aim was for 135th Infantry to attack before midnight on 7 February and to capture Albaneta Farm, so as to protect the right flank of 168th Infantry, which would assault Monastery Hill on the morning of the 8th. As it happened, German counter-attacks fully occupied 135th Regiment, so the 1st and 3rd Battalions of the 168th attacked (but at 0400 hours rather than during the night). The Germans reacted strongly and both sides suffered heavy losses, including the commander of the 168th, Colonel Robert L. Ward, who received a serious leg wound. The 1st Battalion was halted at the foot of Point 444, whilst the 3rd Battalion was pinned down on the barren forward slopes of Point 445. 135th Regiment managed to retake some of the ground it had lost on the northern slopes of Point 593. However, throughout the 9th and 10th the Germans continued their fierce counter-attacks, whilst 36th Division moved up for a further effort. Meanwhile all the battalions of the 133rd were involved in equally heavy fighting in Cassino town. Some progress was made towards Point 165, whilst more ruined streets and more buildings were taken.

During the fighting a platoon of 1st Battalion of the 135th actually reached the walls of the abbey, and took 14 prisoners in a cave nearby. Another platoon of the 168th, under a Captain Jack Sheehy, also reached the abbey walls, before being forced to withdraw as well.

'With 4th Indian Division prepared to follow through the mountains if 36th US Division's attack towards Piedimonte succeeded, or if 34th Division should fail in its assault on Monastery Hill, 36th Division made its attack to capture Albaneta Farm, Point 593 and Point 374 to its south on 11 February in heavy rain. 141st and 142nd Regiments both failed to capture their objectives; the latter tried to neutralize by fire the German strongpoints near Albaneta Farm. It did not, however, occupy the area, and fire from it inflicted considerable casualties on 141st Infantry Regiment as it attacked Point 593. Little progress had been made by midday and the afternoon was taken up repelling two heavy enemy counter-attacks. By darkness, the two forward American battalions mustered less than two hundred men between them. In the early hours of the morning of 12 February, 36th Division was violently counter-attacked on Monte Castellone, Points 706 and 465. The Germans were beaten back, but a further attempt to filter through was made in the afternoon before they finally abandoned their efforts. In its last attack

on Monastery Hill the day before, made in a violent snowstorm, 168th Infantry Regiment had suffered many casualties and made no ground. On the night of the 12/13 February, the relief of the Americans by 7th Indian Brigade of 4th Indian Division began.'[10]

Fred Majdalany, a company commander in 2nd Lancashire Fusiliers who later wrote *The Monastery*, the most evocative book about the Cassino battles, was a member of the British 78th Infantry Division which joined the New Zealand Corps on 17 February. He had first-hand knowledge of the conditions at Cassino and says that 34th US Division's performance:

'. . . must rank with the finest feats of arms ever carried out by any soldiers during the war. When they were finally relieved by 4th Indian Division, 50 of those who had held on until the last, were so cold and numb that they could not move. They were still able to man their positions, but had to be carried out on stretchers.'

Major-General H. Kippenberger, commander of 2nd New Zealand Division, was equally unstinting in his admiration for their bravery: 'the Americans had battled since January with a stubbornness and gallantry beyond all praise' (quoted in the official New Zealand history).

By the end of the first battle (12 January–12 February 1944), the three Allied corps that had attempted to achieve Alexander's grand plan and to break through the Gustav Line were all virtually exhausted. X British Corps on the left had suffered over 4,000 casualties, yet had only a small bridgehead over the Garigliano River to show for all the efforts. Juin's French Expeditionary Corps had achieved brilliant success in capturing Colle Belvedere, but in doing so had completely worn out its men. And the Americans were in no better shape, having suffered similar casualty figures to the British,

Above: Speeding into battle along what looks like a reasonable road is this American M10 Wolverine Tank Destroyer. It mounted a 3in gun in an open-topped turret. The British version (M10 Achilles) had a more powerful 17-pounder gun. *(US Army via Real War Photos)*

crossing the Rapido and fighting in the mountains around Cassino, showing exceptional bravery, but really to no avail. On the other hand, from the German point of view the 'prelude battle' as they called it had been a most profitable one. The Gustav Line had been tested and had held firm. In addition, they now knew where their weak points lay and could plug any gaps as necessary.

It was the end of the first battle and time for the next contender to step into the ring.

Notes
1. Charles Connell, *Monte Cassino, the Historic Battle*.
2. As quoted by John Ellis in *Cassino, the Hollow Victory*.
3. Quoted from 'HQ Malta Study Day papers, 1968'.
4. Martin Blumenson, *US Army in World War II, The Mediterranean Theater of Operations, Salerno to Cassino*.
5. *Ibid.*, quoting from General Walker's diary.
6. According to General von Senger this was the finest combat formation in his corps.
7. The M-2 assault boats were made of plywood with a square stern and flat bottom. They weighed some 410lb and would each hold 12 men plus a two-man boat crew. Designed to be transported in a 'nest' of seven boats per 2.5-ton truck, they were bulky, heavy and awkward to carry.
8. Martin Blumenson, *US Army in World War II, The Mediterranean Theater of Operations, Salerno to Cassino*, quoting from General Walker's diary of 23 January 1944.
9. *Ibid.*, quoting from General Clark's diary of 23 January 1944.
10. Quote taken from 'HQ Malta Study Day papers, 1968'.

Chapter 5

The Second Battle
15–18 February 1944

'The attack by 34th US Division continued to make progress but the enemy was now steadily reinforcing. Leaving 5th Mountain Division to oppose the French he [the enemy] decided to strengthen the mixed group of 44th and 71st Divisions defending Cassino itself and the Monastery with 90th Panzer Grenadiers brought down from the Anzio front. Against these excellent troops II Corps was unable to make progress. It had got into the outskirts of the town and was within striking distance of the Monastery hill; indeed it was only a mile from Route 6 down below, but it was a mile packed with defences held by fanatical troops and broken up by mountain ridges and gullies. The first battle of Cassino was a German success; its retention now was a matter of German prestige.'

So reads Alexander's despatch 'The Allied Armies in Italy from 3rd September 1943 to 12th December 1944' (published as a *Supplement* to The *London Gazette* dated 6 June 1950). It draws a line under the failure of the first series of battles to break through the Gustav Line, which have just been described. Now it was time to try again. The despatch continued:

'I had refused to commit the New Zealand Corps, my *Corps de Chasse*, until it was certain that II Corps could not take the position. The New Zealanders had relieved the Americans south of Route 6 on 6th February to allow the latter to concentrate on the attack, but it was now clear that II New Zealand Corps would be obliged, not merely to debouch through a gateway flung open for them, but to capture the gate themselves. II Corps went over to the defensive on 12th February.'

On his initial reconnaissance, Brigadier Lovett, commander of 7th Indian Infantry Brigade, had noted that the Americans had lost 80% of their effectives. The regiment on Snakeshead Ridge, for example, had only 400 men. And, as will be seen later, they were mostly in a state of extreme exhaustion. As the Indian Division's history, *The Tiger Triumphs*, says:

'Isolated, frozen, battered by night and by day, handfuls of indomitable men clung to positions which they had clawed from the grip of the enemy.'

Orders of Battle for the Second Battle of Cassino

Before outlining Alexander's plans for the 'capture of the gate', let us look in more detail at the orders of battle of the main formations involved, first Allied then German.

Allied Orders of Battle

15th Army Group *General Sir Harold Alexander*

Fifth US Army *Lieutenant General Mark Clark*

Below 15th Army Group and US Fifth Army, was the newly arrived New Zealand Corps (transferred by Alexander on 3 February to under command Fifth Army, from Army Group reserve).

II New Zealand Corps *Lieutenant-General Bernard Freyberg*

Corps Troops
- 3 x field regiments
- 5 x medium regiments
- 1 x light anti-aircraft battery
- 3 x anti-aircraft battalions (US)
- 1 x survey battery

Attached

Combat Command B *Brigadier General F. Allen, Jnr.*

6th Field Artillery Group (comprising four battalions of 155mm howitzers)

Task Force A
- 13th Armored Regiment
- 636th Tank Destroyer Battalion
- 16th Engineer Battalion
- 6617th Mine Clearing Company

Task Force B
- 1st Tank Group
- 753rd Tank Battalion
- 760th Tank Battalion (-)
- 776th Tank Destroyer Battalion
- 48th Engineer Battalion (one company)
- 91st Reconnaissance Squadron (one troop)

2nd New Zealand Division *Major-General H. Kippenberger*

Divisional Troops
2nd New Zealand Division Cavalry Regiment

27th New Zealand Machine-Gun Battalion

2nd New Zealand Division Artillery
4th, 5th & 6th New Zealand Field Regiments (each 24 x 25-pounders)

7th New Zealand Anti-Tank Regiment
(36 x 6-pounder and 12 x 17-pounder)

14th New Zealand Light Anti-Aircraft Regiment
(54 x 40mm)

4th New Zealand Armoured Brigade
18th, 19th & 20th New Zealand Armoured Regiments

22nd New Zealand (Motorised) Infantry Battalion

5th New Zealand Infantry Brigade
21st, 23rd & 28th (Maori) Infantry Battalions

2nd Machine-Gun Company

6th New Zealand Infantry Brigade
24th, 25th & 26th New Zealand Infantry Battalions

4th Indian Division *Major-General Francis Tuker*
then Major-General A. Galloway

Divisional Troops
Central India Horse
6th Battalion, Rajputana Rifles (machine-gun battalion)
4th Battalion Reconnaissance Regiment
4th Field Company Bengal Sappers and Miners
12th Field Company Madras Sappers and Miners
21st Field Company Royal Bombay Sappers and Miners
11th Field Park Company Madras Sappers and Miners
5th Bridging Platoon Sappers and Miners
17th, 26th & 32nd Field Ambulances
15th Indian Field Hygiene Section

4th Indian Division Artillery
1st, 11th & 31st Field Regiments, RA
(each 24 x 25-pounders)
149th Anti-Tank Regiment, RA (36 x 6-pounder and
12 x 17-pounder)
57th Light Anti-Aircraft Regiment, RA (54 x 40mm)

5th Indian Infantry Brigade
1st/4th Battalion, Essex Regiment
1st/6th Battalion, Rajputana Rifles
1st/9th Battalion, Gurkha Rifles

7th Indian Infantry Brigade
1st Battalion, Royal Sussex Regiment
4th/16th Battalion, Punjab Regiment
1st/2nd Battalion, Gurkha Rifles

11th Indian Infantry Brigade
2nd Battalion, Cameron Highlanders
4th/6th Battalion, Rajputana Rifles
2nd/7th Battalion, Gurkha Rifles

Notes
The right flank of US Fifth Army was held by the CEF and US 36th
Infantry Division.

The left flank was held by X British Corps from the Gari and Liri Rivers
to the bridgehead over the Garigliano on the west coast.

Above: German mountain troops moving into their positions near Monte
Cassino. They had had a fair amount of time to prepare their bunkers and
dugouts and would not give them up easily. *(Bundesarchiv 146/771/161/109)*

Not all the troops manning the Gustav Line were involved in
what is now known as the Second Battle of Cassino. In the area
where the New Zealand Corps would be operating, that is to say
that part of the Gustav Line between Cassino Station and Colle
Belvedere where Freyberg's corps attacked, there were a total of 14
German infantry battalions, two tank companies, one medium, one
heavy and four field artillery batteries, and one battalion, plus one
company, of anti-tank guns. According to the official New Zealand
history, opposite 4th Indian Division was *Oberst* Schultz's 1st
Paratroop Regiment, comprising four battalions — two of its own,
one from 3rd Paratroop Regiment (commanded by *Hauptmann*
Kratzert) and the Paratroop Machine-Gun Battalion (*Major*
Schmidt). Opposite the New Zealand Division, Cassino Station
was defended by 211th Regiment, with two of its own battalions
and a third from 361st Panzer Grenadier Regiment, all from
Generalmajor Baade's 90th Panzer Grenadier Division. The New
Zealand history goes on to put these numbers into perspective:

> 'Reconsidered in terms of infantry actually engaged in
> launching or repelling the assault, the odds against the
> Germans almost shrink away. At those points in the German
> lines which it had chosen to breach, the New Zealand Corps
> was far from being able to bring to bear a crushing weight of
> numbers. In the initial heave that was to topple the enemy
> defences, the Indians enjoyed a superiority in battalions of
> perhaps four to three, whilst the New Zealanders fought
> numerically on about equal terms, so narrow were the
> attackers' avenues of approach. The gate was strait and in the
> event the scroll would be charged with punishment.'[1]

The organisation of 90th Panzer Grenadier Division has already
been given in the previous chapter. However, as this was the first
time that any units of the 1st Paratroop Division were involved in
the Cassino battles then this is probably a good place to give details
of *Generalleutnant* Heidrich's crack division which was to be more
intimately concerned with the defence of the monastery than any
other German formation.

German Orders of Battle

(all subordinate formations organised as before — see First Battle)

XIV Panzer Corps

5th Mountain Division

15th Panzer Grenadier Division

44th Infantry Division

90th Panzer Grenadier Division

94th Infantry Division

1st Paratroop Division *Generalleutnant Richard Heidrich*

NB: The entire division did not come over from the eastern part of the front line until 26 February, so it was only Battlegroup Schultz which was involved in the Second Battle

Divisional Troops

1st Paratroop Reconnaissance Section

1st Company – radio company

2nd Company – telephone company

1st Paratroop Artillery Regiment

1st & 2nd Battalions – both equipped with 75-mm mountain howitzers

3rd Battalion – 10-cm light gun – a special type for paratroops

1st Paratroop Pioneer Battalion

1st, 2nd & 3rd Companies – engineers

4th Company – machine-gun company

1st Paratroop Anti-Tank Battalion

1st, 2nd, 3rd & 4th Companies – 7.5cm anti-tank guns (motorised)

5th Company – self-propelled anti-tank guns

1st Paratroop Medical Section

Two medical companies

1st Paratroop Regiment

Staff and reconnaissance section

Pioneer platoon

Cycle Platoon

13th Company – mortar company

14th Company – anti-tank company

1st Battalion

1st, 2nd & 3rd Companies – rifle companies

4th Company – machine-gun company

2nd Battalion as for 1st Battalion

3rd Battalion as for 1st Battalion

3rd Paratroop Regiment

1st Battalion

2nd Battalion

3rd Battalion

4th Paratroop Regiment

1st Battalion

2nd Battalion

3rd Battalion

(Composition of 3rd and 4th Regiments is as for 1st Regiment)

Source: *Monte Cassino* by Rudolf Böhmler

Allied Plans

General Alexander explained his intentions:

> 'My plan now was for 4th Indian Division to capture Monastery Hill while the New Zealanders would seize a bridgehead over the Rapido. The Corps would then exploit up the Liri valley, but this was not to start until weather conditions were favourable enough to allow the movement of armoured forces off the roads.'[2]

At corps level this translated into a detailed plan, which involved the Indians in securing Point 593 from the American mountain bridgehead in the north-west, via Snakeshead Ridge, thus bypassing Cassino town, then going on to take Monastery Hill. The New Zealanders would advance along the railway (in the south-east), seize a bridgehead over the Rapido and capture Cassino railway station, so as to allow the tanks of CC B, 1st US Armored Division, to break out into the Liri valley. There was a degree of urgency to this plan for a number of reasons, the first being the worsening winter weather. Daily the rain, hail and snow followed one another without ceasing, making the already difficult mountainous battlefield into, as one observer put it, 'a wasteland protected by a moat of mud, marsh and flood'. This meant that even existing in such conditions took more and more out of the soldiers on both sides, though at least the defenders had some cover from the elements. Additionally, there was the coming bombing of the monastery which, if it were to be fully effective, had to be carefully phased in with the ground attack. Yet, as we will see, those intimately involved, that is to say the leading troops, knew very little about it.

However, before these plans could be put into effect the soldiers who would be the principal players had to reach their start points. 7th Indian Brigade (1st Royal Sussex, 1st/2nd Gurkhas and 4th/16th Punjabis) had to be concentrated on the lower eastern slopes of Monte Castellone above Cairo village during the night of 11/12 February, before 1st Royal Sussex took over the American forward positions and led the brigade's attack. One of the young officers in 1st Royal Sussex was Lieutenant (later Colonel) John Buckeridge, then commanding 13 Platoon and just 20 years old. He vividly recalled the move forward in a recording he made for the Imperial War Museum Sound Archive:

> 'We came to Cassino from the Adriatic and it was snowing, raining and sleeting. We were moved in six-wheeled vehicles, driven by American maniacs, through the slush and mud. It didn't stop raining. As we turned off Route 6 you could see the monastery, five miles away, perched on top of this incredible cliff dominating everything. The Negro drivers didn't like this. They put their foot down on the accelerator and went like the clappers to dump us off about three miles off the road at a place called San Michele where of course it was raining.'

Having unloaded, the truck drivers left as fast as they could and Buckeridge and his companions had to walk seven miles across the flooded Rapido valley, along muddy tracks in the dark and rain. Eventually they reached the foothills near Cairo, where they had to spend the next 24 hours in the open — no shrubs, bushes or any sort of cover, just acres of granite rockface. And it was still raining and everything was soaking. Buckeridge goes on:

> 'And then they said, "You are going to relieve the Americans." Well, that actually sounded rather good. It was still raining, but we were going to do something . . . During the night we

Above: Men of 1st/4th Essex camp in a ravine near Cassino, whilst in the background is the snow-capped peak of Monte Cairo. *(IWM NA 12252)*

were guided — the Americans sent down a few guides, who guided us up this goat track, and I do mean a goat track — up the sheer side of this mountain. Every now and again you'd slip a few feet and very nearly fall over the side as it was so steep. And you felt your way to the top of what is now called Snakeshead Ridge. And this goat track came out at a place called Madras Circus [*see map*].

'Then the American guides took us on. Now they were in a hurry. My platoon — 13 Platoon — was told that Point 593 was in American hands. Mine was the platoon that was going to take over from the Americans on Point 593, and the rest of C Company, which was our company, was a bit behind me. Therefore I was kind of in the lead. Well, we eventually arrived at a place which I assumed was Point 593 and the Americans who were there were totally exhausted. They had had a hell of a time and we were told quickly, "Well there are your sangars [built-up rock shelters]," because you couldn't dig in — there was no earth. So you built up a shelter with rocks. The guides quickly showed us a few and then they were gone. The Americans were really exhausted. They had fought themselves to a standstill and they had nothing left in them . . . They were either dead or dead on their feet.'

When questioned further about sangars Colonel Buckeridge replied:

'You had got to have cover from enemy observation and enemy fire. And if there was earth then you would dig a trench. But up on the mountain there was no earth. It was sheer granite. But there were rocks and boulders and with these you built a rough shelter for two men. You always had two-man sangars which would give you some shelter from enemy fire, sniper fire and also from any shell splinters . . . But of course it was open to the elements and you had no cover other than your gas cape or a ground sheet which you put over your head to stop yourself getting extra wet . . . When dawn came we realised that the sangars were only 12 to 18 inches high, so you could barely sit up without your head protruding out of the top. Within a short space of time one of my corporals was shot by a sniper, from a place across the ridge, at a place called Phantom Ridge (only some 400yd away), where there were two high points which we called the

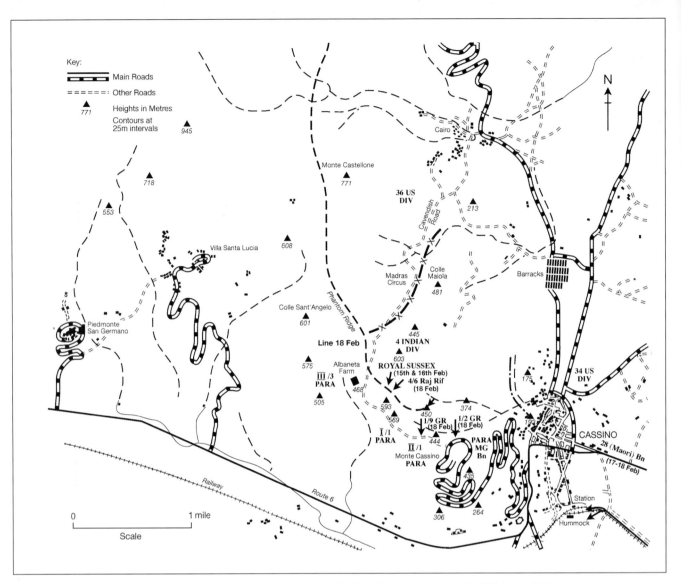

Key:

▬▬▬ Main Roads
= = = = = Other Roads
▲ 771 Heights in Metres
Contours at 25m intervals

Above: Operation 'Avenger', 15–18 February 1944.

"Twin Tits". And an hour later, my own batman sitting in my sangar with me, was killed before my very eyes as close as you are to me now . . . So what we tried to do was to build up the height of the walls, grovelling around on our stomachs, picking up rocks and small boulders . . . that's what we did the next morning as top priority.'

The closest German positions were only 70yd away, so Buckeridge's men had to keep their heads down, use tins to answer calls of nature during the day, and try to observe the Germans through little built-in slits in the sangar walls. In this way they were able to see all the way along the ridge to Point 593 and across the valley, where the snipers were located, and even towards the rear of the monastery itself. After dark, having put out sentries away from their positions in the most likely routes which German patrols might take, they were then able to get out of their sangars and relax slightly:

'Having pushed out sentries as a first priority, you could then think about your food and drink. In the daytime in your sangar you had cold food, if you were lucky, and we did have tins and you had water. You had nothing hot — nothing like modern equipment, where you can actually have self-heating

things. At night you had to go back 200 to 300yd, to bring up food and water and ammunition, from mule trains which had dropped their loads off about 300yd behind our lines . . . we couldn't have survived without the mule trains. You could not get any vehicles up into the mountain at all at that time . . . our mule trains were from Cyprus, Cypriot mules and Cypriot muleteers and they were absolutely invaluable. They were supervised by the RASC [Royal Army Service Corps] and used to spend their nights bringing up all the supplies from San Michele which was seven miles away across the Rapido valley, before first light, seven miles in filthy conditions. The mules were also used for taking down casualties who couldn't walk.'

Next Buckeridge went on to explain the difficulties of the terrain around his positions:

'Snakeshead Ridge was shaped like a boomerang, with Point 593 at its fulcrum. We had to discover where the Germans were, of course, by patrolling at night . . . and it wasn't until

Above: 'Ayo Gurkhali.' Men of one of the Gurkha battalions slog up towards Cassino. *(IWM NA 12054)*

we first attacked them that we appreciated that on Point 593 itself the Germans only had a machine-gun post and some observation posts permanently. They would reinforce the position when necessary, with people who were living behind Point 593, in cliffs and caves. There was a sheer drop behind Point 593 on the German side, and the Germans developed a sheltered place and a track along which they could quickly move to reinforce Point 593 or anywhere else along Snakeshead Ridge that we were threatening . . . Because of the metal studs in our leather boots, walking over granite at night was very noisy, so the first thing you had to do was to try to be as quiet as you could be . . . because strewn all over the top of Snakeshead Ridge were quite big boulders and rocks as well. Snakeshead was really like a razor back, which was only about 20yd wide on the top where it was flat. On one side there was the sheer drop down to a place called Albaneta Farm, and on the other side there were great clefts in the rock face, with sheer rock faces on both sides of these

clefts, so you couldn't just go down and come up and go down and come up again, they were too steep. And the Germans had put in a lot of barbed wire. They had also put in mines, they had put trip wires, they had really blocked all routes along Snakeshead Ridge, other than along the top which is where I was.'

As John Buckeridge mentioned, his battalion swiftly discovered that the Americans were not in possession of Point 593. Not only did the Germans occupy the western side of the feature but also they held the ruins of an old fort near the summit. Their interlocking crossfire was cleverly worked out so that possession of one of the strongpoints was only possible with possession of the others. So, for example, the occupation of Points 450 and 444, immediately north of the monastery, was made impossible by enfilade fire from Point

Above: View of the ruined monastery on Monte Cassino from Snakeshead Ridge — the position occupied by 1st Royal Sussex during the second battle. *(IWM MH 11246)*

593, whilst Point 593 was wide open to fire from Albaneta Farm and Point 575. All this meant that, before an attack could be mounted on the monastery, the Indian division would have to take Point 593, then advance along Snakeshead Ridge (marginally better than trying to negotiate the chaos of ravines, gullies and gorse thickets which lay on its flanks). The plan was therefore for the leading brigade (7th Brigade) to make the assault, with battalions of 5th Brigade being fed into 7th Brigade area as necessary. 11th Brigade would be used as porters, carriers and labourers at the 'sharp end' of the seven-mile supply line, all of which was in full view of the Germans and the last part only negotiable by mule or manpack.

Bombing the Monastery

This had been the plan, but it was about to be changed, to fit in, supposedly, with one of the most controversial incidents of the entire war, namely the bombing of the monastery on Monte Cassino. This has been surrounded ever since by controversy as to whether or not the Germans were using the monastery as an observation and defensive post before it was bombed. Some on the Allied side were clearly in favour of the bombing despite basing their argument on unproven hearsay; others were in no doubt whatsoever, such as John Buckeridge who had a clear view of the rear of the monastery buildings from his platoon positions:

Opposite: Bombing the monastery, 15 February 1944. A Flying Fortress wheels and heads for its base after dropping a load of bombs on the monastery at Monte Cassino. This controversial action has led to heated arguments ever since as to whether or not the abbey was being used by German paratroopers for battlefield observation purposes. In fact the bombing helped turn the abbey buildings into a fortress, but had a morale-boosting effect upon Allied troops under their continual shadow. *(IWM IA 15552)*

'I knew there must have been a base of some sort in Albaneta Farm, although we never went down there and patrolled it. We couldn't get near it. And there was a track on my map which went from Albaneta Farm just below Point 593, to the back of the monastery. I could see this track from my platoon position, just entering the back of the monastery. And I saw Germans, or certainly men in German Army uniform, going in and out of a door. This is before the bombing, in and out of a door which says *pax* [the Latin word meaning "peace"] over the top, p — a — x. And I understand that door is still there, the lintel is still there, which says *pax* . . . This was clearly the route used by the Germans to reinforce their troops in the monastery area, either in the monastery itself, or in their defensive positions which were under the walls of the monastery. And which of course is why they defended the place so rigorously.'

Other arguments were not based on eyewitness observation, as Alexander says in his memoirs, for example:

'There now occurred a curious and slightly comical incident. An American officer on the Intelligence Staff reported that an enemy conversation picked up on the wireless seemed to offer conclusive proof that the Germans were inside the monastery. The intercepted conversation ran: "*Wo ist der Abt? Ist er noch im Kloster?*" ("Where is the 'Abt'? Is it still in the monastery?") "*Abt*" is the German military abbreviation for "*abteilung*", meaning a section. But unfortunately "*Abt*" also means "Abbot" and since "*Abbot*" is masculine and "*Abteilung*" feminine, the conversation referred to the Abbot — if it had referred to the section it would have been: "Wo ist *die* Abt? Ist *sie* noch im Kloster?" Which goes to show that a little knowledge of a foreign language can be a dangerous thing.'

The actual bombing of the monastery would take place on the morning of 15 February 1944, but in fact discussions over the rights and wrongs of doing so or not doing so, can be traced back to early July 1943, when President Roosevelt wrote to Pope Pius XII at the Vatican. His letter contained the following assurance: 'Churches and religious institutions will to the extent it is within our power be spared the devastations of war during the struggle ahead.' Four months later, General Dwight D. Eisenhower, Allied Commander-in-Chief, sent a message to Alexander's HQ 15th Army Group instructing that the ancient Benedictine abbey of Monte Cassino was to be added to the list of protected monuments (in fact it was to be placed at the top of the list after Castel Gandolfo — the Pope's summer residence in the Alban Hills). However, about the same time as this message was sent, the Vatican was also told, via the British Minister to the Holy See, that if the Germans made use of the monastery in their defensive plans, it would be necessary for the Allies to take counter-measures: ' . . . aerial or other, that their own military interests may require'. The German Embassy swiftly assured the Vatican that the abbey would not be occupied 'by regular troops'. The Allies then asked for clarification of the phrase 'regular troops', but an explanation was never given, although, as the fighting got nearer Cassino, the German attitude in the field (at army level and below) was that it would be foolish to forgo such a good observation location. Nevertheless, Kesselring did not waver and continued to promise that German forces would not enter the abbey, but he made it clear that this meant only the main abbey buildings. On 29 December 1943, Eisenhower followed up his president's message with a letter to all commanders in which he emphasised the need to protect monuments with a cultural and historical significance; however, he also stressed that if there was ever a choice to be made between destroying such a monument and sacrificing Allied soldiers, then the lives of the soldiers were far more important, and so the buildings would have to go. He qualified his remarks by emphasising that such a decision must not be taken lightly and that it was the responsibility of all commanders to comply with the spirit of his letter.

Inevitably, mistakes did occur, and in early January 1944, Fifth Army artillery fire damaged the abbey and the Vatican complained.[3] In his report into the matter, Lieutenant-Colonel Robert Raymond, Fifth Army assistant artillery officer, explained that the town of Cassino was regularly bombed and shelled, and would continue to be taken under fire just as long as it was occupied by German troops, but he added (quoted from the official US Army history):

'There are many gun positions and enemy installations in the vicinity of the town, and it is possible that, during an

adjustment, dispersion or an erratic round hit the Abbey. Any damage caused by our artillery fire would be purely unintentional as our artillery commanders understand that neither churches nor houses of worship are to be fired upon.'

Further instructions were then issued to commanders to respect the abbey, despite the fact that '. . . it might well serve as an excellent observation post for the enemy'.[4] Clearly, this was the unspoken conclusion that most soldiers on the Allied side had reached, especially those at the sharp end who saw it constantly glowering down upon them, watching their every move. Then it happened again on 5 February, when a stray round landed inside the abbey walls killing a civilian, whilst a heavy artillery barrage on the same day, fired against nearby German positions, led to some 40 local women leaving their farms and seeking sanctuary within the walls. By 8 February some 100 shells had exploded within those same walls, but none as yet had been deliberate or systematic.

The removal of the art treasures and other precious relics from the monastery has been described earlier. Now many of the monks, and some civilian refugees who had sought safety within the abbey walls, were also evacuated, those remaining being the abbot, five monks and five lay brothers, together with some 150 local civilians. By this time the lower slopes of the hill on which the abbey buildings stood had been carefully incorporated into the German Gustav Line defences. Nevertheless, the monks remained confident that either side would respect their abbey and its immediate environs. On 7 December General von Vietinghoff had asked Kesselring for guidance on how he might use Monastery Hill and the abbey in his defences, warning that in his opinion the preservation of 'extraterritoriality' of the monastery was virtually impossible because it lay within the main line or resistance and loss of both the hill and abbey would '. . . definitely impair the usefulness of the Gustav Line'. Smiling Albert replied a few days later saying once again that he had given his word to the representatives of the Roman Catholic church that no German troops would enter the abbey. The local unit therefore forbade troops to cross a line drawn (figuratively speaking, no doubt) about two yards from its walls and even stationed military policemen to prevent such access. Whilst this ensured that no military personnel came inside the walls, it did not, as has already been explained, prohibit the use of the rest of the hillside around the walls for military purposes.

The Allied views as to whether or not the Germans were using the abbey were thus very mixed, as were the opinions on whether or not bombing it would help militarily. Certainly Mark Clark appears to have firmly believed that such action would not only harm the Allied cause from a moral standpoint, but could also be counter-productive, in that it could produce a more impenetrable barrier and one which the Germans would use to their advantage in their defences. As far as troops on the ground were concerned, as John Buckeridge has already stated, they had no doubts whatsoever that they were being watched from the abbey. As Fred Majdalany put it in *The Monastery*:

'When you have been fighting a long time you develop an instinct for enemy observation posts. You spot quickly where they must be, and you seem to know intuitively the exact moment you start being watched. And it is like being stripped of your clothes. We were being watched now, and we knew it. We were being watched by eyes in the Monastery every inch of the way.'

A test of how this somewhat woolly situation would eventually be interpreted by the Allies finally came in February 1944, when Allied aircraft dropped bombs near the papal estate at Castel Gandolfo, causing damage and casualties. The estate lay within the lines of communication for the German forces attacking the Anzio beachhead and the Commander-in-Chief Mediterranean Air Forces (Lieutenant General Ira C. Eaker) had given the commander of the Tactical Air Force permission to carry out such attacks, when it was, in his opinion (and that of General Alexander), absolutely necessary to do so. Eisenhower's successor — General Maitland Wilson — agreed with this interpretation, and so a principle was established and it would only be a matter of time before Monte Cassino would suffer the same fate. Clearly such an air assault would not be done on its own, as the considerable shock effect on the defenders of a massive air strike would be wasted if not immediately followed up with a ground attack. Such an attack was already in train, but was the timing possible?

First of all it needed someone in the top brass to ask for it to be done and to have sufficient clout to sway any doubters — that person was the most fearless and highly decorated Allied general then serving in Italy, namely New Zealander General Bernard Freyberg. In fact, although he personally agreed wholeheartedly with the proposal, he was actually merely supporting (strongly) a request that had originated with General Tuker of 4th Indian Division. In a message to New Zealand Corps HQ Tuker advocated

that Monte Cassino should either be softened up by aerial bombardment, or turned and isolated.

'To go direct for Monastery Hill without "softening" it properly is only to hit one's head straight against the hardest part of the whole enemy position and to risk the failure of the whole operation.'[5]

In a second message (dated 12 February 1944) he was even more forthright and it is worth while repeating the points he made:

'1. After considerable trouble and investigating many bookshops in Naples, I have at last found a book, dated 1879, which gives certain details on the construction of the Monte Cassino Monastery.

'2. The Monastery was converted into a fortress in the 19th century. The Main Gate has massive timber branches in a low archway consisting of large stone blocks 9 to 10m long. The gate is the **only** means of entry to the Monastery.

Above: Lieutenant-Colonel West DSO, commanding officer 1st/6th Rajputanas, and some of his officers climb the lower slopes of Monastery Hill during a recce prior to their attack. (*Armed Forces Film & Photo Division, MOD New Delhi*)

'3. The walls are about 15 ft high, or more where there are Monks' cells against the walls. The walls are of solid masonry and at least 10 ft thick at the base.

'4. Since the place was constructed as a fortress as late as the 19th century, it stands to reason that the walls will be pierced for loopholes and will be battlemented.

'5. Monte Cassino is therefore a modern fortress and must be dealt with by modern means. No practicable means available within the capacity of field engineers can possibly cope with this place. It can only be directly dealt with by applying "blockbuster" bombs from the air, hoping thereby to render the garrison incapable of resistance. The 1000 lb bomb would be next to useless to effect this.

'Whether the monastery is now occupied by a German garrison or not, it is certain that it will be held as a keep by the last remnants of the Garrison of the position. It is therefore also essential that the building should be demolished so as to prevent its effective occupation at that time.

'I would ask you to give me definite information at once as to how this fortress will be dealt with as the means are not within the capacity of this Division.

'I would point out that it has only been by investigation on the part of this Division, with no help whatsoever from "I" [Intelligence] sources outside, that we have got any idea as to what this fortress comprises although the fortress has been a thorn in our side for many weeks. When a formation is called upon to reduce such a place it should be apparent that the place is reducible by the means at the disposal of that Division or that the means are ready for it, without having to go to the bookstalls of Naples to find out what should have been fully considered many weeks ago.'[6]

Tuker's views were fully supported by his corps commander and the other commanders on the spot. On the evening of 12 February, Freyberg discussed the matter with Clark's chief of staff, Major General Gruenther, who then talked with Clark, who hedged his bets by saying that if it was Freyberg's considered opinion that it was a military objective then he would agree that it should be attacked. Freyberg confirmed this, explaining that the then commander of 4th Indian Division (due to the fact that Tuker was most unwell, Brigadier Dimoline, the division's Commander Royal Artillery was in temporary command) felt that the planned attack could well fail if the monastery was not 'softened'. It is clear that there was also a difference of opinion as to how 'softening' was to be achieved. Freyberg was of the opinion that bombing would damage rather than destroy the abbey and that in any case what he felt was essential was to breach the walls, rather than just flatten the buildings, so that the attacking troops could get through the holes when they assaulted. Unfortunately this was not going to happen because the air forces, which felt they needed to demonstrate their effective support of the ground troops, had already decided to flatten the abbey with many tons of bombs. The date 15 February was chosen as being the day that the bombing would take place — although, as we shall see, this did not fit in properly with 4th Indian Division's ground attack. It was also decided to warn the Italians sheltering in the monastery, so on 14 February, warning leaflets were fired over its walls.[7] From 4th Indian Division's point of view, the ideal time for the bombing was as late as possible on the afternoon of the 16th, so it was a considerable shock to the divisional commander to discover, on the evening of the 14th, that the bombing was planned to take place the following morning. He protested, but by then it was a *fait accompli* and depended merely on the state of the weather as to whether the aircraft would fly or not.

Above: A group of soldiers from the 28th Maori Battalion watches as the bombs rain down on the abbey of Monte Cassino, 15 February 1944. (*US Army via Real War Photos*)

Above:
Collecting wounded under the Red Cross flag. This was a difficult and dangerous job, which the medics on both sides undertook willingly, but was invariably fraught with danger. *(IWM NA 13784)*

Left:
During the battle, Major Reynolds' C Company, 24th Battalion, 6th New Zealand Brigade, having attacked towards Hangman's Hill, was cut off and surrounded. Attempts to relieve the company failed, but it was eventually able to fight its way to safety. *(IWM NA 13782)*

Above: A New Zealand platoon HQ is established in a ruined building in Cassino town. *(IWM NA 13790)*

Tuesday, 15 February dawned clear and cold — clearer than it had been for some days. Shortly after 0930 hours the first bombs began to fall and continued throughout the morning — 142 Flying Fortresses dropping 287 tons of 500lb high explosive bombs and 66.5 tons of 100lb incendiaries (according to the Supreme Allied Commander's report to the Combined Chiefs of Staff). In the afternoon it was the medium bombers' turn to complete the task — 47 B-25s and 40 B-26s dropping some 100 tons of high explosive bombs. As a result the monastery was left a smoking ruin with the jagged remains of the walls rising like rotting teeth on the top of the hillside.

Lieutenant John Buckeridge recalled his view of what happened:

'We were in our sangars, having taken over from the Americans two days previously, minding our own business, when suddenly early in the morning we heard the sound of engines, bombers coming from the Naples direction. And you could see out of the tops of the sangars, because there was no roof on them, and we looked up and saw a great horde of American Flying Fortresses coming directly towards us, from the Naples area up Route 6.

'Looking up, one could suddenly see the bomb doors opening and the bombs come hurtling down, apparently towards us. Most of them luckily landed either on the monastery or near it. But there were overthrows as well. And you could see these darned bombs coming down towards you. Some exploded quite near. We didn't suffer any casualties from direct hits, but we did from granite splinters. Some of the bombs went over the top and hit Albaneta Farm. It was most uncomfortable and we had no warning that they were coming.'

The CO of 1st Royal Sussex, Lieutenant-Colonel Glennie, had also not been told about the bombing before it happened. Now he was in for a second shock that morning, receiving orders that he was to capture Point 593 that night. Little or no time had been allowed for reconnaissance, and the nearest German posts were only 70yd away, with the top of Point 593 just 100yd further on. A silent night attack was almost impossible because of the loose stones which littered the rocky slopes and ridge of their route to the objective. Because of the restricted area, Glennie had decided to attack with just his leading company, C Company (then of 3 officers and 63 men). The men moved forwards as quietly as possible as soon as it was completely dark. They had managed the first 50 or so yards without incident, when suddenly, without any warning, they were drenched with a shower of grenades and withering machine-gun fire. They went to ground immediately, then desperately tried to wriggle their way forwards towards their objective, returning fire as far as they were able. They were soon short of grenades, mainly because two lorry loads of the battalion's allocation had failed to arrive. They continued to try to get forward most of that night, but it eventually became clear that not only would they be unable to make any progress, but that, if they stayed where they were, then none of them would be able to survive come the daylight. Therefore, they withdrew before first light. A head count once they reached their own sangars showed that they had lost two officers and 32 men killed or wounded.

The next day the monastery was again bombed — this time by fighter-bombers — whilst Colonel Glennie was ordered to attack and capture Point 593 again that night with his complete battalion. He immediately asked for a resupply of grenades as they would be essential if the battalion was going to stand any chance of success. Then he made his plan which involved a double envelopment, with D Company, plus a platoon from A Company, attacking Point 593 from the left, while the rest of A Company attacked from the right.

B Company would reinforce D Company on the objective, carrying as much ammunition as possible so as to be in a position to repulse the counter-attack that was bound to follow. What was left of C Company from the previous night would remain in reserve. Zero hour was delayed because the mule train bringing up the grenades was late, and the attack did not eventually get going until after midnight. Even then the battalion had under half its expected resupply of grenades, the rest having again been lost *en route*.

The attack did not start off well. The preparatory artillery barrage, aimed at neutralising the various German positions on the way to the objective, was fired from gun positions that were some 1,500ft below the level of the forming-up area, and had to pass just feet above the men's heads. Unfortunately, a large number of shells failed to clear the ridge and landed in the middle of the troops, causing numerous casualties. This necessitated a hurried reorganisation before the attack could even begin and when it did start, as on the previous night, the leading troops ran into machine-gun fire and showers of grenades. All went to ground, then tried to wriggle forwards as they had done the previous night. A Company on the right was almost immediately stopped by a 45ft precipice that was not marked on the map. When the company tried to edge left to get around it, it found a 20ft-wide, 15ft-deep crevice in front. It was impossible to advance further, so all that could be done was to go to ground again and give covering fire. D Company was more fortunate and managed to get onto the main slopes of Point 593. It immediately found itself engaged in vicious hand-to-hand fighting with the Germans but was unable to dislodge them from their well-prepared positions. Those men of D Company who pushed through to the rear of the German position found themselves going off the edge of a 40ft drop and were either wounded or captured. The battalion ammunition supplies were now beginning to run out for a second time and despite A Company being reinforced by the remnants of C from the previous night's battle, it could not turn the fight in the battalion's favour. By then, too, all the officers in D and A Companies had been wounded and ammunition was running dangerously low.

The battalion made one last desperate attempt to take the objective, but was forced back. In the confusion, some men of D Company were deceived by three green Verey lights that were fired by the Germans, thinking it was their own withdrawal signal to retire through B Company. The attack was then called off, 'the Royal Sussex, practically out of ammunition, being grenaded in the open by Germans in sangars and also silhouetted on the crest for the German Spandaus'.

What was left of the battalion withdrew to its original positions — 10 officers and 130 men, out of a total of 12 and 250 who had been involved that night, were killed, wounded or missing. In just over 24 hours the battalion had suffered a total of 184 casualties out of 328, so well over 50% of its strength had been lost.

This was only the first round; now the rest of the division had to mount their attacks with 4th/16th Punjabis of 7th Brigade designated to occupy the high ground between Points 450 and 444, followed by 4th/6th Rajputana Rifles of 11th Brigade which would then pass through the Royal Sussex positions at midnight, storm Point 593 and, if successful, advance to Point 444 at the monastery end of Snakeshead Ridge. Then at 0215 hours, assisted by the rising moon, 1st/2nd Gurkhas of 7th Brigade and 1st/9th Gurkhas of 5th Brigade would make a direct assault on Monastery Hill, via the ravine and boulder-strewn 'elbow' of Snakeshead Ridge passing to the east of Point 593.

The plan thus subjected the Germans to heavy attacks from three sides of their key positions. However, as the 4th Indian Division's history explains:

'The key to the battle lay in the hands of the two Gurkha battalions. Should the agile hillmen win to the summit, as at Fatnassa and Djebel Garci [in North Africa], success was certain. Should they fail, there could be no victory. As midnight struck on 17 February, 4/6 Rajputana Rifles, heroes of a dozen desperate encounters, flung themselves in a fierce onslaught at Point 593. Yard by yard they closed upon their enemies. Once again a blaze of fire raked the slopes and held the gallant Indians from the close. Major Markham Lee with a handful of men reached the crest and died there. By 0330 hours the attack was at a standstill. Nevertheless, "B" and "C" Companies of 1/2 Gurkhas came forward, formed up on the left and began to work downhill towards Point 444.

'A patch of scrub such as abounded on the ridges loomed in the darkness ahead. There had been no opportunity to reconnoitre this undergrowth, but since it was thin elsewhere and no impediment to free movement, it had not been considered a serious obstacle. A strong body of Germans had, however, crept up and established themselves undetected in this covert within a stone's throw of the Indian positions. A thick seeding of mines with tripwires skirted the approaches;

hidden in the scrub the storm troopers waited with tommy guns at the ready. As the Gurkhas attempted to worm through the copse, the leading platoon blew up on the mines almost to a man. A hail of bullets and grenades followed. Lieutenant-Colonel Showers fell seriously wounded. Two-thirds of the leading companies were struck down within five minutes, yet the hillmen continued to bore in, reaching for their enemies. Naik [Corporal] Bir Bahadur Thapa, although wounded in a dozen places, emerged on the enemy's side of the copse with a few survivors and established a foothold. It was to no avail; in that deadly undergrowth lay dozens dead, many with four or more tripwires around their legs. Only a handful remained to be recalled to their defensive positions at dawn. Stretcher bearer Sher Bahadur Thapa traversed this fearful undergrowth no less than 16 times in order to bring out wounded. He was killed soon afterwards.

'Concurrently "A" and "D" Companies with companies from 1st/9th Battalion in close support, picked their way

around the left flank of the holocaust in the scrub and worked steadily forward in the darkness towards the Monastery. Shortly before dawn "B" Company managed to effect a lodgement on Point 444. Eight hundred yards away a dark defiant height marked the supreme prize. Three companies of the 1/9 GR [1st/9th Gurkha Rifles] closed up. They stood in the midst of a ring of enemies, embedded in the heart of the defences. Fire rained down on them from three sides. Enemy sources afterwards reported an attack repulsed from the Monastery walls, and months later a colonel of paratroopers, captured near Florence, declared that he had led the counter-attack that had destroyed Gurkhas who had penetrated into the fortress itself . . . there are reasons to believe that a small great-hearted group, seven against a city, continued to seek the enemy until death closed on them.'[8]

Fighting continued for most of the night in all areas, but it was obvious as first light approached that those who were near the summit of Point 593 and in the area of Point 444 would not survive for long in the daylight. Therefore, just as had happened on the previous nights, they were pulled back to their starting positions.

The butcher's bill was just as horrific as it had been for the previous attacks, the 4th/6th Rajputanas losing 196 all ranks (including all their company commanders); 1st/2nd Gurkhas lost 11 officers (including their CO) and 138 other ranks, and 1st/9th Gurkhas suffered 96 casualties. So in less than 10 hours the total casualties had been 441 all ranks.

The Maoris Attack

Whilst the brigades of 4th Indian Division were planning their attacks in the hillsides, down in the valley below them 2nd New Zealand Division was also getting ready to open its account, being led off by 28th (Maori) Infantry Battalion, which was preparing to force a crossing over the Rapido and then to capture Cassino railway station. The battalion set off at 2130 hours on 17 February, advancing in the darkness under fire from both Cassino town and Monastery Hill, over muddy, waterlogged fields sewn with mines, until it reached the barbed wire entanglements that bordered the heavily defended station goods yards. A savage assault at about midnight by B Company took the station, although the Germans were still occupying a block of houses just to the north and a small knoll to the south, against which the Maoris' A Company could not make any progress. The Maoris' success depended on the successful completion of the engineers' tasks. Their plan was to open a route to the station before first light. However, their programme was soon behind schedule. A 30ft bridge across the backwater of the Rapido was not open until 2315 hours, more than two hours behind schedule, so the bridging materials did not reach the chosen site on the main river until 0200 hours and, consequently, that bridge was not up and running until 0500 hours. Even then it proved pointless to send tanks along this route as there were two more demolitions further on. 6th Field Company then abandoned work for the day after having several men killed and the rest driven to cover by German mortar fire, which continued despite a smokescreen being laid to shield their operations. The sapper plan had failed, although only by the narrowest of margins.

Now came the Maoris' time of trial. For nearly 11 hours between first light at 0706 hours and last light at 1747 hours, the two companies, weakened by sustaining some 50 casualties, had to face the full fury of the Germans with just their personal weapons, some artillery support and a somewhat undependable smokescreen. They could not be reached by either tanks or heavy weapons during daylight. German attacks began almost immediately after sunrise. At 0715 hours, a German force was seen forming up at the southern end of Cassino town, but was dispersed by accurate artillery fire. The same artillery support was all the

Maoris could call for to try to deal with incessant machine-gun and mortar fire, mainly from Monastery Hill. Smoke, to thicken up the smokescreen, was fired almost continuously, interspersed with high explosive. At about 1015 hours the battalion commander, Lieutenant-Colonel Young, asked again for more smoke, so as to hide the move of a platoon of C Company that he was endeavouring to send up to reinforce the companies at the station. Unfortunately this manoeuvre did not succeed. Later there was a crisis over ammunition re-supply — more smoke shells were required and had to be fetched urgently.

Early in the afternoon, the Germans became more and more aggressive. German troops crossed the Gari via the railway line and closed on the Maoris. Then two tanks drove into Cassino town from the south-west, but were stopped by artillery fire as they tried to reach the station. Then, at about 1515 hours, the Germans mounted a fierce attack, with infantry of 211th Regiment, 90th Panzer Grenadier Division, supported by heavy fire from infantry guns, mortars and machine guns, plus the two tanks seen earlier, and managed to force their way into the station yards. B Company's leading platoon was overrun, whilst the other survivors of the two companies that had been occupying the station managed to escape and somehow to get back across the river at about 1600 hours. They had been out of radio touch with battalion HQ for some time prior to their withdrawal, so no one knew until they got back that of the force of some 200 who had begun the battle, only 66 survived to return — 26 from B Company under their only remaining officer and just 40 from A Company. The remnants of A Company HQ

Above: Kiwi machine gunners in action. The Germans had many strong machine-gun positions, hewn out of the solid rock, whilst the Allied positions were of a more temporary nature. Here a New Zealand Vickers machine-gun section works with a rangefinder to put down accurate, effective fire. *(IWM NA 12552)*

came in about 1900 hours and one wounded officer, unable to walk, dragged himself over the river on the next day.

The results of the first battle in the valley had been just as disappointing as that in the hills. The attacks had so nearly succeeded, but they now had nothing to show for all their bravery. Up in the mountains, Points 593 and 444 had been reached but just could not be held, whilst in the valley the bridgehead had been won, but more time had been needed to deal with the final two remaining gaps in order to get tanks forward up to the railway station and this had proved impossible. It had in fact been touch and go for the Germans as well; only afterwards was it discovered that the Germans had committed all their local reserves in the final attack on the afternoon of the 18th. So near and yet so far.

In addition to failing in their second attempt to break the Gustav Line, the Allies now had to face the righteous indignation of the rest of the world for flattening the historic Benedictine monastery. Whatever the rights and wrongs of the destruction, undoubtedly all the Allied soldiers in the Cassino vicinity must have breathed a sigh of relief that the monastery building was no longer looking down at them. The official Allied view at the time was expressed in an issue of the weekly newsletter for Allied troops in the Mediterranean which was designed to meet the need amongst all ranks for a regular commentary on political and military events, so its contents could be used as a basis for talks. It had this to say on the subject:

'It would have been too much to have expected the German propagandists not to have dined out on the Cassino Abbey affair. Dr Dietrich, the German press chief, recognised it at once as a "piece of cake" and spread it thickly with a sickly mixture of false humanity and bogus culture . . . The fact remains that the unfortunate building crowned a feature of such tactical value that it became an integral part of a locality which had to be defended by the Germans just as it had to be attacked by us. That it became engulfed in the tide of battle was inevitable. What was not inevitable was the cynical German stage management of the affair . . . When, on the previous day, we dropped our warning leaflets the Germans seized their chance for a real scoop and closed the gates to monks and refugees alike. According to refugees no one was able to leave the monastery until our bombs both shattered the walls and killed the German guards.'[9]

An entirely different view was expressed just as forcibly on the German side, by such honest men as General von Senger, who wrote after the war:

'I drove up the Monastery Hill on Christmas morning 1943. I cast a rather superficial view over the large-scale shelling around Monte Trocchio at my feet. Then I changed over to a more peaceful scene, to Holy Mass celebrated in the Crypt by the Abbot in the presence of some dozen refugees from the surrounding country. I was offered breakfast afterwards, as I knew the Abbot by former visits when we were still fighting in Sicily. This was the only visit by a German soldier to the Abbey either since the fighting had approached the Sanctuary or afterwards. Visitors had not even been allowed in before, because all buildings containing treasures were prohibited to soldiers. In the case of Cassino my predecessor had foreseen the need for clearing the treasures from the Monastery in time and had transported them to Spoleto. I had ordered their transference to Rome.'[10]

Clearly von Senger, who was undoubtedly an honourable man, believed that his side had not broken its word and he is certainly supported by this affidavit, signed by the abbot that read:

'I solemnly declare that no German soldier has ever been stationed within the precincts of the monastery of Monte Cassino; that for a while three military policemen were on duty, with the sole object of ensuring that the neutral zone round the monastery was being respected. But these latter were withdrawn 20 days ago.
Gregorio Diamare
Bishop and Abbot of Monte Cassino
Deiber, Leutnant
Monte Cassino, 15 February 1944.'

And in German was added:

'I confirm, as requested, that there never has been and there is now no German soldier in the Monte Cassino monastery.
Gregorio Diamare
Deiber
15 February 1944.'[11]

(So you pays your money and you takes your choice.)

However, also on the negative side was the fact that the Germans now had an almost impregnable position among the ruins of the monastery buildings which they would immediately occupy and hold until the bitter end.

Not far away, on the same day as the second battle for Cassino ended, a climax was reached in the German onslaught on the Anzio beachhead. However, thanks to the firmness of the US 179th Infantry, well supported by heavy artillery, the attack failed and a turning point was reached.

Above: New Zealand troops in action. Here a tommy gunner takes cover behind the wall of a demolished house. *(IWM 13271)*

Reflections on the Second Battle

Some time after the war, Lieutenant-General Sir Francis Tuker wrote a short paper entitled 'Monte Cassino — Memories' which is now held by the Gurkha Museum. It encapsulates his feelings about the attack that caused his division so many casualties. He wrote:

'Although I was taken ill about the 2nd February 1944 and evacuated the next day to hospital, I had some opportunity before I fell ill of examining the situation on the Monte Cairo — Cassino — Liri valley sector of the Fifth Army front,

including in particular of course, around Monte Cassino. It was a strange thing to me at that time how the Higher Command seemed to be losing sight of the object of the operations which the Fifth Army was intending. The object was not necessary at all to attack and capture the Monte Cassino features. The object was so to menace the enemy position on the Gustav Line as to induce him to withdraw from the Anzio front sufficient forces to preclude his exerting any sort of decisive pressure there. It was for Fifth Army to decide what sort of operation would bring about this object. There were two quite reasonable operations in that region that could be undertaken which would threaten the safety of the Monte Cassino feature sufficiently to draw Axis reinforcements from the Anzio front. The first was to move southwards and south-westwards from about Monte Castellone, down the spur, threatening to cut the Highway 6 L of C [line of communication] and isolate Cassino. The second was to go where one could use the whole of one's enormous artillery force to cover the crossing of the Gari River about Sant'Angelo and there establish a strong bridgehead, but not necessarily more than that.

'When 4th Indian first came across from the Adriatic coast late in January, the New Zealand Corps was planning more or less to turn the Cassino feature by using the first alternative, that is to say the operation from the north. That was what we wanted. Very soon, however, for some reason, they started planning to capture Cassino itself, i.e.: the town and the Monastery and Point 593. This of course amounted to a major operation rather than one which would achieve the necessary threat only. We argued that to bring this off would require a combination of both the northern attack and the river crossing. We considered this to be a big undertaking, but within the resources of the 2nd New Zealand, 4th Indian and 78th Divisions, because the Army artillery would have full play for all natures of guns from heavy to field on the Gari crossing. Strangely, the Fifth Army seems to have turned this down and to have insisted that the Cassino features should be taken by direct attack. We pointed out then that there was only one way of taking these features in this way and that was by drenching them with heavy air bombardment over a term of days, followed up by heavy artillery bombardment at dusk and immediate infantry attack early in the night. But, we pointed out, unless the heavy air bombardment could be guaranteed and the garrison reduced to imbecility, the plan of direct attack on the Monte Cassino features should be abandoned and the first course of the northern and the Gari River turning attacks adopted.

'I went on arguing this from hospital by letter through my Divisional headquarters. Those letters are reproduced in the History of 4th Indian Division. The northern threat by the Castellone spur was the best solution, bringing as it would, Highway No 6 by which the whole of the Cassino feature was supplied, under our close observation and fire.

'The outcome, however, was that Fifth Army decided to go on with its direct attack on the Monte Cassino features but they did not apply the essential pressure without which such an attack was bound to fail. That is to say their bombardment by heavy aircraft only put in 500 tons of explosives and that not co-ordinated in any way with the infantry attack which came three or four days later. The air attack should have been 10 times as heavy and should have come up to its crescendo just before dusk when a thousand guns should have taken over and the infantry followed them

Above: General von Senger assists the abbot into a car before taking him to Sant'Anselmo. They stopped on the way at a broadcasting station in Rome, where the abbot made a statement about the destruction of the monastery. *(Bundesarchiv 101/310/892/7)*

closely. As it was, the air attack on the day before the infantry went in at night was a very light and scattered one by fighter bombers. It was almost useless.

'All that I have said here was clearly apparent to us at that time. I remain utterly perplexed as to the reason why the Fifth US Army decided to batter its head again and again against the most powerful position, held by some of the finest troops in the German Army in heavily mined and wired and fixed entrenchments. Without the massive air bombardment, there could be no surprise whatsoever and in my opinion surprise is the one and only principle in land fighting. All the rest are precepts and subsidiary. Historians may bring out one other point but I rather doubt it so I will state it here. A direct attack on the Monte Cassino features meant that we were committed to success: that is, we could not stop short and call it a day without acknowledging complete failure. A direct attack meant that we had to take at least Point 593 and the Monastery or else acknowledge defeat. Thus it was that the Corps went on for six whole weeks hammering frontally at these immensely strong positions and in the end, with 4th Indian Division having lost 4,000 of its best infantry and the New Zealand Division having suffered heavily also, Fifth Army had to acknowledge defeat.

'There is one minor tactical point that I have seen made against the bombing of the Monastery and it is that the building after being bombed would be more easily held by the Germans than in its undamaged condition. It is forgotten that the same tactical argument goes for the British too, for it would be easier for the British to hold after capture against a German counter-attack. Anyway, as soon as the decision was made to attack the Monte Cassino features direct, the Monastery was doomed to destruction.

'I do not claim that by attacking Monte Cassino directly that Fifth Army did not save Anzio. It might indeed have saved our forces at Anzio from being pushed into the sea or from having heavy casualties. We cannot tell. All I do claim is that there were better ways of saving Anzio.'[11]

Notes
1. N. C. Phillips, *Official New Zealand History of the Second World War, Italy*, Vol. 1, *The Sangro to Cassino*.
2. Supplement to *London Gazette*, 6 June 1950 — 'Despatch on the Allied Armies in Italy, 3 Sep 43–10 Dec 44' by FM Viscount Alexander.
3. This was not the first time that the war had impinged upon the day-to-day life of the monastery. Earlier, a Luftwaffe pilot had accidentally flown into — and destroyed — the cables of the funicular that had linked it to the town. From then on any would-be visitor was faced with a six-mile hike up a precipitous, winding, stony road.
4. Martin Blumenson, *US Army in World War II, The Mediterranean Theater of Operations, Salerno to Cassino*.
5. As quoted in N. C. Phillips, *Official New Zealand History of the Second World War, Italy*, Vol. 1, *The Sangro to Cassino*.
6. As quoted by Laurie Barber and John Tonkin-Covell in *Freyberg — Churchill's Salamander*.
7. Drafted by the Psychological Warfare Branch of HQ Fifth Army, they contained the words: '. . . the time has come when regretfully we must train our guns on the Monastery itself'.
8. *The Tiger Triumphs*.
9. Extracted from *Weekly Review of European Events No 17*, kindly supplied by the Polish Institute and Sikorski Museum, Archive Reg No A.XI.67/22.
10. General Frido von Senger und Etterlin 'The Battles of Cassino', an article published in the *Journal of the Royal United Services Institute*, May 1958.
11. Lieutenant-General Sir Francis Tuker, 'Monte Cassino — Memories', paper held by the Gurkha Museum and quoted here by kind permission.

Chapter 6

The Third Battle
15–26 March 1944

The disappointing failure of the second battle left the Allied commanders trying to decide what next they should do in order to break the impasse. There was little point in just committing fresh troops to repeat the past attacks which had failed, unless something new could be added to give them a better chance of success. General Alexander therefore decided to try the effect of really heavy air bombardment. This had been suggested to him by Major General John K. Cannon, USAAF, the commanding general of the 12th Tactical Air Force, who was convinced that, given good weather and by using all the air resources available in Italy, Cassino could, as he euphemistically put it, 'be whipped out like an old tooth'. Although Alexander was not entirely certain it would work, he was prepared to try any way of capturing the positions that would reduce the loss of life other methods had inevitably brought with them. In his report, he says that on 20 February:

Above: German paratroopers take up positions amid the ruins.
(Bundesarchiv 146/7416/56)

'. . . . after discussing the plan with General Clark and General Freyberg, I decided we would next attempt to capture the town of Cassino, after a heavy bombardment, with the New Zealand Division which would then push past the southern face of Monte Cassino, along Route 6, make contact with the Indians north-west of the Monastery and thus encircle the enemy positions. This would give us a big bridgehead over the Rapido and an entry into the Liri valley.'[1]

Whilst the planning continued, the bad winter weather even took a turn for the worse and by 24 February it was raining practically non-stop. It would go on doing so for the next three weeks. The troops who were going to make the attack — to be known as Operation 'Dickens' — waited for the code-word ('Bradman') to start their assault, standing-to each morning in their exposed positions — the New Zealanders in the cold and wet valley, the Indians and the men from Sussex in their equally freezing hillside positions, beset by German sniper fire, Spandaus, 'potato-masher' grenades, mortar bombs and more. It would be the ides of March before they would cross the start line. They would also have a change of divisional commander; on 2 March, Major-General Howard Kippenberger was badly wounded when he stood on a *Schu* mine on Monte Trocchio — one of his feet was blown off and the other so badly mangled that it subsequently had to be amputated. His place was immediately taken by the commander of 6th Brigade, Brigadier (then Major-General) G. P. Parkinson.

The detailed plan was as follows: Phase 1 would be the bombing of Cassino town and then the advance would begin from the north. This had the advantage that it was the least overlooked of the approaches, and enabled the attackers to advance along three reasonable roads (*see map*). However, this approach also meant that the Kiwis would have to tackle, head-on, the bottleneck formed by the end of the town and Monastery Hill, whilst 4th Indian Division would have to attack its objective up a steep mountainside. 6th New Zealand Infantry Brigade and 5th Indian Infantry Brigade would lead, with 4th New Zealand Armoured Brigade in support. In reserve was to be 78th British Infantry Division plus CC B of US 1st Armored Division ready to exploit any breakthrough. (78th Infantry Division had crossed over from the eastern side of Italy in the first half of February, coming under command of the New Zealanders on the 17th.) The New Zealand Corps would begin its advance just as soon as the bombing had ended, seeking to capture Castle Hill (Point 193) at the bottom of Monte Cassino, then the New Zealand Division would move on to clear the town. During that evening, the Indians would take over Castle Hill and use it as a springboard for their advance up Monastery Hill, via Point 165 (the Lower Hairpin), Point 236 (the Upper Hairpin) and Hangman's Hill (Point 435). Initially, the attack was timed to begin on 23 February, but this was dependent upon good weather — first for the bombing, then to allow the ground to become firm enough

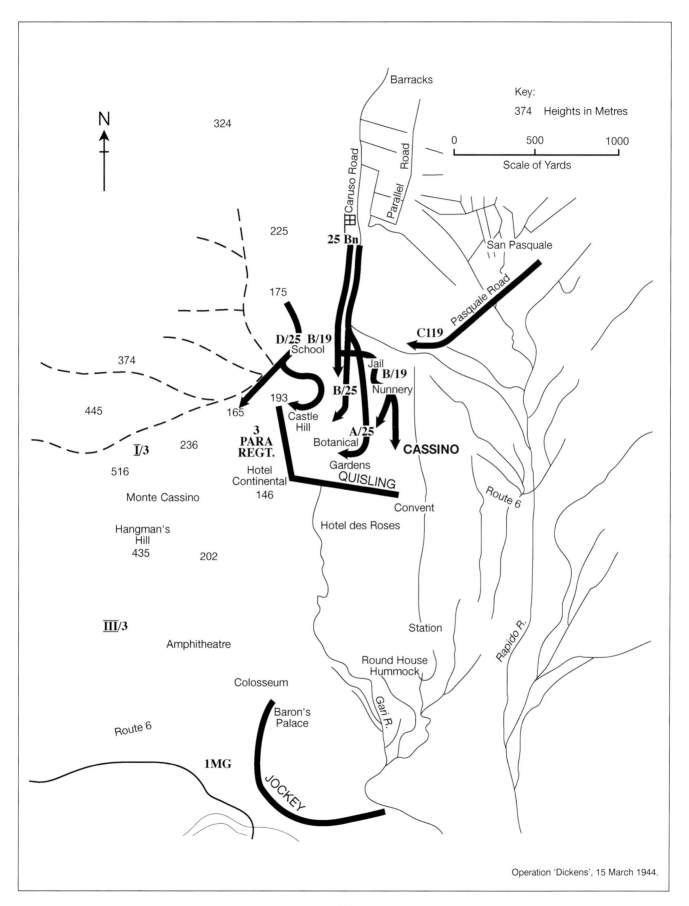

Operation 'Dickens', 15 March 1944.

for tanks, which was estimated to require a period of at least three successive fine days.

Jim Furness MBE, MC, was one of the New Zealand tank commanders waiting for the off. He told me:

Above: A British 5.5in gun blows a perfect smoke ring at Monte Cassino, 8 March 1944. *(US Army via Real War Photos)*

'The attack on Cassino was code-named "Dickens". The start of the attack was held up awaiting favourable weather for the opening aerial bombardment. We put the waiting time to good effect, by studying the layout of the streets, buildings etc, from maps, aerial photographs and ground recces. As I was to lead the tank attack I had to form a clear picture in my mind as to the route we would take, of buildings we would utilise and so on. Then the big day arrived, but not before the Italian kids had been asking: "When is Dickens Day Kiwi?" When we reached the starting point near the old convent, the sight that met our eyes was devastating. Not a single street or building existed — only a vast area of crumbled masonry. The four hour aerial bombardment had completely changed the face of the landscape. The whole panorama was one of devastation and destruction. I couldn't find a route that led to the railway station. I left my tank and scrambled on hands and knees in search of a thoroughfare. Our job was to lead the infantry, but no co-ordinated attack could be developed. We found our way through and over rubble to the station, dealing with targets along the way, but we certainly didn't

help the infantry in the way envisaged in the plan of attack. Ever since that fateful day or days I have felt that we didn't protect the infantry as we had planned.'

Orders of Battle

There is no need to go through two-thirds of the order of battle of the Allied troops taking the foremost parts in the Third Battle, because they were the two divisions of the New Zealand Corps already described in the previous chapter, namely 2nd New Zealand Infantry Division and 4th Indian Infantry Division. However, the British 78th Infantry Division was a newcomer, so its order of battle is given below. Alexander also makes a point of recording at this time the high-level move of HQ Eighth Army from east of the Apennines, so that it would be able to take command of all the British troops (except for the corps on the Adriatic and the two divisions at Anzio) ready to advance up the Liri valley, whilst Fifth Army would advance on a parallel axis through the Aurunci Mountains, and, from Anzio, on to Valmontone to cut Route 6 to the Germans' rear. This advance would not happen, of course, until the weather allowed the opening of the main offensive.

Allied Orders of Battle

15th Army Group *General Sir Harold Alexander*

Fifth US Army *Lieutenant General Mark Clark*

II New Zealand Corps *Lieutenant-General B. Freyberg*

2nd New Zealand Division

4th Indian Division

CC B 1st US Armored Division

78th British Infantry Division

Major-General C. F. Keightley

Divisional Troops

56th Reconnaissance Regiment

17th, 132nd & 138th Field Artillery Regiments

64th Anti-Tank Regiment

49th Light Anti-Aircraft Regiment

214th, 237th and 256th Field Engineer Companies

281st Field Park Company

21st Bridging Platoon

1st Battalion, Kensingtons (machine-gun battalion)

11th Infantry Brigade

2nd Battalion, Lancashire Fusiliers

1st Battalion, Surrey Regiment

5th Battalion, Northamptonshire Regiment

36th Infantry Brigade

6th Battalion, Royal West Kent Regiment

5th Battalion, Buffs (Royal East Kent Regiment)

8th Battalion, Argyll and Sutherland Highlanders

38th Irish Infantry Brigade

2nd Battalion, London Irish Rifles

1st Battalion, Royal Irish Fusiliers

6th Battalion, Royal Inniskilling Fusiliers

Notes

Right flank held by CEF.

Left flank held by 78th (British) Infantry Division along line of River Gari.

X (British) Corps was still holding bridgehead over the River Garigliano.

German Orders of Battle

XIV Panzer Corps

1st Paratroop Division

5th Mountain Division

15th Panzer Grenadier Division

44th Infantry Division

71st Infantry Division

94th Infantry Division

The same duplication from the previous battle also applies to the German order of battle. We have already looked at the detailed order of battle of 1st Paratroop Division, which had now taken over Cassino and the surrounding mountain positions (on 25 February from 90th Panzer Grenadier Division). Some would rate General Heidrich's division as being the best of the German divisions in Italy; certainly it was amongst the most self-confident and aggressive. Its units were located as follows: 3rd Paratroop Regiment (*Oberst* Heilmann) now held Cassino, with its 1st Battalion on Monastery Hill and the slopes running down to Castle Hill and its 2nd Battalion in the town itself, plus three companies of the 3rd Battalion attached — an estimate of the total garrison being about some 500 men. 4th Paratroop Regiment (*Oberstleutnant* Egger) was in the mountains to the north and west of Cassino; 1st Paratroop Regiment was on the southern slopes of Monte Cairo. The division had a fighting strength of about 6,000 men although its total numbers were considerably more, and it was well equipped with plenty of light automatic weapons and anti-tank guns. As soon as it took over the area its men began to improve the already strong defences, putting in more dugouts, shoring up cellars with more concrete walls, siting new machine-gun positions. They also prepared a line of anti-tank gun positions and stockpiled ammunition and supplies in case their supply lines were cut. In short, they prepared methodically and efficiently to hold their positions in a battle in which they would earn the nickname 'The Green Devils of Cassino'.

The Bludgeon of Air Power

At precisely 0830 hours on the morning of 15 March 1944, the first wave of Allied bombers arrived over their target and, according to the *Official New Zealand History of the Second World War*:

> 'As they swept across the blue sky toward the target, the medium bombers of the first wave were watched intently by Allied soldiers who had climbed to vantage points and settled down with binoculars to absorb a sight that they expected to remember for the rest of their lives. In the comparative safety of the hills around Cervaro, the picnic atmosphere was indecent but irrepressible. Here, after many days, was the spectacular promise of release from boredom and deadlock. In the next few hours a whole town would shudder to destruction before one's eyes.'[2]

It had been planned that the bombing would last until noon. Ten groups of heavy bombers and six groups of mediums, some 500 aircraft in all, would drop 1,000 tons of high explosive bombs (1,000-pounders) onto a target just 400yd by 1,400yd in area. It was later estimated that only about 50% of the bombs actually fell within the town boundaries. Near misses landed on Monte Cassino and many in the valley of the Rapido. And of course during the three and a half hours of bombing a number hit Allied troops: there were 44 casualties in American, British and New Zealand artillery areas; 50 men and 100 mules in 4th Indian Division's B Echelon area in the upper Rapido valley were injured or killed; and a Moroccan military hospital and 140 civilians in the town of Venafro, over 10 miles away, but similarly located under the lee of a high hill, were bombed by mistake. Nevertheless, the results in Cassino were quite simply awe-inspiring — not a single building remained undamaged, entire streets had disintegrated into a sea of rubble. *Major* Foltin's 2nd Battalion, 3rd Paratroop Regiment, suffered an estimated 220 casualties, many of them buried under the ruins. And there was more still to come.

Above: The bombing of Cassino town, 15 March 1944. This dramatic photograph was probably taken by a US Army cameraman with a long focus lens. The bombing went on for some three and a half hours and was then followed by a massive artillery barrage. *(Alexander Turnbull Library — DA 9541)*

When the aircraft flew off, the artillery barrage began, over 600 guns taking up the bombardment. Soon the German positions, such as those on Monastery Hill and the surrounding area, were covered with smoke from exploding shells, as were the already ruined buildings in the town. At 1200 hours the assaulting infantry of 25th New Zealand Battalion began to advance, down Caruso Road (*see map*) from their starting point about one mile north of the town outskirts, with B Company moving on the right of the road and A Company moving along the side of the river which ran beside the road. They were accompanied by B Squadron, 19th New Zealand Armoured Regiment, which also moved its tanks down Parallel Road to the left of Caruso Road. The objective of the 25th New Zealand Battalion was to reach Route 6; then the tanks would take over the lead with 26th New Zealand Battalion, heading for the second objective, known as the Baron's Palace, located just where Route 6 turned right round the corner of Monte Cassino, the road forming a semicircle down to the River Gari south of the railway station.

The leading companies of 25th Battalion pushed on into Cassino under cover of the barrage and reached the town gaol. Then, as they advanced further into the town, they were hit by machine-gun and rifle fire from the lower slopes of Castle Hill and the heaps of ruins that had once been a town. They sought cover and rapidly broke into small groups, trying to infiltrate their way forwards. Undoubtedly, they were surprised that so many of the German paratroopers had managed to survive the bombing and shelling, but clearly they had done so by making use of the structures they had put in — the reinforced cellars, the portable steel pillboxes and so on. By the time the attackers arrived they had got a grip of themselves, shaken off their bomb- and shell-induced stupor and were again manning and defending their posts.

There was also worse to come for the attackers. The tanks of 19th Armoured Regiment found their way stopped by a mixture of shell and bomb craters and the piles of rubble that now blocked every street. First Parallel Road was found to be impassably cratered and so all tanks had to switch to Caruso Road, but a deep bomb crater soon stopped them on this route until they managed to find a detour. They did not get into the town until 1300 hours, already 30 minutes behind the infantry. They then managed to worm their way as far as the southern slopes of Castle Hill, but that was as far as they could manage to get. Nevertheless, the Kiwis pressed on in small groups:

'. . . pausing under cover and dashing for fresh cover, exposed to short-range fire, plunging down cavernous craters up to 60ft across and scrambling over piles of debris. Only the pall of smoke made advance possible. Fighting closed to hand grenade range, while mortar bombs and cascades of bombs from Nebelwerfers dropped continuously among the ruins.'[3]

By the middle of the afternoon B Company was still only half-way through the town, and still at least 300yd from its objective on Route 6. However, on the left, A Company had been able to make better headway and had reached the northern branch of Route 6 by 1530 hours. A Company's men went on to capture the post office and then reached the convent, but were unable to break in. A few tanks did manage to penetrate some distance into the town and were able to give fire support to the infantry against various German posts near the convent, but unfortunately most just could not surmount the rubble, some even getting themselves stuck solid in it, as the tank attack ground to a halt.

By late afternoon the whole attack seemed to have lost much of its impetus and it became clear that one battalion was just not enough to clear the town as far as Route 6 and take Castle Hill. At

Above: Castle Hill and the outskirts of Cassino. *(US Army via Real War Photos)*

1600 hours Major-General Parkinson ordered 6th New Zealand Brigade to put in more infantry and this was done, B Company of 24th Battalion setting off at 1700 hours. However, it would be midnight before it arrived at A Company, 25th Battalion. Parkinson also decided, just before last light, to reinforce the assault force further and at 1725 hours 26th Battalion (6th Brigade) was also ordered to advance.

Neal Hopkins was a member of B Company, 26th Battalion, and later recorded his memories of that time:

'Orders came for us to move towards the town and soon we were walking in single file down Pasquale Road towards the river and right into town. Our tanks lined the road, nose to tail, and we realised at once that because of the bomb craters and severely smashed roads, the tanks could not get through. The tank crews looked blandly down at us as we passed. Comments were freely exchanged between we infantrymen and the tank crews. We were quick to tell them that we would "manage it without their help", but after we had left them behind and moved further into the town the situation took on a more desperate meaning. Some tanks did, however, get through, much skill being required to manoeuvre these big vehicles in such shocking conditions. The noise of the odd tank was comforting, although most times at a distance . . . Resistance to us became very evident at this stage and we were withdrawn a short distance to an area near the Post Office, our exact platoon position being alongside the municipal building. The thousands of tons of bombs which had fallen in the four hours of bombing had reduced the area to an unbelievable state, but the rubble was reasonably easy to lift and we made ourselves crude shelters of rock and stone; German snipers were observed in the rubble and Spandau machine guns were firing from the lower slopes of the hill above us. One of my saddest moments came when a burst of Spandau fire killed one of my friends as he scrambled in the rubble only two yards behind me.'

That night the New Zealanders took turns to picket salient points, taking no chances with the Germans, who were trying to infiltrate past their forward posts. Then in the morning they moved back to the post office, as Neal Hopkins recalled:

'In daylight on the 17th March we scrambled back to the Post Office, and I recall taking the spare rations from the pack still on my young friend, whose body had lain beside me since the previous day. The door of the Post Office was ringed with machine-gun and rifle fire as we dashed across the rim of a bomb crater right outside, and I was horrified to see one of our company hanging on some wire which seemed to span the door. Once inside we quickly regrouped and were given orders to make for the Nunnery, some 200yd across open ground. Already the company ahead of us was experiencing heavy going and casualties were starting to rise.

'We each received a small tumbler of rum and, as he handed me the drink, my friend said to me, slapping me on the back, "See you on the other side". We ran out into the open, taking cover where possible. I scrambled under a large steel pylon at one stage and stopped momentarily to help, what I thought was an exhausted soldier, but he was dead, shot through the head — as were so many who did not escape the accurate fire which hissed about our bodies.

'In a state of near fatigue we scrambled into the Nunnery, ready for the next stage in our quest for the ultimate objective which was close to the Railway Station. I stepped over the exhausted form of one of our wireless men, he was really distressed, having run all the way carrying the battery powered radio. He had a long green ribbon draped from the front of his tunic — it was St Patrick's Day. I looked for the fellow who had given us the rum but in vain, he was dead, killed as he ran from the door of the Post Office. I turned to see another companion taking aim at a sniper on a building near at hand and his accurate shot dropped the German into the rubble below. The German paratroopers were good fighters and just as determined as we were.'

Above: A signal section at work on the outskirts of Cassino town, 16 March 1944. *(IWM NA 12901)*

Hopkins has, of course, touched on the basic reason why progress was so slow through the town, namely the courage and determination shown by the young German paratroopers, who were grimly defending every pile of rubble. Typical was *Oberleutnant* Siegfried Jamrowski, who was then commanding 6th Company of the 3rd Paratroop Regiment. His company was one of those garrisoning Cassino town and was caught in the bombing and shelling on 15 March. It took his men a day to dig themselves out and then, in the defensive battle that followed, he led not just his own company but the 8th Company as well, managing to form a new defensive line and thus slowing down the New Zealanders' advance. His initiative undoubtedly prevented the town from falling. He received the German Cross in Gold and later the Knight's Cross for his bravery, and the following year was promoted to command the 4th Battalion. As a matter of record, there were 27 Knight's Crosses (Germany's highest award for bravery) awarded to members of 1st Paratroop Division during the Cassino battles.

Neal Hopkins continued:

'Our thoughts of possible consolidation at the Nunnery were short lived as we pushed on across comparatively open ground in the direction of the Railway Station. Our objective at this stage was to cross the swampy ground beyond the Hummocks. It was feared that our other companies had been in difficulties almost from the start and this became more evident to us by the number of dead and wounded we found, particularly in the vicinity of the Nunnery. Our casualties

were still comparatively light at this stage, but we were soon caught in open ground, by very heavy mortar and Spandau fire from the nearby slopes. Wounded were coming back from the company ahead and I was told that an officer from my home town had been killed. It now became more obvious that we were behind A Company, but already moving to an area to the right of the intended advance — or so we thought at the time. We were to go slightly north of the Railway Station. According to information later disclosed, our casualties for the battalion, at this stage, exceeded the one hundred mark, since the first assault on the town, and we were still endeavouring to overcome the German paratroopers who were so well consolidated, in what was to be stated later, was the finest defensive position to be found anywhere. From the temporary shelter of the railway embankment we crossed over into open ground once again, but because of the smoke and haze, I cannot recall exact distances, but our numbers seemed very small to advance into such unknown territory.

'Others of our company were killed as we spread out and took what cover we could find. Mortars continued to tear at the ground all around us and the six-barrelled Nebelwerfer mortar never gave up. I was on the left of our platoon position and was soon joined by one of our company, whom I think, had been held up farther back helping the wounded. He scrambled past me to what appeared to be a shallow drain, some 20 paces to my left. The concentration of fire was so intense that I felt we could not escape from this treacherous position. I clutched the ground with my hands. It was a moment or two before I realised that the mortaring had stopped and by the sounds ahead it was clear that the enemy were moving closer.

'Suddenly orders were shouted to retire a short distance to the shelter of some half-demolished houses. As we moved back I called to the friend in the ditch but there was no reply. I edged over to see if he needed help, but he had gone. He had probably moved before I did. I never saw him again, but found out later after the war, that he had jumped into the ditch and had been taken prisoner by a group of Germans.

'From the protection of the houses we stopped any enemy advances and, although unable to see clearly, we could detect movement by snipers, worming their way towards us. Our automatic weapons were in better positions now, even though we were surrounded, and we had a better chance of holding out . . . The severe casualties inflicted on the enemy were very satisfying and there were no more full scale attacks. Some of our company were despatched to give support to A Company, 13 of whom had finally gained the Hummocks. For three days we held out without too many incidents, except for spasmodic Spandau and mortar fire. On the 22nd we moved to yet another position in the town, I think we were more forward and nearer the Continental Hotel.'

Whilst in this position Hopkins' section was occupying a badly damaged house that, from its contents, had clearly belonged to a music teacher as there was a damaged piano, sheets of music and music books everywhere. Close to this house was a very disturbing sight — the protruding barrel of a German 88mm gun:

'It was positioned behind some rubble and concrete. As we could observe no movement around the gun we assumed that it was inoperative. From about 40yd out it pointed straight at us and had a menacing appearance. We watched it very closely but, being unable to get near it by day or night, we took the only way out and ignored it. On about the second day, when those of us who were not on picket duty and in a somewhat exhausted state, rested, the gun was fired. The shell burst through the wall, hit the floor and buried itself into the opposite wall of the room, leaving about eight inches of its length sticking out. It had hit a steel helmet on the floor leaving a massive crease right across the top, then passed between two of my companions who were sitting side by side. Nobody moved for what seemed an age — surprise, fear and utter amazement showed on all our faces. Then, a great sigh of relief. Had the shell been a live one then we would all have been blown to bits, fortunately, however, it was a dud.

'We pushed the piano across the hole in the wall, then proceeded to break through the opposite wall of the room in order to get into another part of the house. This took us some hours with our picks as the wall was at least two feet thick. We finally made a hole big enough to just get through. The Germans then set up a Spandau and fired consistently through the hole in the wall where the shell had hit it and the piano was gradually reduced to matchwood.'

Hopkins' battalion was clearly in a holding position while the next phase was planned, which was to send in the brigade's Maori battalion. Later, on 23 March, 26th Battalion was withdrawn back about two miles and its place taken by the 5th Battalion, The Buffs.

'It was a great relief to be away from the constant noise of mortars and of shelling. We were all desperate for sleep.'[4]

Despite the setbacks in Cassino town, there was one bright spot for the New Zealanders in. D Company 25th Bn had managed a skilful attack on Castle Hill, 16 Platoon climbing up a virtually sheer vertical face below Point 165, arriving completely unexpectedly and thus unopposed and capturing Point 165, taking 23 paratroopers prisoner, including a company headquarters. The remainder of the company then made a determined assault on Castle Hill (Point 193) and, despite heavy machine-gun fire, succeeded in taking the fort and most of Castle Hill itself by 1645 hours, 15 March. There was some delay in getting this information back to battalion HQ, so the intended relief by 5th Indian Brigade was also delayed:

'When night came, it was one of almost impenetrable darkness. The clouds obscuring the moon brought rain. For hours after 1830 it teemed down, chilling and soaking the troops to the bone and turning craters into ponds. Paths, always devious, became treacherous and the men of 25th New Zealand Battalion groped forward, sliding in the mud and blundering into great cavities. Eventually, one by one, the companies appeared out of the night and consolidated in the vicinity of Route 6. The difficulties of co-ordinating and orienting an attack in the blackness of the night postponed further efforts until dawn.'[5]

Above: Captured in the fighting. In the first of these two photographs a Gurkha brings in a German paratrooper whom he has taken prisoner. *(IWM NA 13279)*
In the second, a group of British soldiers captured by the paratroopers is assembled in one of the ruined buildings in Cassino town. *(Bundesarchiv 101/577/1921/14)*

Meanwhile, the relief of D Company on Castle Hill had begun, troops of 5th Indian Infantry Brigade closing up as soon as the darkness came. The Indians had been given three tasks:

- 1st/4th Essex to take over Castle Hill and Point 165, which were just above the lower hairpin on the road up to the monastery.
- 1st/6th Rajputana Rifles would then pass through the Essex battalion along the monastery road, aiming to hold between two bends in the road — the northern one being at Point 236, the southern at Point 202 (*see map*).
- From this firm base 1st/9th Gurkhas would then move over the upper slopes to Hangman's Hill (Point 435) — a knoll that sprouted out of the stony hillside, only some 300yd from the south-east wall of the monastery buildings.

When all these three tasks had been successfully achieved, then the final assault on the monastery would be made by 1st/4th Essex, together with as many Gurkhas as were available.

Unfortunately, the terrible weather, the difficult terrain and the tough German resistance all contributed to delays in achieving the relief of 25th New Zealand's D Company, which had been optimistically timed for 1930 hours, but was not actually completed until gone midnight. By then, the leading elements of C Company, 1st/4th Essex, were established in the castle, A Company held the approaches to the castle from the town outskirts, and D Company held Point 175, across the ravine from the castle. B Company was in reserve along the hillside to the north and S Company plus Battalion HQ were near Point 175.

One of the Essex men was Corporal Bill Hawkins, and he told me that the climb up Castle Hill was the most difficult time of his life. He recalled in a private letter:

'If we could have seen our position in daylight and seen where we were going it would have been much easier. But in the dark and rain you were slipping and sliding and hoping that you were going in the right direction . . . If you looked up and there was a gun flash, then you could see a structure up in front of you, so you knew you were heading somewhere in the right direction. But you couldn't be absolutely certain . . . we just carried on moving up the hill . . . the shellfire was terrific and the sniper fire continuous. You put your foot forward, thinking you were going to put your next foot forward as well, only to find a boulder in the way, so you then had to get round the boulder the best way you could. It was a terrible climb up to the Castle.'

Part of the way up he realised that he couldn't see his platoon commander in front of him and in fact did not see him again until after the war. Later it transpired that the officer had been wounded in the foot and evacuated.

'We finally made it into the Castle and I was taken by a New Zealand Sergeant, who pointed to a little dug-out where he'd been with another New Zealand soldier. Another NCO and myself took up the position they had just vacated and I assume that everybody else was doing the same. You couldn't see a thing, because it was still dark, but you could hear people moving about . . . Sniper fire seemed to be coming from many directions, so although you assumed that the front was in front of you . . . it was all strange to us, we'd got to find out everything . . . On the morning of the 16th, when the mist began to clear, was the first time I realised what position I was in, in the Castle. I was looking right down on

Above: Corporal Bill Hawkins of 1st/4th Essex took part in the third battle. The photograph was taken in Italy later in 1944, after he had been promoted to sergeant. *(W. Hawkins)*

Cassino Town high street. In the distance was the railway, with the railway station on the right hand side, to our right. We could see all the town from up there. That was in the early hours of the morning. From then on, if you put your head up you got sniped at — they seemed to be everywhere.

'The Castle was the first main position that the Allies captured, it never returned to German hands again. It was held onto and was a jumping off point for various patrols and so on. It had been well blasted. There was a turret and an outer wall, but a lot of it was knocked down and broken . . . just boulders and rocks, lumps of concrete. The men who had managed to get up into the Castle — from Able and Charlie Companies took up whatever defensive positions they could and continued to fire at any targets they saw . . . we were very vulnerable there, in as much as it was going to be very difficult to get supplies up to us for a start, with the enemy fire going on all round us and the snipers. It was difficult getting ammunition, which was the main thing really, ammunition and grenades were the most important things to get, and rations at the same time . . . And men were getting wounded all the time.'

There will be more from Bill Hawkins later.

Following on behind the Essex battalion were the men of 1st/6th Rajputana Rifles, squashed together on the narrow, twisting, congested dirt road, and making slow progress. They were suddenly in chaos when a heavy German artillery barrage came down on their two rearmost companies, throwing them into confusion as they scattered to find cover. It would take until morning for them to reorganise. However, the two leading companies (A and B) of the Rajputs reached the castle at about 0245 hours, and immediately A Company started across the hillside to try to capture Point 236, just above the second hairpin. Meanwhile, 1st/4th Essex reported that Point 165 together with a building known as the 'Yellow House' had been taken. Having helped the Essex men to consolidate on Point 165, the Rajputs moved against Point 236. As their history *The Tiger Triumphs* relates:

> 'Much hung on the capture of this position. Except for the Monastery it was the last strongpoint which gave observation on to the roads to the north along which the attacking troops must advance. It dominated the slopes of the Monastery Hill in both directions and could bring flanking fire to bear on any forces which endeavoured to pass below or to climb above it. This valuable position was found to be strongly held. When the Rajputanas had closed to within 150yd, a blaze of small arms fire swept the slope. The attack broke down and it was necessary to withdraw to the Castle and to reorganise before renewing the assault.'

Above: Wounded in the fighting. An injured Indian soldier is stretchered out from the fighting on 16 March 1944. *(IWM NA 12893)*

'A Battle on the Stalingrad Model'

> 'Dawn broke on a wild scene. The New Zealanders, like the Indians, found the air bombardment to have been too thorough. Huge craters had filled with rainwater, and with the streets obliterated the Kiwi armour could not break in to mop up. Those paratroopers who had lived through it all emerged from their shelters full of fight. A battle on the Stalingrad model developed. Bombers and snipers were laboriously cleared from a few square yards at a time. On the hillside above the town the Essex and the Rajputana Rifles experienced equal difficulty in establishing a perimeter around Castle Hill. Every shattered wall, every cellar window, seemed to harbour a paratrooper. Of "C" Company of the Gurkhas there was neither sight nor sound. They had vanished into the blue and were off the map. It seemed

fantastic that a complete company could disappear on a few acres of hillside . . . Then, shortly before noon came some electrifying news. Corps artillery had asked if it was safe to lay a shoot on Hangman's Hill. The New Zealanders had reported that they could see figures around the outcrop and a little later a faint wireless message came through. The lost company of 1/9 Gurkhas was firmly established on the crest. By one of those freaks of fortune which so often alter history, Captain Drinkall and his men had threaded their way past two battles in the darkness, passing along the narrowest of corridors between the fighting at the hairpin bends and the strongpoint of the Continental Hotel. Across the rocky slopes the Gurkhas had worked steadily forward, clambering silently and weaving their way through a mass of enemy defences. They were unsupported and alone in the midst of the enemy. An hour before dawn they scrambled up the last few hundred yards, flung themselves at the crest and secured only a less prize than the Monastery itself. This exciting success made it imperative that whatever the risk this gallant company must be supplied and reinforced.'[6]

Hangman's Hill

This stirring action deserves more telling than the few short paragraphs given in the official history, so I am grateful to the Gurkha Museum for allowing me to quote from its archives.

> 'We began by moving down the valley to the old Essex area. From there we would be loosed to the attack by the Brigadier. It was only a move of about 800yd but it was one of the most difficult things we did. It was a pitch black evening. It was raining again. For some reason or other the normal nightly moves for the French on Castellone and for the Cavendish track were not diverted from the track down which we had to go. The confusion was hellish. We pushed and shoved our way against a stream of Moroccan muleteers, Madrassi

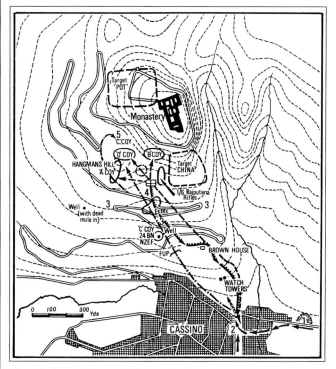

Above: Action on Hangman's hill 15-25 March 1944

Above: Supplies being airdropped onto Hangman's Hill by low-flying aircraft. Unfortunately many of them fell into German hands. *(Armed Forces Film & Photo Division, MOD New Delhi)*

pioneers and what have yous. We won. At last the whole battalion got into its right place. Enquiries at Brigade HQ which was just beside our position showed that the Kiwis were where they should have been, but that the takeover at the Castle was taking longer than expected. Taking into consideration the state of the weather and the ground in the town, this was not to be wondered at. At a quarter to midnight the Brigadier told the battalion to set off and wished us good luck, and at five minutes after midnight we started. We went in single file, C Company leading, followed by D, then Battalion HQ, B and A Companies and last of all the Carrier platoon, which was to form a little admin post to supply us, on the edge of town. Each company and Battalion HQ had with it a porter party formed from men of the Mortar, Anti-tank and Carrier platoons, strengthened by a newly arrived party of reinforcements who had not yet been allotted to companies. These porters, by reason of the burdens they had to carry, had to go unarmed.

'We went down the nullah [dry watercourse] to the old barracks and then turned down the main road to Cassino itself. The rain had now stopped and the night was getting lighter. When we reached the little quarry just north of the town we came up against the tail of 1/6 Raj Rif [Rajputana Rifles] and some New Zealand tanks. Beyond this place the road was blown and the track into Cassino lay over the fields. The Raj Rif did not know what the situation was. Their three coys [companies] had gone into the town and as yet no reports on their progress had come in. Since our movements were dependent on theirs we waited for a while to see if any news would come. By two o'clock in the morning nothing had come so 1/9 GR [1st/9th Gurkha Rifles] set off into Cassino. After a few yards of good going we got into the town itself. The place was in an unbelievable mess after the bombing. There was no vestige of a road or a track, only vast heaps of rubble out of which peered the jagged edges of walls. The whole of this mess was covered by huge deep craters that needed hand and foot climbing to get in an out of. There was no question of following any landmarks so laboriously picked off the air photos. We could only make for that part of the jumble that seemed to be nearest the Castle. It was slow going too.

'When we got to the top of the town we found the track to the Castle. Since it was being shot up by a machine-gun post about 20yd above our heads, and since we planned to go to our objective by a route that ran through the top of the town and out onto the hillside well below the Castle, we did not attempt to go up the track. Instead, we turned left into a narrow gully that ran between the broken walls of two houses. After squeezing through this for a little way we came upon a little open space where two ways led in the direction we wanted to go. C Company, under Micky Drinkall, were directed along the lower of the two and filed away into the darkness. In order to get the battalion onto a wider front, when D Company came along they were directed up the higher of the two ways. They had only gone a few yards when they were fired on then grenaded by a Bosche in a hole immediately above them. The head of the company recoiled a little and then they began to try to get at the Bosche. A few men, there was not room to manoeuvre more, tried to climb around the rubble and get behind and above the enemy. They made little progress in the unstable sea of rubble. At this time it was noticed that the eastern sky was lightening with the dawn.

'To be caught with the battalion in single file, hemmed in a narrow gully, in daylight would have been disastrous. It was therefore decided to shake out into daylight fighting formation. This was done by spreading out the battalion in an arc across the whole of the northern tip of the town. D Company was on the flank nearest the Castle, then B in the centre of the town and on the left nearest to the Rapido was A. Battalion HQ was put between D and B in the basement of what had once been a house of some size. It had been realised that the Germans in Cassino were by no means all dead or dismayed and so each company had to clear its own area and then try to work forward. By the time all were in place it was full light.

'At about this time there came into our lines a Sapper officer of one of our Sapper & Miner companies, who, with a New Zealand tank sergeant, had been given the task of making the recce for a tank approach to the road up to the Monastery. They had done their recce right in the middle of German held Cassino and had even been into the Hotel

Above: For 10 days and nights during the battle 1st/9th Gurkhas held their objective on Hangman's Hill, despite being cut off and having to be resupplied by air. Here fresh chapatis, made near the supply aerodrome, are packed into containers. *(Armed Forces Film & Photo Division, MOD New Delhi)*

Continental, the keystone of the enemy defences. They had had many desperate adventures in which the Kiwi was killed and they in turn killed Germans. This most gallant officer told us of the unbroken German strength in the town and of the deep defences in the Continental. There was little we could do about it, so off he went to Brigade to pass on his important news to those above.

'With the daylight came a good deal of incident. A little group of D Company, high up above near the Castle track, saw Germans creeping out of a whole well to the rear of A Company. A sniping competition was begun and keenly followed by an enthusiastic audience. Each Ted (short for the Italian word tedescaccio [*sic*], meaning "Kraut") as he emerged was shot. On the face of our perimeter there began a fusillade of small arms fire and grenading and the pot was stirred up with a good deal of mixed mortar and shell fire. Mingled up with the battalion were a good many other folk. There was Battalion HQ of the 1/6 Raj Rif and their one uncommitted coy. There were oddments of the Essex, Gunners and Signallers who had lost themselves and a good deal of tidying up and sorting out was needed. During this process a large shell brought down a huge avalanche of stones and rubble right on the heads of 1/6 Battalion HQ putting it out of action at a stroke. It was the cruellest luck. When that mess was cleared up there remained no one except the MO to command the battalion.

'About the same time B Company reported that there was a platoon of New Zealanders in their midst. They were all down in a cellar having a well earned rest. The entrance to the cellar was guarded by one man, completely unconcerned and competent. This platoon told us that they had captured the Castle and had then come down to join the rest of their battalion in the town. It is a measure of the New Zealand quality to realise that one little platoon had captured that almost inaccessible stronghold by itself and had then gone on for more. The Kiwis told us the situation on their front which was that most of their companies had got to where they were supposed to go, but now they were stuck with the Bosche all around them. They and we could make little progress and the state of the town itself denied us the possibility of getting tanks in to help.

'While the battalion was getting sorted out in the town no news of C Company had come in. Then about 11 o'clock rumours that our men had been seen on Hangman's Hill began to circulate, in the mysterious way that they do. Shortly after A Company, whose wireless sets were less screened by the hills than Battalion HQ, reported that they were in touch with C and that they were in fact on the objective and that for the present they were all right. The movements of C Company were quite incredible. After leaving the battalion they had wormed their way in single file through the labyrinth of rubble. They were challenged by Bosche who, however, did nothing about it. They called in at

Above: In full view of the enemy, Gurkhas collect their supplies of ammunition, food, water and medical equipment. They were often sniped at or mortared during such collections. *(Armed Forces Film & Photo Division, MOD New Delhi)*

the tradesmen's entrance of the Hotel Continental and had then struck up the hill. When they got to the line which had been chosen as the start line from the air photos they divested themselves of their small packs, as had been arranged, so they could climb and fight the better; these packs contained their food and water and should have been retrieved by a porter party had all gone as arranged. In fact, of course, they were lost for good.

'On the climb the coy got divided and the coy commander, Micky Drinkall, who, with only a few men climbed up to the hill on the south side, came round the west edge of the peak and neatly surprised the garrison who were situated on the little lip between the Hill and the Monastery. That was the end of them. The rest of the coy, under Jem [Jemadar] Kharakhbahadur, uncertain where anyone else was, went for the peak from the north and the two parties linked up on the Hill and held it. A fine example of daring, of everybody knowing the plan and carrying it out.

'Down in the town the unpleasantness continued. Bosche kept popping up where they had no right to be and frequent little excursions had to be made to round them up right behind our own front line. A Company had a lot of men buried in rubble brought down by shellfire and there was a steady drain of casualties from snipers. The stretcher bearers had a tough time collecting the men under the Red Cross flag and carrying them out over the craters and mess. It was here that we got our first realisation that these Germans were respecting the Red Cross.'[7]

A Symbol of Resistance

On the German side things were just as difficult. Despite all the efforts of the paratroopers, by the evening of the 15th, two-thirds of the town was in Allied hands. Nevertheless, the paras were still hanging on grimly to the rest of the ruins and, just as long as they could retain the railway station and the town centre, Cassino remained unconquered. As Rudolf Böhmler put it: 'Cassino had become the symbol of the German paratroops' will to resist.' And it was much the same on the surrounding hillsides. 1st/4th Essex had relieved the Kiwis on Castle Hill; in fact the whole sector of 2nd Company, 3rd Paratroop Regiment, was now in Allied hands and the company had virtually ceased to exist, only a solitary survivor managing to reach the monastery with his news. It then appeared for a while that the way to the monastery lay wide open, especially when the Rajputanas advanced towards Point 236. However, as we have already seen, they were held up by the right wing of 3rd Paratroop Company and also came under fire from their own artillery. Thus, after suffering grievous casualties — including all their officers killed or wounded — they had to abandon their attack. Next came the Gurkhas' assault which, as just recounted, reached the rugged slopes of Hangman's Hill. However, the machine guns of the German paratroops inflicted heavy losses on them. They soon had to take cover on the reverse slopes of the hill,

Above: This wounded German paratrooper cannot be medevac (medically evacuated). Instead, after being bandaged, he can only snatch a hasty cigarette during a brief lull in the battle. *(Bundesarchiv 101/577/1921/13)*

and were then pinned down there by accurate artillery fire. Then, at dawn on 17 March, an assault platoon of the 1st Battalion, 3rd Paratroop Regiment, under Sergeant-Major Steinmüller, stormed and recaptured Hangman's Hill. However, the Gurkhas launched an immediate counter-attack and pushed the Germans off the hill and back into the monastery. This New Zealand Corps penetration had caused considerable worry to both the German XIV Corps and Tenth Army headquarters, which urged General Heidrich to restore the situation immediately with another counter-attack. However, he decided that he would first try to destroy the infiltrators by fire rather than risk more heavy casualties in an assault. And this appeared to work well.

The Gurkhas' Advance

Plans were now put into effect to move the remainder of the 1st/9th Gurkhas up to join Micky Drinkall's gallant band on Hangman's Hill that night. The battalion set off from the town not a little apprehensive about what would happen to the area it had cleared, as it would be left to just a handful of Kiwis (in fact just one platoon) to prevent the Germans from infiltrating back. However, that was not their problem, so, having warned those concerned, they set off.

'The battalion climbed steadily and slowly up the track to the Castle. We left behind only the Aid Post, an important point later, since we thought they could work better under cover than on the hillside. When we got just below the Castle we met a man who told us that the south side of the walls was covered by enemy snipers in the old watch tower of the mediaeval wall which joins the Castle to Cassino town. Since there appeared to be a way round the north wall we went that way. Here there was complete peace. There was a goat track along the edge of the precipice and we walked along it enjoying a wonderful view of the moonlit hills adorned by occasional bursts of tracer fire and Verey lights. At the far end the battalion halted and then we went into the Castle to find

out what was going on. It was hard to tell and all we could be sure about was that the Essex held the little group of houses just west of the Castle and that C Company (ours) was on Hangman's Hill. We decided to set off across the hillside, each coy directed on its original objective, i.e.: D on the top of the peak with C Company; A down the southern face of the hill and B across the face of Monte Cassino and to the north of the peak.

'As we set off we were annoyed by being shelled by our own tanks from Route Six. They shot off their 75mm guns at the mountain and nearly hit us. We had this trouble again and there was no way we could stop it. The enthusiastic can be a sore trial to others. We had been shelled quite a bit while on the track above the town and we got machine-gunned from the hairpin bend of the road next below the Monastery. That informed us that the place was not held by our own troops, as it should have been. Apart from that we had little trouble as we climbed across and up to the Hill. One coy met and despatched a couple of Bosche from a strong point in a culvert under the road, who were apparently taking a moonlight walk. It was as well they were as they would have been difficult to get out of the culvert.

'Things now began to hot up. D Company's arrival at the Hill coincided with a mortar stonk which was followed by a most determined attack by the enemy onto the peak. The attack began on the south side and spread round the base of the crag to the north side. It was covered by the fire of enemy in the Monastery garden and in the roots of the Monastery walls. The attackers showered grenades on to the rock as they advanced. It was desperate work whilst it lasted. C Company, most gallantly led by Micky Drinkall, now wounded and with a broken leg, fought like tigers. There were many examples of individual gallantry, but the Bosche began to get a lodgement on the crag. At the critical moment D Company arrived and, led into a wild charge by Sammy Samuels, they drove the Bosche back and cleared the hill. They then settled down to consolidate the position and were soon after joined by B Company on their right and A Company below them. Such stores, mostly ammunition, as there were, were put into the right places. C Company were replenished and the casualties — a large number alas — were brought down off the crag and put into a culvert under the road just below Battalion HQ. The work of the unarmed carrying parties in all this necessary work was beyond praise. It was carried out under mortar and sniper fire, but it was done quickly and well. The battalion now dug itself in. The men made little sangars and burrowed in under the base of rocks or made themselves secure in cracks in the crag. Word was sent to Brigade HQ that we were settled in. A most pleasantly worded message of praise came back from the Brigadier.

'All this had been taking place in the early dawn. As the light strengthened our Gunners began to put down a smokescreen across the face of Monte Cassino. The screen was designed to, and effectively did, blind the eyes of the German OPs in the Monastery, as to what was going on in the town below. We, only 50 or so yards away from those same OPs, were the point of origin of the screen. The empty shells and the base plugs and the canisters all fell onto us. The empty shells and the base plugs were enough to kill a man and the reeking canisters choked us with the foul smelling smoke. We suffered many casualties from these causes, including Tony Hobbs, the adjutant. We got our battery commander to ask, first persuasively then abusively to have this nuisance abated.

Above: Both sides employed snipers — this one is a New Zealander and he is using a Lee Enfield No. 4 Mk 1 (T) which had a special cheek stock and was fitted with a No. 32 telescopic sight. *(IWM NA 13384)*

But as the battles in the town needed the screen our pleas were not heeded. The only thing to be said for the screen was that it did reduce the amount of sniping and mortaring which the Germans in the Monastery directed against us. The screen was kept up for the best part of a week.

'At about eight o'clock there fell on the town below us the full barrage of all available Allied artillery. How many guns there were is not known, but there were a lot. This tremendous bombardment went on for hours. It was odd to be on the enemy side of it. To have been in it must have been hell. The bombardment was followed by an attack by the New Zealanders. We saw some of it through rifts in the smokescreen. In particular we watched the attack on and the capture of the railway station by their tanks. We watched and saw, far away as if it were no concern of ours, two of the tanks brewed up as they went along the causeway to their objective.

'In the meantime we had our own problems. The enemy we had always with us. Sniping, mortaring and shelling went on and on and on. We also had other problems. The most pressing was water. We had long ago drunk our bottles and we had to find a source of refilling. We sent out little search parties. One of these reported a large bomb crater on the hillside which the rain had filled with water. This we used and the water was quite sweet. Food we had none as we had eaten our day's ration but we expected to get sent up some rations after dark. At two o'clock in the morning of the 18th of March, a party drawn from 4/6 Raj Rif came to us over the hill from the Castle. They brought with them a little food and some ammunition. There was enough food for everyone to get a little but by no means a full meal each. The Raj Rif had to come as a fighting force and that fact reduced the amount of payload they could carry. By the time that delivery had been made it was getting light and it was too light for the maintenance party to return, so we kept them with us and gave them a line to hold on our north flank, facing back towards the Castle.

'In the dawning came a contact officer of C Company 24th NZ Bn, a lad called Lloyd. He told us that they were going to try to clear Cassino from our side, the west. We wished them luck. We saw them on the spur below us and heard the reaction of the Tedesci to their attempts. We then saw them take up position on the spur and reckoned that they were not able to get on. During the morning we watched through the smokescreen the battle in the town. In the early afternoon, the smokescreen lifted. A little later we heard the hum of aircraft and saw about a dozen American fighter bombers coming towards us. They swooped down and dropped bundles on parachutes on to our position. It was the first attempt to supply us by air, which our Brigadier had arranged for us. Like all subsequent drops this one was only partially successful. This implies no criticism of the pilots who could not have shown greater skill and dash. But to land parachute bundles on a position one hundred yards square, set on the almost vertical side of a cliff is beyond the skill of any man. On this first occasion a few bundles landed in our place, these we quickly opened and found the contents to be ammunition. This gave us plenty and we never had any more anxiety on this score. The covers and parachutes also came in very handy as bedding for our large number of wounded. The packing of the bundles included empty water cans which we found very useful for drawing, distributing and storing water. When the aircraft had dropped their loads, the Germans mortared each one that we had not been able to get and so we left those to be fetched in after dark. Some bundles floated away far beyond our reach and we never recovered them.

'That night a maintenance party of the Raj Rif came to us. They came early and although they could not carry much, they had thought of everything and brought a little of each. There was food, ammo, signal stores, medical stuff, cigarettes and, best of all, two BOR [British Other Ranks] signallers from the div signals. These two brought a 22 set[8] with them and at last we had some real communications with the outside world. On the way up we had lost our brigade set and had had to make do with our gunner's set and our own 18 sets,[9] with which our sig officer, Doc Evans, did marvels. It was also during this night that Lincoln Gordon our LO [Liaison Officer] to Brigade made the trip back to HQ to give the Brig a true picture of our situation. It was no small feat to make that arduous trip and return in one night. When the Raj Rif party went back they took with them our wounded. We were mighty glad to get them off as many had been lying in the culvert with nothing but the most elementary treatment since the morning of the 16th. It was a good example of Gurkha stoicism that, in spite of their wounds, the lack of treatment, the cold and lack of shelter or food, no man complained and all were appreciative for the little that could be done for them. But that stoicism was to be more conspicuously displayed before we had done with Hangman's Hill.'[10]

That night, the battle began again around the Castle Hill area, where 1st/4th Essex prepared to extend its perimeter, supported with fire from a number of New Zealand Sherman tanks. Unfortunately, due to the angle of fire, some of the 75mm shells from the tank guns went over the crest and struck the walls of the castle, burying some of those who were forming up ready to

mount the attack. It had now also become virtually impossible to move in and out of the castle gateway without drawing heavy fire from fixed machine guns on the surrounding hills. Nevertheless, preparations for the attack continued. Down in the town the New Zealanders were unable to make much progress, any movement immediately drawing enemy fire. 25th Battalion HQ was out of touch with all its companies apart from C Company, which was in the gaol where there was a telephone. 26th New Zealand Battalion, which was waiting for the first objective to be taken before attacking towards the railway station, had a similar frustrating day until the afternoon, when one of its platoons managed to clear the paratroopers out of the convent. Three tanks of A Squadron had managed to reach the convent along Route 6, using a Bailey bridge that had been erected over the Rapido by some US engineers. The arrival of these tanks was probably the most encouraging event that day, because most tank movement was so severely limited. Nevertheless, the overall plan remained for the New Zealanders to synchronise an attack on Cassino railway station with the Indian attack on the monastery, to be followed by a tank thrust up Cavendish Road, which ran from Cairo (*see map in Chapter 5*), to the west of Colle Maiola and Snakeshead Ridge, to the rear of the Monastery. That was to be on the morning of the 16th, but it was postponed until the 17th, when it was decided that 25th New Zealand Battalion, supported by A Squadron, 17th Armoured Regiment, would lead the attack, then 26th Battalion would take the railway station and 24th Battalion the area around the Colosseum. However, the problem was that there were only nine of the squadron's tanks in the town and six of these could not advance until numerous bomb craters had been filled in and debris removed — the negative effects of the air strike were certainly coming home to roost.

Up in the hills, the situation around Castle Hill was deteriorating. The Germans had perfect observation and could follow all the moves made by the attackers. Sensibly, they waited for dawn, then a battalion from 1st Paratroop Regiment attacked down the spur from the Monastery, aiming at Castle Hill. Companies of 1st/4th

Essex and 1st/6th Rajputanas, which were engaged in a relieving operation at the hairpin bend, were overrun and virtually destroyed. The attackers swept on and reached the walls of the castle, but were then stopped by the garrison who:

'. . . like knightly defenders of old, lined the walls with their men, exchanging showers of grenades and bursts of tommy gun fire at point blank range. A paratroop prisoner in the castle courtyard watched this exciting clash with a professional eye. When his comrades fell back baffled he congratulated Major Beckett of the Essex on a most soldierly performance and in token of his appreciation presented the Essex officer with his fur-lined paratrooper gauntlets.'[11]

Corporal Bill Hawkins was right in the middle of this action:

'The Germans came right up to the castle walls and the grenades came in from all round us. We had [No] 36 Mills Grenades, but the German grenades had long wooden handles and they could throw them quite some distance. They were throwing them up, to drop in the castle. If we wanted to shoot at them, then you had to put your head over the parapet and look down over the top of the wall, so you were quite exposed. It was a difficult place to defend really. We lost our company commander. He was killed by a sniper. They were very good at what they were doing and must have been in very, very good positions. We also lost two platoon commanders and our second in command. He was buried under the wall, but we managed to get him out. There was a terrific amount of shelling, hitting and blasting the walls, with some landing inside, then there was this noise of rocks tumbling and a section of wall tumbled down on 10 or 11 chaps, including the platoon commander and three NCOs. There were several attacks on the castle but we managed to keep them out. The only ones who actually came into the castle were prisoners or wounded.'

The German attack on the castle had been beaten off, but not without grievous loss to both sides, including the Essex CO, who fell to a sniper's bullet. Two companies of 1st/4th Essex, which had been on their way to support the Gurkhas on Hangman's Hill, were caught on the bare hillside at first light and sustained heavy casualties. They tried to withdraw, but were badly mauled, only a handful managing to reach the comparative safety of the castle walls. The battalion ceased to exist as a fighting force and had to be withdrawn, its place being taken by 6th Royal West Kents, from 78th Infantry Division. The task given to this battalion was to take over the castle and positions on Castle Hill as its regimental history relates:

'The troops moved off in MT [motor transport] on the morning of the 19th to a harbour at San Michele, while Col Bryan and the Company Commanders went forward to Castle Hill to view the ground. As they were doing so, the CO of 1/4 Essex who was handing over the positions to them, was sniped and badly wounded. Ten minutes later, as they walked back down the hill Maj Birch and Capt Weatherly were killed. The loss of these two company commanders at this stage was a severe blow. In the evening the battalion moved forward behind an advance guard to the Cairo area, and after dark, one company took over the Castle, while the reminder of the battalion took over positions on the hill . . . All day on March 20th the positions held by the battalion were shelled and mortared spasmodically. That night, to assist the renewed New Zealand attack on the Monastery, Col Bryan received orders to assault a yellow house some 120yd away from the castle walls. In order to do this the troops had to debouch from one of the castle entrances which was covered by German fixed lines of fire, and then deploy on the rocky slope of the hill. The space was so small that only one company could be used. D Company

(Maj Wakefield) was selected to carry out the attack. The first platoon succeeded in leaving the Castle and it was approaching the yellow house when a mine exploded and killed four men and wounded the platoon commander. Undeterred, Sgt Norman, who had also been wounded, remained at the head of his platoon and led it up to the objective. Maj Wakefield then brought up the other two platoons, but just as they reached the area of the yellow house more electrically detonated mines exploded and caused more casualties. By this time machine-gun and mortar fire was sweeping the confined area. There was considerable confusion and Maj Wakefield moved about amongst his men, encouraging them to press home the assault. But the enemy fire was too heavy. As dawn broke the troops were ordered

Above:
Lieutenant Jim Furness MBE, MC. This photograph was taken in Tel Aviv in February 1943, whilst he was attending a tank commanders' course. *(J. Furness)*

Left:
Jim Furness with his tank crew. *Back row:* Stan Furling (*left*) and Lindsay Myles; *front row, from left:* J.F., Bill Forbes and Leo Strong. *(J. Furness)*

back to the Castle to reorganise. A counter-attack came in immediately and, although it was beaten off, the attempt to capture the yellow house was abandoned.'[12]

Meanwhile, down in Cassino, the New Zealanders were pressing on with their battle for the station and, remarkably, some tanks were able to get through. Troop leader Jim Furness MBE, MC, recalled:

'My favourite patron saint, St Patrick, on that memorable day of March 17th 1944, saw to it that I would never forget his anniversary. I feel that I had more than my share of good luck and near misses, but I didn't realise until 20 years later as I will explain: Two German officers, one of them Gunter [*sic*] Rabiger, of the elite German Paratroop Division, were visiting my home town, Blenheim, and I was invited to meet them. The battle for Cassino came up for discussion and it was during this that Gunter solved the mystery for me — why did

my tanks get through an anti-tank road block when about six others following me for support met serious trouble? Gunter was in charge of an 88mm anti-tank gun in the basement of the Hotel des Roses a mere 500yd away. They saw my tanks stop at the roadblock — a perfect target as they had intended. My radio operator and I, under a smokescreen, got out and lifted the mines, testing each one to ensure that it had not been booby-trapped. However, their gunner was away attending to a call of nature and he had the keys of the gun turret in his pocket. He returned to see my tanks on their way to Cassino railway station, which was just a smoking skeleton at this stage. But he was able to destroy or disable five of the six tanks following me. I felt proud to have been able to claim a valuable piece of overseas real estate — a flattened railway

Above: Aerial view of the crossroads leading from the flattened town (*right*) to the railway station and Hummocks (*left*). The road was blocked at Q by rows of anti-tank mines. At the top of the picture is the Hotel des Roses in which a German 88mm anti-tank gun was concealed. The two leading tanks got through after lifting the mines, but only one of the next six sent in to support them made it. The rest were knocked out by the 88mm and are marked with circles and numbered 2 to 6. *(J. Furness)*

station and yards that it was . . . After three days and nights at the Railway Station, my tanks were withdrawn for the crews to have a "breather". Then after a couple of days I was asked to take my tank back into the mass of rubble which had once been Cassino town, where the German snipers had played havoc with our ground troops. It wasn't safe to stay overnight in those conditions so, as darkness closed in, I headed for base. Everything was going to plan until the tank began slowly to topple sideways. We hadn't seen the deep bomb crater ahead and down we went, ending upside down and very uncomfortable. The five of us in the crew made an ignominious exit through the escape hatch. The artillery put down a thick smoke screen to assist us in our trudge back to our lines. But the effect was not entirely what we wanted. One of our crew was subject to bouts of asthma and the smoke brought on an attack. We took turns at carrying him until we were out of the thickest screen and we all reached base "tired but happy".

But this wasn't the end of the drama for me. I hadn't been back in base long when I discovered I had left my pistol draped over the tank radio, which was in the rear of the turret. I feared all kinds of repercussions, even court martial, for leaving my weapon behind. Under cover of darkness, I sneaked back to my tank and with great relief found my pistol where I had left it. But I was annoyed to discover that after vacating the tank, an "unscrupulous" enemy had raided our tucker box attached to the rear of the tank. Gone were all kinds of goodies, and most tragic of all was the sizeable container of rum. An interesting sidelight to my tank in a crater episode was provided by a newspaper report I saw after I had come home. I knew my tank had not been recovered before I left Cassino, as I had seen the double set of tracks forming the road surface, the road had been built right over the tank. Back home towards the end of 1944, I read in my local newspaper that in the reconstruction of the highway through Cassino, a Sherman had been pulled out of a deep bomb crater and was now back in service again — minus the rum ration of course.'

Mr Furness went back to Cassino for the 50th anniversary in 1994 and helped unveil a plaque at the rebuilt railway station (actually 'pocketing' the covering flag to bring back to Blenheim and present it to the local Returned Services Association, which now has it on display with a suitable inscription).

During the final phase of the third battle, on the 18th, General Freyberg had decided to put in a fresh Maori battalion at first light the next day, to attack the Continental Hotel, whilst 1st/9th Gurkhas and 1st/4th Essex would storm the monastery. In order to help the infantry in their assault on the abbey, there would be a tank

Right:
Jim Furness's caption reads: 'I took this pic when I arrived at Cassino Railway Station, March 1944. I had a small camera strapped around my neck.'
(J. Furness)

raid from the rear, down Cavendish Road which the sappers had been working on for some weeks. So, as H-Hour approached, everyone got ready, the Maoris preparing themselves for their 200yd dash — not a great distance, but of course it was 200yd which had defied the other battalions for the past four days, so it was not going to be easy. Meanwhile the two columns of tanks readied themselves for their approach that would bring them to the back door of the monastery. Down in the Rapido valley the gunners made ready to give their supporting fire to both attacks, whilst on Hangman's Hill, the Gurkhas were ready to attack, but were still waiting anxiously for the Essex men to join them (they had been delayed when fire from the New Zealand tanks had overshot the crest and hit the castle, as already explained, burying a number of men who were forming up to the attack).

Then, just at the critical moment, the Germans had launched their counter-attack. Covered by withering machine-gun fire a paratroop battalion came racing down the mountainside, taking the Essex and Rajputs, who were still completing their relief, entirely by surprise. Despite the fact that the German took many casualties — one estimate was over 150 out of a starting force of 200 — they still pressed home their attack and stopped the Essex and the Rajputs in their tracks.

Elsewhere the Maoris had been halted in their assault on the Continental Hotel. The attack had started at first light but petered out by midday without making any real progress. In the mountains the tanks had also started off well but, when they reached the end of the road, had found the rough mountain tracks just too difficult and had been able to advance only in single file. Then, as they got near to Albaneta Farm, they came under heavy fire and ran into a minefield. Without infantry support, they had been forced to withdraw. Unfortunately, what had begun as a worthwhile gamble had not come off.

By the afternoon of the 19th, all the different parts of the battle had begun to peter out, the initiative passing once again to the Germans. Now it was a question of consolidating the gains which had been made, rather than hoping for new ones. The costs of the battle had been staggering — in the Second and Third Battles of Cassino, the New Zealand Division had lost 1,600 men, while 4th Indian Division had suffered over 3,000 casualties. Neither would ever be the same again; indeed, 4th Indian was now virtually non-existent. As the Indian history comments:

'There is a fierce chagrin that the two best divisions in the British Army, forming a corps that seemed a perfect combination, should have achieved nothing.'

Nevertheless, it goes on to say that there was in fact light at the end of the tunnel, because spring was just around the corner and, 'The disappointment of friends, like the vaults of the enemy alike had less than 50 days to live.'

A Final German Comment

The Third Battle was undoubtedly another victory for the defenders, so it is only fair to close this chapter with a final comment from their corps commander, who wrote:

'The battle raged for a fortnight in the town and on the steep slopes between what had once been the Abbey and the town. Often it looked as if the enemy, having penetrated into so many strongholds in the defence system, might well turn the tide against the defenders. But the two tactical handicaps for the attacking side remained the same all throughout the battle; infantry could not follow the bombing instantaneously — it had to be withdrawn for the bombing two or three miles back.

Secondly, tanks could not follow nor bypass the infantry. Their movements were slowed down by the huge craters leading into Cassino and on to the few bridges. The craters were not only those of bombs but also those of the shelling which had gone on for months. It was — as Hitler later said to me — the only battlefield that resembled the ones of World War 1. And, indeed, wandering along the path across the battlefield to reach a battalion command post reminded me of the Somme in 1916, the same surface all covered by clods or ploughed by shelling, no wall, no tree unhurt, no human being to be seen, but hell ablaze with the crack of explosions and the particular smell in the air of hot iron and newly turned soil.'[13]

Above: Exhausted Indian troops of 4th Indian Division are pictured as they come out of the line at Cassino. *(IWM NA 12895)*

Notes
1. *Supplement* to the *London Gazette*, 12 June 1950.
2. N. C. Phillips, *Official History of New Zealand in the Second World War, Italy*, Vol. 1, *The Sangro to Cassino*.
3. Quoted from the Malta Study.
4. Neal Hopkins, 'Some of my experiences during the Cassino campaign'.
5. Quoted from the Malta Study.
6. *The Tiger Triumphs.*
7. Extract from a contemporary account held at the Gurkha Museum (Ref: 9GR 429).
8. The WS 22 radio could transmit either speech or morse, over a range of 10 or 20 miles respectively. The two BOR signallers had certainly done a good job, because the 22 Set was supposed to be a three-man load.
9. The WS 18 was a short-range manpack set with a 6ft rod aerial and a range of only 2.5 miles on RT (voice).
10. Quoted from 9/GR/4, held at the Gurkha Museum, by kind permission.
11. *The Tiger Triumphs.*
12. Lieutenant-Colonel H.D. Chaplin, *The Queen's Own Royal West Kent Regiment, 1920–1950.*
13. General Frido von Senger und Etterlin, 'The Battles of Cassino', *Journal of the Royal United Services Institute*, May 1958.

Chapter 7

Operation 'Diadem', the Fourth and Final Battle:
11–18 May 1944

'Soldiers of the Allied Armies in Italy . . . you have drawn into Italy and mauled away many of the enemy's best divisions which he so badly needed to stem the advance of the Russian armies in the East . . . The Allied armies are now assembling for the final battles on sea, on land, and in the air to crush the enemy once and for all.

'From the East and the West, from the North and the South, blows are about to fall which will result in the final destruction of the Nazis and bring freedom once again to Europe, and hasten peace for us all. To us in Italy has been given the honour of striking the first blow.

'We are going to destroy the German Armies in Italy. The fighting will be hard, bitter and perhaps long, but you are warriors and soldiers of the highest order, who for more than a year have known only victory . . . So with God's help and blessing, we take the field, confident of victory.
H.R. Alexander, General
'Commander in Chief Allied Armies in Italy'[1]

Alexander's finest hour

Undoubtedly, the fourth and last battle of Cassino, Operation 'Diadem', was General Alexander's masterpiece of planning, meticulous in every detail, though of course that did not automatically mean that everything would go 'according to plan'.

Below: The Italian front, 11 May 1944.

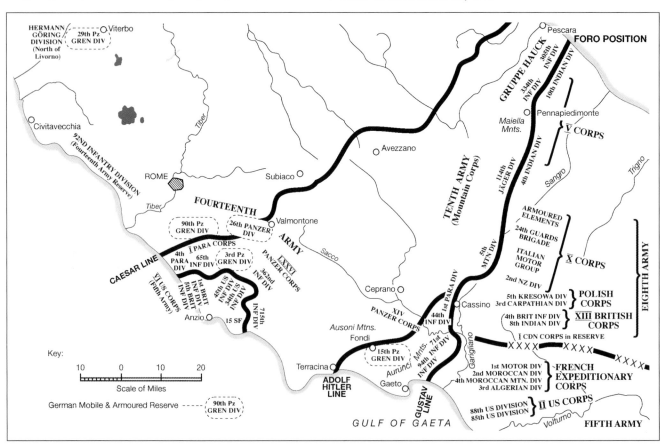

Above: The planners at work. Major-General Charles Keightley (*right*) of 78th Infantry Division, and Lieutenant-Colonel Hodgson, CO 3rd Welsh Guards of 1st Guards Brigade, hard at work prior to the final battle. *(IWM NA 13592)*

The Germans were difficult and dangerous enemies with many advantages from being in such a good defensive position, so it was never going to be easy. However, it was going to happen at a time and at a place of Alexander's choosing, and was not so dependent as before upon pressures from above, where almost every waking moment was now focused on the preparations for the Normandy landings. The good weather meant that Alexander would be able to deploy a large number of troops and thus have the requisite high level of superiority in men and weaponry as was required for success against the well-protected, determined and experienced enemy. This was normally reckoned to be at least three-to-one in infantry, together with a full complement of supporting arms and services.

In outline terms, 'Diadem' had three main elements:

- On the right flank, the Eighth Army would break into the Liri valley, take Cassino and advance towards Rome astride Route 6.
- On the left flank, the Fifth Army would drive towards Rome using Route 7 as its centre line.
- At the appropriate time, the forces in Anzio would debouch from their beachhead, cutting off any Germans withdrawing before the main advance. (This part of the plan falls outside the scope of this book.)

General Alexander's primary aim was to 'destroy the right wing of the German forces' rather than to capture Rome, which was, as far as he was concerned, a side issue, albeit a desirable one. However, its capture would unfortunately become the one and only goal to be achieved in the eyes of one of his senior commanders, General Mark Clark of US Fifth Army, giving it an importance that would inevitably detract from the stated aim.

Achieving the desired three-to-one superiority was not going to be easy because at the time there were only five more Allied divisions in Italy than there were German — 28 Allied to 23 German — so it was necessary to carry out extensive movement of troops so that superiority could be achieved. Alexander had to carry out this regrouping without the Germans finding out, so the move of the Eighth Army troops across from the east coast took place with the utmost secrecy. In addition, in order to achieve surprise, an ingenious deception plan was initiated, based upon encouraging the Germans to believe that the Allies had accepted the fact that the Gustav Line was just too strong to be broken, and that the coming summer offensive was going to take the form of another amphibious assault, this time to the north of Rome. Remarkably, the deception plan was a resounding success. In addition, the Allies continued Operation 'Strangle', the highly effective large-scale interdiction programme, begun by the Mediterranean Allied Tactical Air Force in the spring, against German rail, road and sea communications, so as to stop the flow of supplies to the southern Italian battlefront.

Alexander's plan required the concentration of some 16 divisions — eight-plus from the Fifth US Army and eight from the Eighth Army. These were deployed as follows:

Element One

The Polish Corps (3rd Carpathian and 5th Kresowa Infantry Divisions) would capture Cassino, then push on down the slopes to Route 6.

The British XIII Corps (4th and 78th [British] Infantry Divisions, 8th [Indian] Infantry Division, and 6th [British] Armoured Division) would force an entrance to the Liri valley, cross the Rapido, then, once across, one half would wheel right and link up with the Poles on Route 6, whilst the other half pushed on to the Hitler Line.

Above: Polish Corps commander General Anders arriving at General Keightley's HQ before the battle. (Keightley is shaking hands with Anders' interpreter.) *(IWM NA 13676)*

Above: Meanwhile the Germans await the Allied attack. Inside a ruined building German defenders prepare alongside a 7.5cm StuG 40 (assault gun, based upon the PzKpfw III tank chassis) which gave front-line troops an effective, hard-hitting anti-tank weapon. *(Bundesarchiv 101/578/1928/23a)*

Element Two

On the left II US Corps (85th and 88th US Infantry Divisions) and the French Expeditionary Corps (1st Motorised, 2nd Moroccan, 3rd Algerian and 4th Moroccan Divisions plus some 12,000 Goums) would attack through the Aurunci Mountains between the sea and the Liri valley. On the right, the French were to advance north of the Garigliano to Ausonia, then up the Ausente valley to Pontecorvo on the Hitler Line. On the left, II US Corps would push west across the grain of the country and along the coast to Gaeta.

Element Three

VI US Corps in the Anzio pocket was on orders to break out when necessary from the beachhead to Valmontone and cut Route 6.

This left a further four divisions immediately available/in reserve: two in the Canadian Corps (1st Canadian Infantry Division and 5th Canadian Armoured Division); and one each in the two Army Reserves: 6th South African Armoured Division (Eighth Army Reserve) and 36th US Infantry Division (Fifth Army Reserve). The Allied troops also had massive forces of artillery, aircraft and armour backing them up — some 1,600 guns behind both armies, 3,000-plus aircraft in support, and some 2,000 tanks at hand. H-Hour for the attack was fixed for 2300 hours on 11 May 1944.

Opposing them the Germans had the following groupings: 44th Infantry and 1st Paratroop Divisions in the Cassino area and elements of 15th Panzer Grenadier and 305th Infantry Divisions in the Liri valley; 71st Infantry Division plus elements of 44th Infantry Division in the coastal area; 94th Infantry Division in the Aurunci Mountains — one division; the rest of 15th Panzer Grenadier Division was in reserve near the coast, while 90th Panzer Grenadier Division was in Tenth Army Reserve.

Orders of Battle

We start as with each of the other three battles, with the Orders of Battle. To save too much repetition, only those of the Allies are shown and I would ask the reader to refer to previous chapters for the German orders of battle. (Only those forces actively engaged in the fourth battle are shown in detail.)

Allied Orders of Battle

(See previous chapters for fuller details of forces introduced in the First, Second and Third Battles)

Allied Armies Italy *General Sir Harold Alexander*

Eighth Army *Lieutenant-General Sir Oliver Leese*

II Polish Corps *Lieutenant-General W. Anders*

Corps Troops

6th Light Artillery Regiment

9th Artillery Regiment

10th & 11th Heavy Artillery Regiments

2nd Polish Armoured Brigade

1st, 2nd and 6th Kresowa Armoured Regiments

3rd Carpathian Division

Divisional Troops

1st, 2nd & 3rd Carpathian Field Artillery Regiments,

3rd Carpathian Anti-Tank Regiment

3rd Carpathian Light Anti-Aircraft Regiment

1st, 2nd & 3rd Carpathian Engineer Field Companies

3rd Carpathian Field Park Company

12th Podolski Lancers

1st Carpathian Rifle Brigade

1st, 2nd & 3rd Carpathian Rifle Battalions

2nd Carpathian Rifle Brigade

4th, 5th & 6th Carpathian Rifle Battalions

5th Kresowa Division

Divisional Troops

4th, 5th & 6th Kresowa Field Artillery Regiments

5th Kresowa Anti-Tank Regiment

5th Kresowa Light Anti-Aircraft Regiment

4th, 5th & 6th Kresowa Engineer Field Companies

5th Kresowa Field Park Company

12th Pozanski Lancers

5th Wilno Infantry Brigade

13th, 14th & 15th Rifle Battalions

6th Lwow Rifle Brigade

16th, 17th & 18th Rifle Battalions

XIII British Corps *Lieutenant-General S. C. Kirkman*

4th British Infantry Division *Major-General D. Ward*

Divisional Troops

22, 30th & 77th Field Artillery Regiments

14th Anti-Tank Regiment

91st Light Anti-Aircraft Regiment

7th, 59th & 225th Field Engineer Companies

18th Field Park Company

3rd Bridging Platoon

4th Reconnaissance Regiment

2nd Northumberland Fusiliers (machine-gun battalion)

10th Infantry Brigade

2nd Battalion, Bedfordshire and Hertfordshire Regiment

2nd Battalion, Duke of Cornwall's Light Infantry

1st/6th Battalion, Surrey Regiment

12th Infantry Brigade

2nd Battalion, Royal Fusiliers

6th Battalion, Black Watch

1st Battalion, Royal West Kent Regiment

28th Infantry Brigade

2nd Battalion, King's Shropshire Light Infantry

2nd Battalion, King's Own Regiment

2nd/4th Battalion, Hampshire Regiment

78th British Infantry Division *Major-General C. F. Keightley*

Divisional Troops

56th Reconnaissance Regiment

17th, 132nd & 138th Field Regiments

64th Anti-Tank Regiment

49th Light Anti-Aircraft Regiment

214th, 237th & 256th Engineer Field Companies

281st Field Park Company

21st Bridging Platoon

1st Battalion, Kensingtons (machine-gun battalion)

11th Infantry Brigade

2nd Battalion, Lancashire Fusiliers

1st Battalion, East Surrey Regiment

5th Battalion, Northamptonshire Regiment

36th Infantry Brigade

6th Battalion, Royal West Kent Regiment

5th Battalion, Buffs (Royal East Kent Regiment)

8th Battalion, Argyll & Sutherland Highlanders

38th (Irish) Infantry Brigade

2nd Battalion, London Irish Regiment

1st Battalion, Royal Irish Fusiliers

6th Battalion, Royal Inniskilling Fusiliers

8th Indian Infantry Division *Major-General D. Russell*

Divisional Troops

3rd, 52nd & 53rd Field Artillery Regiments

4th Anti-Tank Regiment

26th Light Anti-Aircraft Regiment

7th, 66th & 69th Engineer Field Companies

47th Field Park Company

17th Indian Infantry Brigade

1st Battalion, Royal Fusiliers

1st/12th Battalion, Frontier Force Regiment

1st/5th Battalion, Gurkha Rifles

19th Indian Infantry Brigade

1st/5th Battalion, Essex Regiment

3rd/8th Battalion, Punjab Regiment

6th/13th Battalion, Frontier Force Regiment

21th Indian Infantry Brigade
5th Battalion, Royal West Kent Regiment

1st/5th Battalion, Mahratta Light Infantry

3rd/15th Battalion, Punjab Regiment

6th British Armoured Division *Major-General V. Evelegh*

Divisional Troops
12th Royal Horse Artillery

152nd Field Artillery Regiment

72nd Anti-Tank Regiment

51st Light Anti-Aircraft Regiment

5th & 8th Engineer Field Squadrons

144th Field Park Squadron

8th Bridging Troop

6th Reconnaissance Regiment

1st Guards Brigade
3rd Battalion, Grenadier Guards

2nd Battalion, Coldstream Guards

3rd Battalion, Welsh Guards

26th Armoured Brigade
16th/5th Lancers

17th/21st Lancers

2nd Lothian & Border Horse

I Canadian Corps *Lieutenant-General E. Burns*

1st Canadian Infantry Division

Divisional Troops
1st, 2nd & 3rd Field Artillery Regiments

1st Anti-Tank Regiment

2nd Light Anti-Aircraft Regiment

1st, 2nd & 3rd Engineer Field Companies

2nd Field Park Company

1st Reconnaissance Regiment

1st Canadian Infantry Brigade
Royal Canadian Regiment

Hastings & Prince Edward Regiment

48th Highlanders of Canada

2nd Canadian Infantry Brigade
Princess Patricia's Canadian Light Infantry

Seaforth Highlanders of Canada

Loyal Edmonton Regiment

3rd Canadian Infantry Brigade
Royal 22ieme Regiment

Carleton & York Regiment

West Nova Scotia Regiment

5th Canadian Armoured Division

Divisional Troops
8th Canadian Horse Artillery

17th Field Artillery Regiment

4th Anti-Tank Regiment

5th Light Anti-Aircraft Regiment

1st & 10th Engineer Field Squadrons

4th Field Park Squadron

5th Reconnaissance Regiment

5th Canadian Armoured Brigade
2nd Armoured Regiment (Lord Strathcona's Horse)

5th Armoured Regiment
(8th Princess Louise's New Brunswick Hussars)

9th Armoured Regiment (British Columbia Dragoons)

11th Canadian Infantry Brigade
Perth Regiment

Cape Breton Highlanders

Irish Regiment of Canada

Army Reserve
6th South African Armoured Division

Fifth US Army *Lieutenant General Mark Clark*

II US Corps *Major General G. Keyes*

85th (US) Infantry Division

Divisional Troops
328th, 329th & 910th Field Artillery Battalions

403rd Medium Artillery Battalion

310th Engineer Battalion

337th Infantry Regiment

338th Infantry Regiment

339th Infantry Regiments

88th (US) Infantry Division

Divisional Troops
337th, 338th & 339th Field Artillery Battalions

913th Medium Artillery Battalion

313th Engineer Battalion

349th Infantry Regiment

350th Infantry Regiment

351st Infantry Regiment

VI US Corps *Major General L. K. Truscott*

3rd US Infantry Division

34th US Infantry Division

36th US Infantry Division

45th US Infantry Division

1st US Armored Division

1st (British) Infantry Division

5th (British) Infantry Division

1st Special Service Force

The French Expeditionary Corps[1] *General Alphonse Juin*

Corps Troops

Armour – Tank Group
7th and 8th Tank Destroyer Battalions

Engineers Group
201st & 202nd Pioneer Regiments;
180th Engineer Battalion

Artillery
Levant Colonial Artillery Regiment (155-mm gun)
63rd Algerian Artillery Regiment
(1st, 2nd & 3rd Battalions 105-mm howitzer,
plus one naval battery 155-mm gun)
32nd, 34th & 40th Anti-Aircraft Weapons Battalions

Medical
401st, 405th & 415th Evacuation Hospitals
422nd & 425th Field Surgical Hospitals
1st, 2nd & 3rd Mobile Surgical Fmns
531st Ambulance Company
541st & 542nd Veterinary Ambulance Companies

Pursuit Corps *General E. Larminat*

1st Motorised Infantry Division *Major General Diego Brosset*
(arrived in Italy in April 1944)

Divisional Troops
1st Marine Reconnaissance Battalion
1st Engineer Battalion
1st Artillery Regiment (1st, 2nd & 3rd Battalions
105-mm howitzer; 4th Battalion 155-mm howitzer)

1st Motorised Infantry Brigade
1st & 2nd Motorised Infantry Battalions Foreign Legion
22nd Motorised North African Infantry Battalion

2nd Motorised Infantry Brigade
4th, 5th and 11th Motorised Infantry Battalions

4th Motorised Infantry Brigade
21st & 24th Motorised Infantry Battalions
Pacific Marine Motorised Infantry Battalion

2nd Moroccan Infantry Division *Major General André Dody*
(arrived in Italy end of November 1943)

Divisional Troops
3rd Spahi (Moroccan) Reconnaissance Battalion
41st Anti-Aircraft Automatic Weapons Battalion
87th Engineer Battalion
63rd Algerian Artillery Regiment
(1st, 2nd & 3rd Battalions 105-mm howitzer;
4th Battalion 155-mm howitzer)

Regimental Groups
4th, 5th & 8th Moroccan Infantry Regiments
(each three battalions)

3rd Algerian Infantry Division
Major General Joseph de Goisland de Monsabert
(arrived in Italy end December 1943)

Divisional Troops
3rd Spahi (Algerian) Reconnaissance Battalion
37th Anti-Aircraft Automatic Weapons Battalion
83rd Engineer Battalion
67th Algerian Artillery Regiment (1st, 2nd & 3rd Battalions
105-mm howitzer; 4th Battalion 155-mm howitzer)

Regimental Groups
3rd & 7th Algerian Infantry Regiments;
4th Tunisian Infantry Regiment

Mountain Corps *Major General Guillaume*

4th Moroccan Mountain Division
Major-General François Sevez (arrived in Italy in February 1944)

Divisional Troops
4th Spahi (Moroccan) Reconnaissance Battalion
33rd Anti-Aircraft Automatic Weapons Battalion
82nd Engineer Battalion
69th Algerian Artillery Regiment
(1st, 2nd & 3rd Battalions 105-mm howitzer;
4th Battalion 155-mm howitzer)[2]

Regimental Groups
1st, 2nd & 6th Moroccan Infantry Regiments[3]
1st, 3rd & 4th Groups of three Tabors of three Goumiers[4]

General Reserves
7th Regiment Chasseurs d'Afrique
8th Regiment Chasseurs d'Afrique
64th African Artillery regiment

Notes
1. Not included is the fifth re-equipped division, the 9th Colonial Infantry Division of West African origin which was used to storm Elba.
2. Those operating with Goumier groups retained their 65mm mountain guns (mule pack).
3. All Regiments contained specially trained ski recce sections.
4. These included ten mule companies of Tunisian muleteers and 300 mules.

The Battle Begins

At 2300 hours on 11 May 1944, the 1,600 guns of the Allied artillery opened up with a 40-minute bombardment against every known German headquarters, gun battery and defensive position. Operation 'Diadem' was about to commence. Strangely enough, although the Germans really must have been expecting the Allies to resume their assault now that the good weather had arrived, it was clear that they did not suspect that 12 May was going to be D-Day, some of their key senior officers being absent from the front when 'Diadem' began. Not unlike Rommel, who had been absent from North Africa when the Battle of Alamein began, the Tenth Army commander, General von Vietinghoff, had gone to Germany to receive a decoration for valour from Hitler and was away on 11/12 May 1944. General Westphal (Kesselring's exceptionally able chief of staff), General von Senger (the brilliant XIV Panzer Corps commander) and his chief of staff were all away either on home leave or sick leave. The Allied planners could not have chosen a more opportune date and time to attack.

As the artillery blasted away, the men of II US Corps and the French Expeditionary Corps began moving up the lower slopes of the hills that led to their objectives. Forty-five minutes later the soldiers of the Eighth Army began their attack, XIII Corps moving towards its intended crossing sites over the Rapido River. One of these was Major George Knight MC, a company commander in 2nd/4th Hampshires of 28th Infantry Brigade. He recalled in a private letter:

'At precisely 2300 hours the barrage began and all across the front as far as we could see and hear, became alive. I was called to the field telephone by Bn HQ and told to go to see what state the bridge building had reached, some half a mile to our front. Pete (my batman) and I reached the approach track and found a mass of RE [Royal Engineers] vehicles, and as we walked towards the river, we thought it prudent to get into the ditch alongside the track, as things were rather lively. Soon we were stepping over dead bodies and then, so closely were they packed, actually on them. Reaching the CO by the river's edge

I commented on the scale of casualties the company had suffered. "They aren't casualties," he replied, "They are just taking cover!" Pete and I walked back over them and there wasn't a single movement! In response to my query as to where was the water's edge, the CO rattled a chain and a mass of bullets flew over our heads, together with shell and mortar fire.'

More from George Knight later. However, first some reminiscences from the sapper in charge, Lieutenant-Colonel A.P. de T. Daniell MC, then a field engineer company commander, who recalled:

'The long awaited assault on Cassino and the German "Gustav" Line was to be on May 12th. Our part of the operation was to be known by the code-name "Honker" — the cry of the homing wild geese . . . On 10th May we had a free day which we gave over to washing clothes, letter-writing and chores. It was a lovely day, I remember writing home so well. But the following day was devoted to briefing every member of the team, sappers, fusiliers and drivers all included. This was done with the help of three visual aids. The first was a most excellent model of the river, including our bend and the hinterland behind it, built up by Lt Notley almost entirely from aerial photos. In addition, we had sufficient vertical photos for every man to study. And thirdly, perhaps the most useful of all, we had a set of low-angle oblique air photos of the river line looking towards the Bosche.

'That night the team moved to a lying up area just behind Trocchio, about a mile from the river. The whole area was in fact part of the Divisional Gun Area. When I remarked on it some of the gunners said: "Oh Yes, we usually get plastered about 10pm." Just the time when the team was due to arrive!'

Fortunately that night there was no shelling, so the team was able to dig in undisturbed. Next day Daniell joined them with the division's Commander Royal Engineers (CRE), who wanted to wish the men good luck — and the Germans decided to shell them!

'We had 80 shells — 10 rounds of gunfire from two batteries. And the incredible thing was that not a soul was hurt . . . while our kit, motor-cycles and the two trucks we had with us were riddled. So we took it as a good omen and said our luck was in . . . H-Hour came and down by the river the flashes made it as light as day, while all one could hear was the continuous swish of shells passing overhead. Meanwhile, the old Bosche, cunning fellow that he always was, did not retreat under the barrage, but instead came forward to the line of the shingle bank of the river with machine guns. It was, originally, a still night with natural mist hanging over the river. But to add to the general confusion, the Bosche thickened up this natural mist with smoke till it was an impenetrable fog some hundred yards or more wide.

'Into this thickest of pea-soup fog the infantry advanced on a wide front carrying their boats in good order, straight towards the river. "W" or "Water Hour" was three-quarters of an hour after "H" Hour. But once in the fog they were lost. Some went right, some went left and nearly all went around in circles, coming back out of the fog into unfamiliar surroundings. Meanwhile, the Bosche who could not see either, fired his

Spandau machine-guns intermittently into the fog as well as mortaring spasmodically all along the river. All this fire was unobserved and therefore not very dangerous, but in the fog extremely frightening. A few of the boats did get across. But their main intention on landing was to get inland and seize their objectives, which they did all too easily as there were no Bosche anywhere near. But they did not clear the enemy off the far bank nor were we able to get anyone to do this vital though invidious chore. I did not want to use sappers for this, as we had hardly enough for our engineer tasks as it was.

'Half an hour later after "W" Hour, I set up my Bridge HQ at the top of the approach track and at the same time the old bulldozer trundled down the track. This seemed to enrage the Bosche, who directed all his available fire in the direction of the sound. This brought the bulldozer to a standstill, wounding the driver, but not until he had almost got to the bank. Thereafter, every time he started up a hail of bullets arrived. Next the Sappers arrived with the first of the lorries. But nothing could be done in that awful fog with bullets whizzing overhead. We simply had to get some chaps across to deal with those Spandaus.'

It was then that the CRE arrived and he and Daniell tried to find some officers or warrant officers, but could find only dejected parties of infantry 'milling around with their boats'. Meanwhile, however, one of Daniell's officers had swum across the river with a

Above: A German mortar detachment prepares for action. There are three 8cm schwerer Granatwerfer 34 going into action here. Although it entered service in 1934, this remained the standard German infantry mortar throughout the war and was a very sturdy and popular weapon. *(Bundesarchiv 101/577/1923/34)*

Above: Men and vehicles stream over the Bailey bridges across the River Gari. The bridges had to be covered by a heavy smokescreen as they were under continuous German fire. *(IWM NA 14809)*

Above: On the other side of the hill a British heavy mortar detachment swings into action, covering their ears as they fire their first salvo. It is 13 May 1944. The massive artillery barrage began at 2300 hours on the evening of 11 May, so the attack is now well under way. *(IWM NA 14732)*

rope and secured both ends to trees, passing it also through the bow fairlead of an assault boat which made a foolproof ferry. He then found an infantry officer, who raised a platoon and went off to clear the German machine guns, but soon returned having got hopelessly lost in the fog.

'All this time, of course, the bridging lorries had been arriving, strictly according to time-table, and were merely piling up at the top of the track. I stopped them eventually, but not until at least 20 out of the 32 had arrived. During this time Chubb was able to do a bit of improvement to the track, but even that was under difficulties and several track material lorries were hit on the hill down to the river.'

One can imagine how the state of chaos continued to build up as the night wore on. By dawn absolutely nothing had been achieved. When daylight came, they were all in full view of the monastery — caught like sitting ducks. Fortunately, Daniell was able to contact the CRE on the radio and when he explained the situation, was told to get everyone back to the relative safety of the lying-up area. One can imagine the relief as he passed the word around and started to move everyone back individually and in small parties, whilst he and his officers walked slowly back together. 'No one spoke a word, our tails could not have been lower.' All the planned bridge building for Operation 'Honker' had thus come to naught. Not one of the field companies had managed to complete its tasks. The bridgehead was never secured in sufficient strength to make that possible. However,

Above: This bridge was about 1,000yd from the main River Gari bridge and was built in two days, under continuous German fire, by 214th Field Company, RE, of 78th Infantry Division. *(IWM 15042)*

undeterred, the CRE decided to make another all-out effort on the night of the 12th/13th. He selected the original 225th Field Company site, code-named 'Amazon', as the place to build the bridge. Each of the three field companies (225th, 7th and then 59th) would work in relays, each relieving the other, as first one then the next became too exhausted to continue effectively. They were building an orthodox 80ft Class 40 Bailey bridge. Work began in earnest soon after 1700 hours and there followed a hectic night, during which the sappers sustained numerous casualties both whilst carrying out their engineer tasks and whilst having to go hunting persistent machine gunners. Eventually, as every single sapper was required for engineer work and there was still a danger of the Germans rushing the bridge, a covering party was established. Then a column of friendly tanks was heard approaching the bridge site, long before the bridge was completed. Its arrival would have caused chaos, and also brought down German fire. In fact, the column proved impossible to stop in time. It was eventually halted only a short distance off and its presence caused the bridge site to be heavily shelled. Nevertheless, the bridge was built by 0400 hours, but with the last four bays decked only and the decking of the other bays piled on the last bay to act as a counterweight. Every available man was needed to help the D4 bulldozer to give it all a 'good push' and launch it across the river. However, at the critical moment the bulldozer decided to give up the ghost. Fortunately someone remembered the tank column, so whilst one of his officers went to fetch the leading tank, Daniell explained on the radio about the latest hold-up. Eventually, despite everything, he and his men managed to open 'Amazon' to traffic and by 0500 hours the leading squadron of 17th/21st Lancers tanks was across.[2]

George Knight later recalled:

'Our battalion crossed the river via "Amazon" bridge, a few miles nearer Cassino. We were due to make a "two company forward and two in rear" attack with artillery and tanks, but had some hours to wait until zero hour. We lay down and enjoyed the warm sunshine and all the activity that was going on around us. There was the occasional sniping and I gave permission to two fellows to "sort him out" but not to loose off a lot of ammunition. Eventually we moved off in extended line and passed through the forward companies at the first objective, and went on to secure the others. On our left, some 200yd away were the remnants of a square wood, which from previous experience I believed to be held heavily by the enemy. Sure enough we were fired on again from there and I directed my reserve platoon into it, with orders to join up with us again beyond. Meanwhile I ran over to the nearest tank and pressed the button [on the infantry/tank telephone which was located inside an armoured box on the rear of the tank] for attention. Getting none, I lobbed a lump of earth into the open turret and a head popped up with a: "What the Hell?" I shouted: "Fire on that wood!" He shot off three or four rounds and I saw my fellows collecting the surrendering Germans. We then pressed on to our final objective taking many prisoners.'

Above: Men of the 6th Inniskillings pass through positions taken by the 2nd London Irish Rifles. *(IWM NA 15063)*

'Personal message from Lt-Gen S.C. Kirkman commander XIIIth Corps to Maj-Gen A.D. Ward, GOC 4th Inf Div (dated 18 May 44): "Now that Cassino has fallen to your division I would like to let you know how well I consider they have done. The assault across the Rapido was undoubtedly a most formidable undertaking, as the river, so aptly named, is swift and deep and the defences were well prepared and strong. The overrunning of the enemy's positions was a magnificent effort, the work of your Sappers on the second night was first class, and the building of the bridge which allowed you to pass over your tanks was a turning point in the battle. Each subsequent advance which you were asked to do has been quickly and successfully carried out. What has been achieved will long be remembered as a credit to the 45th Division."

'*S. C. Kirkman*, Lt-General, Commander'

A Victoria Cross for the Hampshires

After the epic night's work by the sappers, other infantry battalions, supported by tanks, were switched to cross by way of the Amazon bridge. As George Knight has already explained, these included 2nd/4th Hampshires which advanced over the bridge in brilliant sunshine and a heavy German barrage. The Hampshires' regimental history recalled how:

'Three hundred yards across the river the Battalion found what cover it could in shell-holes and small ditches while Col Fowler-Esson co-ordinated his plan with the troop leader of the 17th/21st Lancers (with Sherman tanks) and with the Gunners. The plan was for the Battalion to wheel left along the river and then proceed towards their original objectives. Zero hour for the advance was 14.30 hours, preceded by a 15-minute artillery concentration on the first objective. As the battalion waited in the scanty cover they were under constant high explosive fire, but spirits were high. The company commanders disregarded the German fire and walked round encouraging their men.

'At 2.30 on the afternoon of 13th May the 2/4th Battalion was ordered to advance. The companies stood up, formed into extended line and, with fixed bayonets, walked grimly forward beside the river, accompanied by the Sherman tanks of the 17th/21st Lancers.'

The history goes on to recount, as George Knight has already done, the storming of the wood and the capture of 73 prisoners. On the battalion went, crossing the River Pioppeta by wading across, although the tanks were unable to cross as the route over was blocked. The Germans were nonplussed by this resolute flank attack and, finding themselves now squeezed between the river and the Hampshires, they began to surrender in considerable numbers. B and D Companies advanced up the slope beyond the River Pioppeta and having topped the ridge (which was their original objective) pressed on. It was now that Captain Richard Wakeford came to the fore. Accompanied only by his orderly and armed only with a revolver, he was leading B Company on the right. He reached the objective first, killed a number of Germans and when his company caught up with him, handed over some 20 prisoners.

'The success of the Battalion was such that there was no stopping them and Col Fowler-Esson, who was with the leading companies throughout, kept them going. A strong-point in a house in the line of advance was vigorously defended, but Capt Wakeford once more led "B" Company in the assault with grenades and tommy guns. He was himself twice driven back by grenades, but with a final rush he reached the window and flung in his grenades. Five Germans surrendered at once; a sixth came out as though to surrender and suddenly shot one of "B" Company. He was immediately disposed of.

'By five o'clock in the afternoon the companies had taken up positions well beyond their objectives on Brown Line. The

Above: Lieutenant (Temporary Captain) Richard Wakeford of the 2nd/4th Battalion, Hampshire Regiment, who was awarded the Victoria Cross for gallantry on 13 May 1944, in the hills near Cassino. *(IWM HU 2056B)*

whole operation was a fine example of a set-piece attack with infantry, tanks and artillery co-operating to the finest degree. It was like a model exercise at a battle school. At the cost of comparatively slight casualties, the Battalion had cleared Brown Line across the whole front of the 28th Brigade's sector and beyond. The Battalion were in the highest spirits; they had taken some 200 prisoners and the battlefield was scattered with German corpses. Thus ended the first phase of the attack on the Gustav Line.'

Once the Germans recovered, the company positions came under concentrated artillery fire, but fortunately casualties were light. Phase 2 of the operation began the following morning at 0245 hours with a silent attack (that is, without a preparatory or accompanying artillery barrage), the battalion advancing in extended order, keeping direction by means of tracer bullets fired over the men's heads along the axis of advance. Despite poor visibility, the line of march was maintained. There was confused fighting on both flanks but by midday fighting on the battalion front had almost died down. At this stage total losses were only some 50 killed, wounded and missing. The third phase was to take the Red Line and this time the battalion ran into very heavy defensive fire, losing more than 100 men in two minutes. Nevertheless, despite the 'inferno of fire' the advance was maintained, up the slopes and on towards the objective.

'It was at this point that Captain Wakeford came so splendidly to the fore. He was already wounded in the face and arms, but he led "B" Company up the slope on the left of the battalion, keeping them under perfect control through withering fire. Half-way up the hill his company came under heavy Spandau fire; Capt Wakeford organised and led a party which charged and silenced the machine gun. As the

Above: Men of the Durham Light Infantry file past what is left of the Hotel des Roses in Cassino town, which earlier housed a German 88mm anti-tank gun *(see previous chapter)*. *(IWM NA 14999)*

Above: Cassino town is taken. A Guardsman brings in two German prisoners through the ruins below Castle Hill. *(IWM NA 14991)*

Captain Wakeford's orderly, Private J.C. Baxter, also fought with conspicuous gallantry, especially during the last desperate charge up the hill. Although NCOs and officers were falling all around him, he gathered a group of leaderless men together, including a number of Bren gunners, rallied them and led them onto the objective, then allocated them fire positions. When the Germans began to shell the newly won positions, he organised stretcher parties to carry away the wounded. He was awarded the Military Medal, whilst Company Sergeant-Major Pullinger nearby was also like a man possessed, moving from platoon to platoon in his company, rallying the men, despite considerable personal danger, only taking cover when the position was properly consolidated. His citation spoke of a '. . . notable example of the standards tradition has set for the British warrant officer'. So there was indeed much gallantry that day.

The French attack

'Order of the Day, 11 May 1944
    'French Soldiers of the Army of Italy, a vital battle which will hasten victory and the liberation of our country begins today. The struggle will be all-inclusive, implacable and fought to the bitter end. Called to honour our colours we will conquer as we have already conquered, thinking of martyred France who waits and watches us. Forward!
Alphonse Juin, General'

As explained in a previous chapter, by early May 1944 the CEF contained some 105,000 officers and men, a massive corps that was in strength equivalent to nearly five divisions. It had already shown its fighting prowess on Colle Belvedere and now bore the brunt of the offensive launched by US Fifth Army to break

company advanced again mortar bombs were bursting among the men and Capt Wakeford was wounded in both legs. But he still led on, reached the objective, organised and consolidated the remainder of his company and reported to his CO before submitting to any personal attention. For his extreme gallantry Captain Wakeford was awarded the Victoria Cross, and the citation ends with the words: "During the seven-hour interval before stretcher bearers could reach him his unwavering high spirits encouraged the wounded men around him. His selfless devotion to duty, leadership, determination, courage and disregard for his own serious injuries were beyond all praise."[3]

Below: The allies break through the Gustav and Hitler Lines, 11–23 May 1944.

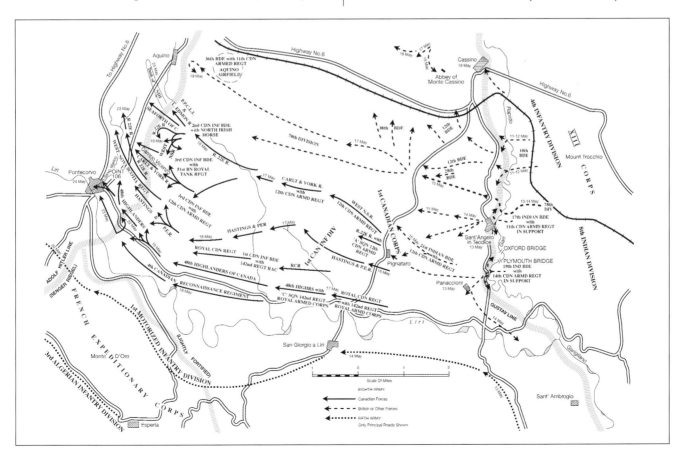

Above: French tanks also pushed forward. Here a column is led by a Howitzer Motor Carriage M8, which mounted a 75mm howitzer in an open-topped turret on an M5 light tank hull. *(IWM NA 15530)*

Above: These French troops of the same column examine a captured Nazi flag. *(IWM NA 15329)*

through the Gustav Line. This was the type of fighting in which the French colonial troops were experts — basic hand-to-hand combat, night operations and other low-level actions that were well suited to the mountainous country. Even their lack of motor transport and their preferred dependence on pack mules became an advantage in such rugged conditions. They had some 10 companies of mules, each comprising over 230 men (mainly Tunisians) and 300 animals, whilst the division's integral artillery (69th African Artillery Regiment) was equipped with 65mm mountain guns that were carried by pack mule. As General Alexander explained in a post-war interview, on 11 May the French attacked with splendid *élan* and 'drove like the wind' across the mountainous terrain between the Liri River and the Tyrrhenian Sea. Showing themselves quick to exploit each local success, 'possibly quicker than US and British troops', they succeeded 'to the surprise and elation of the Allied Command' in overrunning the German positions, inflicting a heavy toll in casualties and prisoners.[4] In just three days they had not only completed the breakthrough but had outflanked the German positions in the Liri valley. Their sensational advance came as a major surprise to the Germans and, having broken through, they pursued relentlessly, continuing their advance through the mountains south of Rome. 'French troops fighting splendidly with our American material' is how General Devers reported the situation in a message to General Marshall on 15 May 1944. General Mark Clark was equally enthusiastic about the French success, as he wrote in his autobiography *Calculated Risk*:

'Meantime the French forces had crossed the Garigliano and moved forward into the mountainous terrain lying south of the Liri River. It was not easy. As always the German veterans reacted strongly and there was bitter fighting. The French surprised the Germans and quickly seized key terrain including Monte Faito Cerasola and the high ground near Castelforte. The 1st Motorised Division helped the 2nd Moroccan Division to take Monte Girofano and then advanced rapidly north to San Apollinare and San Ambrogio. In spite of the stiffening German resistance, the 2nd Moroccan Division penetrated the Gustav Line in less than two days' fighting.

'The next 48 hours on the French front were decisive. The knife-wielding Goumiers swarmed over the hills, particularly at night, and Gen Juin's entire force showed an aggressiveness hour after hour that the Germans could not withstand. Cerasola, San Giorgio, Mte D'Oro, Ausonia and Esperia were seized in one of the most brilliant and daring advances of the war in Italy and, by May 16, the French Expeditionary Corps had thrust forward some 10 miles on their left flank to Monte Revole, with the remainder of their front slanting back to keep in contact with the British Eighth Army. For this performance, which was the key to the success of the entire drive on Rome, I shall always be a grateful admirer of Gen Juin and his magnificent FEC.'

The CEF eventually went on to Siena, which it captured on 3 July, then, as its leading elements were approaching Florence, the order was issued for their withdrawal and regrouping behind the front lines. By 23 July the relief of the CEF was completed. It was of course being replaced by other Allied units so that it could start getting ready for Operation 'Anvil', the forthcoming assault on Southern France. During its time in Italy, the records show that the CEF sustained about 30,000 casualties (5,900 killed and over 24,000 wounded). It had taken over 8,000 prisoners.

Above: From the northern edge of Cassino town a GI looks over the rubble, towards the ruins on Castle Hill and Monastery Hill towering behind it. *(IWM IA 24313)*

II US Corps Pushes On

South of the French, II Corps was also moving with considerable speed. 85th US Infantry Division captured Formia on 17 May and then Gaeta just two days later. 88th US Infantry Division, which was fighting in the mountains like the French, took Itry on the 19th. Thus the whole southern sector of the Hitler Line, known as the 'Dora' extension, was being overrun before the Canadian Corps, whose task it was going to be to break the line, had even begun to approach it in the Liri valley. To try and fill the gap Kesselring attempted to move 26th Panzer Division, which had been 'coast watching' in the vicinity of Rome — thanks to the Allied cover plan which had hoodwinked him completely.

North of the CEF, on the Eighth Army's left flank, XIII Corps was striking for Aquino, whilst the Canadian Corps prepared to assault Pontecorvo early on the 23rd. The Canadians had a hard battle and lost a fair number of men and tanks before they achieved a breakthrough, taking some 500 prisoners. The Hitler Line was broken and the Allies could resume their advance up Route 6.

At the same time as the Eighth Army was making its set-piece attack on the Hitler Line on the 23rd, the force in the Anzio beachhead was launched; two days later it was within striking distance of Valmontone and the following day astride the German withdrawal route. However, the hoped-for encirclement would not happen. General Truscott was ordered to change his plans and to head, on Clark's direct order, straight for Rome. This allowed the German Tenth Army to escape from the Allied trap and General Clark to celebrate the capture of the Holy City on 5 June — just a few hours before the Allies landed in Normandy.

And the Poles

But to return to the main story and the final capture of the Monastery.

> 'Order of the Day — 11 May 1944
> 'Soldiers!
> 'The moment for battle has arrived. We have long awaited the moment for revenge and retribution on our hereditary enemy.
> 'Shoulder to shoulder with us will fight British, American, Canadian and New Zealand Divisions, together with French, Italian and Indian troops.
> 'The task assigned to us will cover with glory the name of the Polish soldiers all over the world.
> 'At this moment the thoughts and the hearts of our whole nation will be with us.
> 'Trusting in the Justice of Divine Providence we go forward with the sacred slogan in our hearts: God, Honour, Country.
> '*Wladyslaw Anders*, Lt-General
> 'Commander, II Polish Army Corps.
> '11 May 1944'[5]

Anders' plan was to attempt to overcome the mutually supporting German positions around Snakeshead Ridge by attacking all the German positions simultaneously. Whilst the Poles had some advantages over the other national forces that had already tried and failed to take the Cassino redoubt — for example, the better weather — they still faced probably the most difficult task of all the attackers, impeded as they were by rocks, boulders, impenetrable thickets and savage, unrelenting machine-gun fire.

'As the evening faded into darkness of night on May 11 all was quiet. Suddenly the guns roared, echoing from mountain

to mountain and filling the valleys with the sound of thunder. From one coast of Italy to the other the offensive had begun. For 40 minutes Allied artillery pounded the German artillery positions. At 11.40 the Polish gunners turned their fire upon the positions of the enemy infantry. At 1 a.m. two Polish divisions attacked.'

That is how General Anders begins his account of the Polish part in Operation 'Diadem' in his book *An Army in Exile*. The plan was for his corps to tackle the heights around Cassino, with a view to isolating the monastery feature by seizing the adjacent heights, then pushing on down the slopes to Route 6. Here is how the attack is covered in a Polish report written for the British Historical Section of HQ Central Mediterranean Forces on operations of II Polish Corps 11–25 May 1944:

The attack of the 5th Kresowa Division (11–12 May)

'The Division's plan for the capture of Colle S. Angelo Ridge was straightforward. While 6 Lwow Brigade covered the right flank on Mte Castellone and held the attention of the enemy on Passo Corne by fire and by a feint attack, 5 Wilno Brigade advanced two up, 13 Bn right and 15 Bn left, with Phantom Ridge as their first and Colle S. Angelo Ridge as their final objective. 18 Bn, placed under command of 6 Lwow Brigade, was to follow 15 Bn; but in order to avoid congestion, 18 Bn was not to leave its forming up point until 15 Bn had taken and cleared its first objective and had begun the advance on Point 575. 14 Bn held the start line. An MMG [medium machine-gun] company, 26 x 4.2in mortars and a troop of tanks supported the attack.

Above: Polish troops in action. Here two Polish infantrymen are attacking using hand grenades. They are throwing Mills 36M grenades which weighed 1.7lb and had a variable delay fuse of 4–7 seconds. *(IWM MH 1984)*

'6 Lwow Brigade's feint, which was made by patrols with a maximum display of fire support, was successful and the enemy duly reacted by putting down defensive fire on the brigade front. 5 Wilno Brigade's plans, however, began to go awry from the start. The greater part of the German artillery and mortars survived the counter-battery bombardment, the chief effect of which was to sever the German telephone communications; as these were put in order, the enemy's fire rapidly regained almost its full intensity. Sufficient of the German guns and mortars were able to come into action at the start of the advance to slow it down very considerably; by 0230hrs, when 13 and 15 Bns reached the foot of Phantom Ridge, after taking twice as long as anticipated, they had suffered 20% casualties and, with their communications already becoming disrupted, control of the attack was slipping.

'Nevertheless, both battalions gained the crest of Phantom Ridge, but once there, they found it impossible to proceed, because of the intense fire from all types of weapons, and very costly to remain. On the extreme right, on reaching the crest and the saddle [map reference] 826227, the commander of the two right-hand companies of 13 Bn found his troops withering away under intense frontal and flanking fire, so ordered a withdrawal to the hummock (Pt 706) on the southern end of Mte Castellone, where they joined forces with the left flank of the 6 Lwow Brigade. The two left-hand companies of that battalion engaged the enemy field works at close quarters on reaching the top and partially cleared them, but were finally pinned down by automatic fire. On the left 15 Bn also began to clear the Germans out of their sangars, but dense thorn-scrub as well as rocks and boulders greatly added to the difficulties of night-fighting and prevented proper clearance of the ridge. Two companies nevertheless managed to thrust past the enemy positions and reached Pt 517's small spur 300yd on and almost half-way to the final objective. There they were heavily engaged by small arms fire and their commander, finding himself well ahead of the remainder and out of touch, ordered a retirement to the forward slope of Phantom Ridge.

'18 Bn was waiting to move off at 0300hrs, by which time 15 Bn was expected to have finished clearing the first objective and to be resuming its advance. Communications within the brigade had by then broken down entirely, however, telephone lines had been cut, wireless sets destroyed or their operators killed by shelling, and communications by runner were impossible. The Brigade commander was himself without news of forward troops and 18 Bn had communications with neither. Seeing 15 Bn apparently beginning the second phase of its advance and supposing, therefore, that the ridge had been duly cleared, OC 18 Bn decided to keep to the original timings and gave the order to advance. By 0630hrs, 18 Bn had joined 15 Bn on Phantom Ridge causing much congestion. German shelling and mortaring grew steadily heavier and the damage caused by

the initial counter-battery was repaired and casualties were rising. About the time of 18 Bn's arrival, the Germans mounted a counter-attack from behind Pt 517, which was successfully beaten off, however, by the two forward companies of 15 Bn on the western slopes of the ridge. The enemy still held some positions among the rocks and bushes, though they were being reduced and altogether the situation was confused.

'The Divisional commander reviewed the position in the course of the morning and, appreciating from such scanty information as was available that, although they had incurred heavy losses and were still disorganised, two and a half battalions were still on the intermediate objective, decided to press the attack and to commit 16 and 17 Bns from 6 Lwow Brigade. Before 1500 hours, which was the time set for renewing the attack, however, he received orders to withdraw.

'Meanwhile CO 18 Bn withdrew at 1300hrs of his own accord. Seeing his troops suffering heavily under the German fire without apparent advantage and being unable to call down defensive fire or to consult the Brigade Commander, he gave the order to retire to the start line. Some troops of the other two battalions mistook this for a general withdrawal and fell back also, leaving the two forward companies of 15 Bn and part of two companies of 13 Bn to hold Phantom Ridge from which they too withdrew, in accordance with orders received from Corps, the same evening without substantial further loss.'

Above: Poles belonging to the 3rd Carpathian Infantry Division struggle up a steep slope towards the monastery, dragging ammunition supplies with them as they move ever closer to the last German stronghold. *(IWM MH 1978)*

Above:
The Poles had to winkle German paratroopers out of some of their positions. However, there were only a handful of wounded paras left in the shell-torn buildings when the Poles eventually reached the monastery. *(IWM MH 1983)*

Opposite top:
Victory at last. The top of the monastery is crowned by a rudimentary Polish Lancers pennant (made from parts of a Red Cross flag and a blue handkerchief), plus a Union flag, 18 May 1944. *(IWM MH 1680)*

Left:
From their positions among the ruins of Castle Hill, Guards Bren gunners cheer the fall of the town and monastery. *(IWM NA 14987)*

Opposite:
Polish soldiers resting in the monastery catacombs after the battle, 18 May 1944. *(IWM NA 15143)*

The attack of the 3rd Carpathian Division (11–12 May)

Unfortunately the attack by the other Polish division was equally unsuccessful. Major Zdzistaw Kirakowski was serving in one of the infantry regiments in the Carpathian division. He remembered much of the action:

'At one o'clock we moved to the attack and as soon as we had crossed the road we encountered German bunkers and that is when it started. It is difficult to describe. No one wants to remember shouts and shooting and killing, that's something dreadful which you do because you have to. If you don't do it to them then they will do it to you. I will always live with the memory of shooting a German who was throwing a hand grenade at me — he fell on his own grenade and I was all covered in his blood — I still dream about it. OK — but it was necessary.

'We moved towards Pt 593, initially there were 25 of us, with three machine guns. We captured the hill but by the time we got there we had only one machine gun and two boxes of ammunition, each containing 250 rounds. It was still very dark. The 2nd Battalion moved on to the next Hill — Pt 563 I think — while we stayed on 593 most of the morning and used up most of our ammunition. We were "sitting ducks" as the Germans could see every one of us. By now there were just three of us left and one machine gun. Eventually I was wounded and a friend of mine pulled me out. Once we ran out of ammunition we decided there was no point staying — if I told you that we threw stones you wouldn't believe me, but that's what we did and eventually we had to withdraw from the hill. As we moved the Germans threw hand grenades and one exploded in front of me and I was covered in small pieces of shrapnel — they were superficial wounds really. However, it also pierced some ammunition boxes I had on my back and pierced into my right arm and sort of nailed it so I couldn't move it . . . I was wounded again, this time in the legs, so my friend helped me back. There was just three of us then and I was badly wounded and had lost a lot of blood.'[6]

Eventually Major Kirakowski reached hospital and was there when the news came that Monte Cassino had been taken by Polish troops — he said that he 'jumped for joy'.

Sadly, the Carpathian Division, just like Kresowa Division, had flung itself at the Germans, then been fought to a standstill on Point 593 and Phantom Ridge and was now down to just a handful of survivors who were slowly being picked off as they lay out in the open, until, at long last, they were ordered to withdraw. The Poles had lost heavily and were back where they had started. Nevertheless, it would soon be time to try again, but not before a rest to reorganise and to resume artillery and mortar barrages onto the German Parachute Division positions.

General Leese visited General Anders on the afternoon of the 12th and said that he felt the Poles had more than carried out the task he had set them and had been of great assistance to the British XIII Corps, which had been attacking in the Liri valley as we have seen. Thanks to this assistance XIII Corps had been able to cross the river and establish its bridgeheads and to bring up further reinforcements of men and equipment. Leese agreed with Anders' intention to mount a second attack, but felt that its timings should be co-ordinated with the progress made in the Liri valley as he did not want General Anders to fight an isolated battle.

Above: A Polish soldier sifts through German equipment in one of their underground bunkers. *(IWM NA 15159)*

Above: After the battle: Polish dead being moved from the battlefield for proper burial. *(IWM NA 15138)*

The Poles spent the interval between the first and second attacks by carrying out aggressive patrolling of the German positions, regular artillery bombardments, local attacks and so on. The new co-ordinated attacks for both corps would be timed to start at 0700 hours on 17 May. The corps plan called for 20 minutes of counter-battery and counter-mortar fire, followed by a further 40 minutes of concentrations onto the German infantry positions. Then the infantry of both divisions would go in.

Undoubtedly, the pressure was beginning to tell on the Germans, because what had altered more than anything was their strength. They had suffered heavy casualties in the first attack and had then begun to draw on their reserves to stem the Allied advance in the valley. It was estimated that the forces facing the Poles now consisted of three battalions, two of which (2nd Battalion, 100th Mountain Regiment, and 1st Battalion, 3rd Parachute Regiment), both in the line, were weak. The third was being held in reserve.

The Poles got off to a good start, and on the first day captured Phantom Ridge, Sant'Angelo, Hill 593 (apart from its northern portion) and the Gorge. The next day they had to make use of the battalions who had been involved in the first battles on 12 May and were therefore much reduced in strength. They also used Polish commandos, part of the Poznan Lancers and two small new battalions, that General Anders had organised from men from the anti-tank regiment, drivers, workshop personnel and suchlike. 'I estimated, however, that the Germans must be quite as exhausted as we were, or even more,' wrote Anders later in *An Army in Exile*, 'so that in the next day's fighting, therefore, our attack, even if less powerful than our first effort, would achieve definite success.'

And he was quite correct. Clearly the critical moment had been reached. Both sides were exhausted and apparently neither was capable of making any further effort. However, as General Anders guessed, at a moment like that 'the one with the stronger will, who is able to deliver the final blow, wins'.

Above: Generals Alexander and Anders salute the Polish colours after their historic victory at Monte Cassino. *(IWM NA 15352)*

'The mist-shrouded slopes of Monte Cassino were uncannily quiet on the morning of 18 May 1944. Then, shortly before 10 o'clock, soldiers wearing the battledress and distinctive disc-shaped steel helmets of the British Army heard a bugle playing from within the bomb- and shell-blasted ruins of the monastery that still towered above them. Few of the combat-hardened soldiers who heard it were unmoved, for it was sounding their country's traditional military call, the *Hejnal*. A rudimentary flag, improvised from parts of a Red Cross emblem and a blue handkerchief, flew from the ruins. It was the pennant of the 12th Podolski Lancers, the Reconnaissance Regiment of the 3rd Carpathian Rifle Division, which had ordered a patrol to investigate the suspiciously quiet monastery. The 12th Lancers had cautiously entered the ruins to find its German paratroop defenders gone, leaving only a handful of their wounded behind.'[7]

The fortress that had so long blocked the road to Rome had fallen.

There were to be many congratulatory messages sent to General Anders by all the other Allied commanders. However, what he considered to be their highest reward was one from the soldiers of the Polish Underground, who sent him the following telegram (as he put it, 'by roundabout ways through London'):

'Soldiers of the Polish Underground Army pay tribute to the fallen and surviving combatants of the victorious battle of Monte Cassino. Your glorious fighting gives to us the strength to carry on with our tenacious struggle. Commander Home Army, 24.5.44.'

For the record, the Poles lost 281 officers and 3,503 other ranks in the fighting, of whom over one third were killed — more D-Day Dodgers who would 'stay in Italy'.

Notes
1. Message from CinC Allied Armies in Italy to his troops, May 1944.
2. Quotations taken from an article: 'The Battle for Cassino, May 1944' by Lt-Col A. P. de T. Daniell MC, TD, Royal Engineers.
3. Extracts taken from: 'The Hampshire Brigade in Italy' chapter of The Regimental History of the Royal Hampshire Regiment. There was another Victoria Cross awarded during Operation 'Diadem' — to Fusilier Arthur Jefferson of the Lancashire Fusiliers, for knocking out an enemy tank on 16 May 1944 during an attack on the Gustav Line, with a hand-held PIAT (Projector Infantry Anti-Tank).
4. Field Marshal Alexander to Dr Sidney T. Matthews during an interview in Ottawa 10–15 January 1949; see *Rearming the French*, page 178.
5. Message from Gen Anders to his troops, 11 May 1944, from *An Army in Exile*.
6. Imperial War Museum Sound Archive No 20930.
7. Janusz Piekalkiewicz, *Cassino: Anatomy of the Battle*.

Above: The ruins that once were the Benedictine monastery of Monte Cassino. It would rise again in all its glory after the war. *(IWM C 4363)*

Above: Commander of the victorious Eighth Army, General Leese (*centre*), walks through the ruins of Cassino town after the battle. *(IWM NA 15096)*

Above: The moonscape that once was the little town of Cassino. Jagged walls and water-filled bomb craters are all that remain on the battlefield. *(IWM NYP 25219)*

Above: Another view of Cassino, May 1944. The inevitable 'MINES' notice warns everyone to keep off. *(IWM MH 1516)*

Above: A few hours after the capture of Cassino the bulldozers were at work, clearing the famous Route 6 through the town. These men belong to 11th Field Company, South African Engineer Corps. Note the 40mm Bofors gun there to give the sappers air cover whilst they work. *(IWM NA 15087)*

Above: This South African engineer bulldozer is working near where the railway station once stood in Cassino. The red flag warns of the danger that mines may be set off during the work. *(IWM NA 15089)*

Above: Just as soon as the route is cleared the Allied armour begins to rumble forward. *(IWM NA 15709)*

Above: A group of German grave markers in the shadow of Monte Cassino. *(IWM NA 15026)*

Above: This sign set up on the outskirts of Cassino town provides testimony of how dangerous were the uncleared ruins long after the battle was over.
(US Army via Real War Photos)

Chapter 8
Return to Cassino

What Remains of Cassino and the Battlefield

'It makes no difference from which direction you approach the town of Cassino, it is the Abbey on its hill overlooking it that draws the eye first. It was rebuilt as a copy of its predecessor, on and incorporating the ruins, by the Italian State immediately after the war. The other belligerents made no contribution.'

That is how Colonel Tom Huggan OBE, late of the Royal Tank Regiment, now working in the British Embassy in Rome, began a letter to me, in reply to mine asking for his help in describing what the average visitor could hope to see of Cassino and around the battlefield, some 60 years after the fighting had ended and peace had returned to those war-torn hills. He continued:

'If you wish to share the soldiers' point of view it is as well to start south of Cassino on Route 6, the "strada provinciale", ideally when it is cold and raining. Then you could appreciate just how much the Abbey controls the area. And as it took time and four bitter battles to overcome, how easily it became an object of loathing to the Allied generals, the staff officers and, above all, to the soldiers who attacked again and again in the mud and cold, under the German gunfire. This may help you to understand why the Abbey was destroyed, even if you personally, might have been loath to give the order.

'A suitable starting place for your visit could be Mignano Monte Lungo, 12km south of Route 6. Here the first Italians in British battledress, with British weapons and equipment, fought their first battle on the Allied side. There is a museum and, on the west of the road, a cemetery where their dead are buried. Following the road northwards, always under the Abbey's watchful eye, you come to the two villages of San Pietro, the first on the roadside is the more recently built, while the original one, now deserted, presents a somewhat eerie feeling to the visitor, as though the inhabitants were still in their houses, Post Office, etc.

'Continuing along Route 6 you come to Sant'Angelo in Theodice where in addition to the fighting there was an experimental river crossing, using a bridge fixed on top of a Sherman tank, that was launched into the river — the outcome is not known. The village square has memorials to American units and the rebuilt bridge leading to the Abbey is dedicated to the French. Standing on the bridge you can see the ground over which the GIs of 36th (Texas) US Infantry Division attacked so bravely, but unsuccessfully, under continual heavy fire from the secure enemy positions, in thick fog, over flooded and mined terrain, in an abortive attempt to cross the Rapido . . . this was the subject of a post-war US Congressional inquiry [as explained in Chapter 4]. You will have probably already seen the next prominent feature, Monte Trocchio, on the south of the road at a bend. The feature afforded excellent observation to whoever occupied it, and will do the same for you if you can find a way through to the top — there are no public roads and even on foot you could find yourself trespassing.

'It is possible to call in at the Commonwealth War Graves Commission Cemetery next, but that of course depends on how you have arranged your visit. It is signposted on the outer eastern edge of Cassino town and is on the road to Sant'Angelo. This can be an emotional experience and some may prefer to delay their visit until later. The Cemetery, like all CWGC cemeteries, is immaculate, and the lines of headstones and the flowers, laid out under the watchful eye of Saint Benedict's Abbey, give even the most hardened pilgrim cause for reflection. Here lie 4,266 servicemen of the Commonwealth; 284 of the burials are unidentified. On the pillars are commemorated over 4,000 Commonwealth servicemen who took part in the Italian Campaign, who have no known graves. Wheelchair access to the cemetery is possible, but may be by an alternative entrance.

'The town of Cassino was rebuilt as soon as possible after the war in order to provide shelter for those returning and for refugees, and as a result is in no way picturesque. There are a few sights to catch the eye such as some World War Two armoured fighting vehicles in the main square in front of the Town Hall (Il Commune). There is also a bookshop that specialises in books about the Italian campaign. The shop is owned by Mr Federico Lambertini who speaks English and is a mine of information concerning the four battles. He is often absent helping TV programme makers. There is also the Hotel des Roses, in whose garage a German self-propelled gun sheltered when not engaging targets.

'You should now be able to see the Castle on its hill north-east of the Abbey, on the edge of the zig-zag road that leads up to it, known as the Rocca Janula. It is currently being restored and when completed it will be open to the public. The restorers are using different coloured material for the new sections. There has been a castle there since about AD940 and it has been destroyed and rebuilt many times in the course of defending the town from raids by the Saracens and Lombards, who were always on the lookout for the plunder which the Abbey and town offered. During the World War 2 battles it was the scene of two incidents of chivalry — one being the presentation by a captured German paratrooper of his gloves to the British commander, in recognition of his brave defence.[1] The other incident concerned a German attack on the Castle that destroyed part of the wall, burying both Germans and British under the debris. There was an immediate ceasefire without negotiation and all lent a hand to dig them out. Indeed, it is said that, as in other wars, the combatants met relatively frequently (albeit unofficially) to arrange for the recovery of casualties. One such rendezvous point is the cave in the hillside just before the last bend in the road at the top.

'Around this bend there is a road going straight to the Abbey, and from it another road leads right downhill to a fenced car park from which there are two gates. The gate on

Above: Castle Hill, surmounted by the castle. This is currently being restored using different material so that the restored parts will be evident. *(Signals Museum)*

the right is the entrance to the Polish Cemetery, where 1,052 soldiers from the 2nd Polish Corps are buried, commanded in death as in life by General Wladyslaw Anders, accompanied by his Chaplain Monsignor Gawlina, both of whom asked to be buried there. This Cemetery and the Abbey are naturally places of pilgrimage for Poles and it is very rare not to find at least one Polish registered vehicle in the car park.

'The other entrance is normally barred by a padlock, the key to which is kept by the Abbey Information Officer, in his office at the entrance to the main building. The locked gate leads to the Abbey lands and is not readily available. Official groups can obtain permission by getting in touch *before* visiting, by letter or fax, preferably in Italian (fax: +39 (0)776 312930) addressed to: His Most Reverend Excellency Bernardo D'Onofrio, L'Abbazia di Monte Cassino, Frosinone (FR), ITALIA. It is also possible to obtain guides for a tour of the Abbey, but do specify the language — however, they are not always available.

'This locked gate should, if you obtain access, lead on to a roughish track, used by the Abbey staff, agricultural workers and the few people who live on the Abbey land. Cars can use it, but drive slowly. After about 200m there is a junction — to the right leads to the Polish Memorial Obelisk on Point 593, which is sited on the bend of Snakeshead Ridge. The Obelisk carries an epitaph to the fallen and next to it is a cement model of the battlefield, which will help to get yourself oriented. In the hillside around the Obelisk you can find the caves and foxholes that were used by defenders and attackers alike. Souvenir hunters may find German MG 42 belt links, or .303 cartridge cases, but *be very wary* as explosives do not become harmless with time and may still be there, despite the most rigorous clearing up the area has

undergone. Returning down the road, at a bend, you will find a working farm named 'Doctor's Farm' — this is where a Polish First Aid Post was established, which cared for the wounded regardless of nationality. A little further down and you are back at the junction, turn right and this track will take you past Albaneta Farm and a small shrine in memory of the Poles who captured it at tremendous cost. Albaneta Farm is currently a cattle byre, but in fact was already a Monastery when the Abbey was young. Colle Angelo, 50m above you, sports another memorial and the side of Snakeshead Ridge shows where ammunition bunkers and caves have been destroyed. Further on there is another working farm and a further bumpy track unsuitable for all except an off-road vehicle, which leads to the head of Cavendish Road. Here there is a Polish Sherman tank, its one track welded into a crucifix, its turret lying where it was blown off all those years ago. Cavendish Road provides a track leading up on to the Abbey lands. It was originally constructed by Indian Army Sappers, under fire and behind camouflage nets. This road nearly allowed the New Zealand armoured regiment to succeed in surprising the German defenders. The commander of the leading tank was knocked out by a defender, whom he met, quite by chance, years later at a Cassino reunion. They formed a friendship that only death dissolved.

'If you can move to get a view to the north you will see the imposing bulk of Monte Cairo. This was part of the 34th US

Above: View of the rebuilt town and monastery — the distance between the two is greatly foreshortened by the camera. *(Signals Museum)*

Above: This view of part of the town together with the twisty road up to the monastery gives a far better idea of the height the latter is above the former. Also visible on the far side of the monastery is the Polish Cemetery. *(Signals Museum)*

Infantry Division's objective during the First Battle, and as you walk over the ground you can well appreciate its importance to the belligerents as it looms on the horizon. It would take three more battles before the Polish Corps included its occupation in the successful attack on Snakeshead Ridge where the Polish Obelisk is located. They would also win, at long last and after so much bitter fighting, the prize of the Abbey of Monte Cassino.

'The German dead are buried in what is the principal German War Cemetery for the south of Italy. This is on Colle Marino, in the village of Cairo at the foot of the mountain of the same name. Here there are buried over 2,000 soldiers, gathered from the battlefields. For curiosity's sake if you are going to visit the spot, you will pass near to the "Barracks" which figure in many of the battle accounts. These still remain Italian Defence Ministry property though not in use. You may look in vain for the River Rapido on the opposite side of the road, as it has now been restricted to pipes — presumably so as to avoid the flooding that caused such difficulty to the US 34th and 36th Divisions.

'The Free French of General Juin's CEF played a significant part in the battles and their appearance gave rise to many tales and a prize winning film. Perhaps the presence of so many North African troops recalled the tradition of Saracen raids, in turn providing the "Bogeymen" for mothers to frighten their children, with the children shouting in warning: "*Mamma Mamma li turchi* (literally: the Turks)", an expression still used in play. The French Military Cemetery is at Venafro, some 20km from Cassino.

'The American fallen were, for the most part, taken for burial in the USA; however, there is an impressive cemetery at Nettuno, south of Anzio, near the beaches where the forces of US VI Corps landed in January 1944.'

Memorials and Museums

'There are not so many memorials, the cemeteries with their ordered rows of headstones serving as reminder enough. However, as already mentioned, there are memorials to American units in the square at Sant'Angelo and a French plaque on the bridge nearby over the Rapido. Then there are the Polish monuments, such as the tank at the start of the Cavendish Road and a little further on towards the Abbey, a memorial to another Polish unit. There is also the Cross on Phantom Ridge, just north-east of the largest Polish monument, the Obelisk on Snakeshead Ridge (Point 593).

'At the time of writing, no War Museum exists in Cassino, although there is continual discussion on the subject. There is

an Archaeological Museum (tel: +39 (0)776 301168) open daily 0900–2000 hours, which displays Roman material collected from the Cassino area, beginning at the end of the 1700s, then begun again at the start of the 20th century. Apart from the Italian Museum at Monte Lungo, the next nearest War Museum is to be found at Anzio in the Villa Communale (tel: +39 (0)698 30883). There is also an extensive museum of weapons and rural occupations, agricultural tools and equipment at Latina called the Museum of 'Piano Delle Orme' (tel: +39 (0)773 258708). It also has a working example of a Sherman DD amphibious tank, salvaged off the Salerno beaches, where it had 'drowned' during pre-Normandy landing trials. The Abbey Museum and Pinoteca has a rich display of treasures; typically it has gold and silver works of art, processional crosses, miniature missals, robes and vestments, as well as the art displayed in the Pinoteca. The archives and library are not normally open to visitors, but they contain documents and books of immense value.'

Tourist Information

Cassino town can be reached by train from Frosinone. Its main attraction, the Abbey of Monte Cassino, is open daily 09.30–12.30 and 15.30–sunset. Buses that scale the mountain up to the abbey run from Piazza San Benedetto twice daily.

There are two tourist offices in the town: *Piazza de Gasperi 10* (opposite side of the square to the train and bus stations), open Monday–Saturday 08.30–13.30 and 15.30–18.30, Sunday 08.30–13.30; tel: +39 (0)776 25 692; and *Corso della Repubblica*

Above: Another view of the monastery towering above the Cassino War Cemetery, which is on the road on the eastern side of town, signposted to Sant'Angelo. *(Commonwealth War Graves Commission — Col 12665 (32A))*

Above:
Another view of the
Commonwealth Cemetery
at Cassino, showing the
Cassino Memorial.
(Brigadier J. Chapman)

Above:
The Italian Cemetery at Monte Lungo.
*(Commonwealth War Graves
Commission — Col 12665 (24a))*

Right:
Close-up of the inscription on the
memorial at the Polish Cemetery.
(Brigadier J. Chapman)

Above: This memorial is at the head of Cavendish Road and comprises a knocked out Polish Sherman tank, with its turret blown off and one of its tracks welded into a crucifix. *(Brigadier J. Chapman)*

Above: German war memorial to their dead at Cassino. *(Mrs D. Elsby)*

23, open Monday–Saturday 09.00–12.00 and 16.00–19.00. A list of inexpensive hotels is available from both tourist offices.

One of the cheapest and best guides to the battlefields is Issue 13 of *After The Battle* magazine. Clearly it would be sensible to purchase this before visiting Italy, but I am told that it is also on sale in Cassino, at Mr Lambertini's bookshop. It contains excellent short descriptions of all four battles, plus some reprints of the Staff College Cassino Battlefield Tour notes and maps.

A GI remembers his visit:

'I stopped the car and we all got out. Before us was a valley walled in by steep mountains, with the abbey built high up on one of them. The clouds had lifted and the sun shone brilliantly on the wet, green landscape. Fruit trees bloomed on the floor of the valley and behind them were the towering blue hills and the gleaming abbey. Nancy and the girls were impressed, for this view is perhaps the most awe-inspiring sight in Italy. But I could hardly believe what lay before me. I had last seen a valley where nothing grew, and a town and abbey reduced to grey, shattered rubble, a place where wretched and desperate men moved fearfully from one sheltered position to another, where scarcely a minute went by at any time of the day or night without an artillery shell landing, a place of death and utter desolation.'

That is how Harold L. Bond opens his description of his arrival at Monte Cassino in 1962, whilst on holiday with his family, 18 years after he had fought there in command of an infantry mortar platoon in the US 36th Infantry Division. Monte Cassino had haunted his mind over the intervening years, since he had been evacuated one cold, wet afternoon in late February 1944. He continued:

'I recognised the familiar landmarks, but I was having trouble bringing them into focus. Moreover, when I had last been here I had no children, nor had I even met Nancy. Now she and I and our four girls stood together before this place where I had nearly been killed, a place where men from almost every continent in the world had struggled and died. And it was spring and peaceful, and we were all healthy and alive.

'The abbey, I saw, had been completely rebuilt of warm, Travertine stone, and once again it dominated the entire scene. It is a gigantic building, and the mountain on which it sits rises steeply from the level plain. Behind it to the right rise higher mountains, and in the distance is huge Mount Cairo, covered in snow. The town of Cassino originally was situated at the foot of Abbey Hill, with some of its houses and hotels perched on the lower slopes. The town now before us had been built farther out in the plain. The brightly coloured stucco houses and wide streets gave one the sense that peace and order had always reigned here, but Nancy and the girls had seen pictures of the ruined Cassino, so I was not the only one in the family who could understand the transformation when life returned to the wasteland left by the war.

'The highway darts straight from the shoulder of Trocchio across the plain and into the town. During the fighting, it was impossible to cross this stretch of road in the daylight, but this day we drove across it with the girls chattering about lunch and wondering if the could buy gelato (ice cream) in Cassino.

Right: The reburial of five soldiers of the now disbanded York and Lancaster Regiment, July 2003. They had been discovered during building work at Minturno and, as the CWGC Cemetery there was full, they were buried at Cassino CWGC. The Rev. Jonathan Boardman, Anglican Padre of the British Church at Rome, took the burial service. *(Colonel T. Huggan)*

As we travelled down the wide avenue of the new Cassino we saw flowers blooming in the parks. Trees had been planted along the streets, but the newness of the town seemed strange.'[2]

The 45th Anniversary, May 1989

'Never thinking at the time that I would survive what turned out to be the final Battle of Cassino, its 45th anniversary loomed this year and I decided that I would like to attend the ceremonies to mark the occasion.'

This is how Lieutenant-Colonel B. D. H. Clark MC, GM, the then Chairman of the Royal British Legion, Republic of Ireland, and subsequently joint founder, with Herr Jupp Klein, of the Monte Cassino International Veterans Association, began his reminiscences in 1989. He continued:

'. . . so I contacted a travel company, who booked me in. However, since the Falklands War the British Government has funded the Royal British Legion to run worldwide pilgrimages and the National Chairman (Elect), Mr David Knowles, knowing that I had taken part in the fighting at Cassino in 1944, invited me (and Brenda, who had been in Italy with the Red Cross & St John) to lead a Legion pilgrimage at Maggie Thatcher's expense.

'I had been on two previous pilgrimages to Europe — Berlin and Arnhem — and at first had wondered why widows had wished to visit their husbands' graves after over 40 years; especially those who had remarried. However, I soon discovered that, until they had stood in front of the headstone, part of their lives had never been finally concluded. Once they had visited the grave, it was like the

solving of an equation. The women who accompany these pilgrimages are a splendid lot of girls, from the vintage that had been blitzed in London, Coventry, etc. Indeed, some of them had lived more dangerously than their husbands in administrative jobs at base.

'On May 14th, the pilgrimage participated in a Service of Remembrance and Reconciliation in the Commonwealth War Graves Cemetery to which many people came. After the Address, given by the former Dean of Bristol Cathedral whose CND line was not well received by the majority of British soldiers present, the Order of Service indicated that the Exhortation — "They shall grow not old . . ." would then be given. However, the individual nominated "froze" and there was a hiatus. The courier with my pilgrimage urgently drew my attention to this and said: "You'd better go and do it, colonel." So the Irish Infantry plugged the line as usual and I climbed the steps to the Cross of Remembrance.

'It was quite an experience, on turning to the microphone, to face an audience of thousands of old soldiers — British, Irish, Scots, Italians, New Zealanders, French, Indians and Pakistanis, Canadians, Americans, Poles etc . . . and Germans. However, my memory did not fail me, as I recited Laurence Binyon's lines and, after remaining at the salute for the Last Post and continuing at attention for 'The Flowers of the Forest' played by a piper of the Queen's Own Highlanders, I returned to the foot of the steps to retrieve my Poppy wreath, preparatory to laying it after the British Ambassador to Rome, Sir Derek Thomas KCMG. Out of the corner of my eye I spotted the leader of the German delegation. I approached him discreetly and, in German, asked him if he would like to accompany me so that we could lay our wreaths at the same time. He agreed and we stood before the Cross

together — former enemies — he with a comrade beside him who helped carry their large wreath.

'At the end of the Service, the man who should have given the Exhortation came up to me and said: "God sent you." I didn't tell him that it was not God, but Piers Storie-Pugh. The leader of the German delegation then came and thanked me for my gesture. His name was Jupp Klein, formerly of the German Paratroop Engineers, a holder of the Iron Cross and other decorations. He asked me if I would lay a wreath on behalf of the British Eighth Army at their Soldatenfriedhof (War Cemetery) near the village of Cairo, 3km north of Cassino, that evening. I replied that I would be honoured to do so and laid the wreath, not far, in fact, from where our old Battalion HQ had been.

'After the service an old paratrooper drew my attention to the fact that Winston Churchill had said that there were probably no better infantry than the Fallschirmjäger. I replied that I totally agreed — but that some of us were as good. Another of the German paras asked if he could take a photograph of me. After he had done so, he grinned broadly and said he had been waiting for 45 years to have another shot at me. Who says the Germans have no sense of humour?

'I am now in close touch with Jupp. He and his wife, Elisabeth, are to visit us in Ireland next year and, not long ago, I received a German Paratroop Engineers card from Saarbrücken signed by Jupp and about 50 of his former comrades and their wives.'

In May 2004 a further offical anniversary service was held at the Commonwealth Cemetery at Cassino, to mark the 60th anniversary of the Battle of Monte Cassino. More than 2,700 people attended, including many veterans of one of the most devestating battles of World War 2.

Were there Germans in the Monastery?

Finally, a short reminiscence made by John Clarke, Secretary of the Monte Cassino Veterans Association, about a visit he made to Cassino in March 1994, as the organiser of the association's 50th anniversary trip. He had flown out to Italy, together with a travel agent, who was also a member of the RAF Association, in order to check on the suitability of the hotels in Cassino:

'When I arrived in Gaeta I was contacted by the second in command of the NATO base in Laterina, who asked if he and his RSM could join us when we visited Cassino, and if possible visit the Monastery.

'I agreed and the next day we went straight to the Monastery and on arrival, I met the only surviving monk from the bombing of 25 February 1944. He was Augustino Sacameno, who was a friend of mine. Augustino agreed to take us on a tour of the monastery which is not available to the general public.

'We went down into the mountain to the Chapel of St Benedict, which remains as it was in the 16th century. The four of us were guided by Augustino who showed us the famous murals on the walls next to the chapel. Suddenly, he pointed to a square with steps going upwards and said: "This is where 300 people sheltered during the bombing including some Germans." Seeing my amazement at his statement, he smiled and repeated: "including some Germans". His statement was also heard by Ken Foulkes of the RAF Association and the lieutenant-colonel and RSM from the NATO base, whose names I cannot remember.

'On my return to the UK I told *Soldier* magazine of Augustino's remarks which they printed. Then a month later, the editor of *Soldier* magazine phoned me to say that he had received word from the Monastery that said that Augustino had never made such a statement. The editor told me that he had checked with Ken Foulkes, who confirmed he had heard Augustino's remarks.

'Another interesting result of the visit was the secret doors adjacent to St Benedict's Chapel. Augustino would not explain where they went or what they were for. I truly believe that these tunnels were discovered by the Germans and used to take supplies to the paras in Cassino town. I have no proof, but some of the villas in the old Cassino town had deep cellars where the tunnels could have exited.'

Notes
1. See Chapter 6 for a fuller account of this incident.
2. Harold L. Bond, *Return to Cassino*.

Below: A View inside the spectacular monastery at Monte Cassino that has been completely rebuilt. *(Brigadier J. Chapman)*

Bibliography

Books

Anders, Lieutenant-General W., *An Army in Exile*, Macmillan, 1981

Barber, Laurie, & Tonkin-Covell, John, *Freyberg — Churchill's Salamander*, Century Hutchinson, 1989

Blumenson, Martin, *US Army in World War II, The Mediterranean Theater of Operations, Salerno to Cassino*, Office of the Chief of Military History, US Army, 1969

Blumenson, Martin, *Mark Clark — The Last of the Great World War II Commanders*, Congdon & Weed, 1984

Böhmler, Rudolf, *Monte Cassino*, Verlag E. S. Mittler & Sohn, 1956

Bond, Harold L., *Return to Cassino*, J. M. Dent & Sons, 1964

Brett-Smith, Richard, *Hitler's Generals*, Osprey, 1976

Chaplin, Lieutenant-Colonel H. D., *The Queen's Own Royal West Kent Regiment, 1920–1950*, Michael Joseph, 1954

Churchill, Winston S., *The Second World War*, Vol. V, *Closing the Ring*, Cassell, 1952

Clark, General Mark W., *Calculated Risk*, Harrap, 1951

Connell, Charles, *Monte Cassino, The Historic Battle*, Elek Books, 1963

Daniell, D. S., *Regimental History of the Royal Hampshire Regiment*, Vol. 3, Gale & Polden, 1955

Delaney, John P., *The Blue Devils in Italy*, 88th Infantry Association Inc, New York, 1947

Ellis, John, *Cassino, the Hollow Victory*, Andre Deutsch, 1984

Forty, George, *Fifth Army at War*, Ian Allan, 1980

Forty, George, *Land Warfare — The Encyclopedia of 20th Century Conflict*, Arms & Armour, 1997

Hougen, Lieutenant-Colonel John H., *The Story of the Famous 34th Infantry Division*, first published 1949; reprinted by Battery Press, 1979

Huff, Staff Sergeant Richard A. (ed.), *A Pictorial History of the 36th Division*, 36th Division Association; reprinted by Battery Press, 1979

Huff, Richard A. (ed), *The Fighting 36th, A Pictorial History of the 36th Division*, The 36th Division Association

Inter-Service PR Directorate, *The Tiger Triumphs*, GHQ New Delhi, 1945

Jackson, General Sir William, *The Battle for Italy*, Batsford, 1967

Kay, Robin, *Official History of New Zealand in the Second World War 1939–45, Italy*, Vol II, *From Cassino to Trieste*, Historical Publications Branch, Department of Internal Affairs, 1967

Keilig, Wolf, *Die Generale des Heeres*, Podzun-Pallas Verlag, 1983

Kurowski, Franz, *Knight's Cross Holders of the Fallschirmjäger*, Schiffer, 1995

Majdalany, Fred, *Cassino — Portrait of a Battle*, Longmans, Green & Co, 1957

Majdalany, Fred, *The Monastery*, John Lane, The Bodley Head, 1945

Mitcham, Samuel W., *Hitler's Legions*, Leo Cooper, 1985

Morris, Eric, *Circles of Hell — The War in Italy 1943–45*, Hutchinson, 1993

Parker, Matthew, *Monte Cassino*, Headline, 2003

Phillips N.C., *Official History of New Zealand in the Second World War 1939–45, Italy*, Vol. I *The Sangro to Cassino*, Historical Publications Branch, Department of Internal Affairs, 1957

Piekalkiewicz, Janusz, *Cassino: Anatomy of the Battle*, Orbis, 1980

Pujo, Bernard, *Juin, Maréchal de France*, Albin Michel, 1988

Robson, Walter, *Letters from a Soldier*, Faber & Faber, 1960

Smith, E.D., *Even the Brave Falter*, Robert Hale, 1978

Smith, E.D., *Battles for Cassino*, Ian Allan, 1975

Trevor-Roper, H. R. (ed), *Hitler's War Directives 1939–45*, Sidgwick & Jackson, 1964

Truscott, Lucian K., *Command Missions*, Dutton, New York, 1954

Vigneras, Marcel, *Rearming the French*, from the US Army in WWII series, Washington Office of the Chief of Military History, US Army, 1957

Studies

1968 — British Troops Malta Study in Italy — now held by Royal Signals Museum (916.3 Italy)

Battlefield Tour of the Italian Campaign 1943–45, Salerno to Monte Cassino — held by the Defence Intelligence and Security School

Library Papers (from the Polish Institute and Sikorski Museum)

A.XI.67/5 — British Historical Section HQCMF Report on operations of 2 Polish Corps 11–25 May 1944

A.XI. 67/22 — ACMF: Copy of Weekly Review of European Events, No 17

Library Papers (from the Gurkha Museum)

Contemporary Account of Hangman's Hill action (Ref 9GR 429)

Copy No 1 (1.C.) — 'Monte Cassino — Memories' by Lieutenant-General Sir Francis Tuker

Copy No 2 (1.D.) — '4th Indian Division at Cassino' by Lieutenant-General Sir Francis Tuker

Letter written by General Tuker dated 26 May 1965 to 'Taffy'

Interview Papers from Cassino veterans of the Irish Brigade (from J.R. Doherty, Esq, FIRSO, MRHistS)

Account of attack on Sinagoga Farm by Major Desmond Woods MC, 2nd London Irish Rifles

Notes for a lecture on the final battle of Cassino given to the Military History Society of Ireland by Lieutenant-Colonel Brian Clark MC, GM, late adjutant 1st Royal Irish Fusiliers

Reminiscences of visiting Cassino for the 45th anniversary of the battle, also by Lieutenant-Colonel B. Clark

Account of the attack on Sinagoga Wood by Major Mervyn Davies (later Sir Mervyn) 2nd London Irish Rifles

Account of a platoon of 1st Royal Irish Fusiliers' involvement in the final battle for Cassino by Lieutenant (later Lieutenant-Colonel) Jim Trousdell

Account by Rifleman John Ledwidge, 2nd London Irish Rifles

Miscellaneous

Supplement to *The London Gazette* of 12 June 1950 (MOD Whitehall Library)

Senger und Etterlin, General Frido von, 'The Battles of Cassino', *RUSI Journal*, May 1958

'Some Experiences during the Cassino campaign, Italy 1944' by Neal Hopkins 26th New Zealand Infantry Battalion (private ms)

After the Battle, Issue No. 13

Army Quarterly, October 1945. Article by Col H. Piatkowski, II Polish Corps

Various recordings from the Imperial War Museum Sound Archive:

No 20905 — John Buckeridge, Royal Sussex

No 20906 — Edward Grace, Gordon Highlanders

No 20907 — 'Bill' Hawkins, unit not specified

No 20908 — 'Gordon' Shakespear, 1st/2nd Gurkhas

No 20930 — Zdzistaw Kirakowski, Polish Carpathian Div

Index

Figures in italics refer to illustrations

Airfields
  Foggia — 16
Air Forces
  German (Luftwaffe)
    1st Paratroop Panzer Div *Hermann Göring* — 12, 15, 23, 54, *54*, 61, 70, 72, 76
Alexander, General Sir Harold — 10, *13*, 23, 25, *28, 29*, 89, 100, 120, *142*
Allen, Col Frank A. — 41
Allfrey, Lt-Gen C. W. — 31
Anders, Gen Wladyslaw — *30, 31*, 32, *122*, 135 *et seq*, *142*, 149
Anti-aircraft guns
  Bofors 40mm — *16, 145*
'Anvil', Operation — 30, 46, 134
Anzio — 25, 49, 52, 54, 72 *et seq*, 99, 135, 152

Armies and army units (see also under
    Regiments, units etc)
  Allied
    15th Army Group — *13*, 16, 27, 30, 88
    21st Army Group — 16

  British
    Eighth Army — 12, 31, 73, 126, 134 et seq, 155
    V Corps — 31
    X Corps — 25, 31, 68 *et seq*
    XIII Corps — 15, 31 *et seq*, 121, 126, 131, 135, 139
    Royal Army Service Corps — 84
    1st Airborne Div — 15
    6th Armoured Div — 73, 121
    7th Armoured Div — 16, 46
    5th Div — 69, 72
    46th Div — 15, 72 *et seq*
    56th Div — 15, 69 *et seq*
    94th Div — 69 *et seq*
    23rd Armoured Bde — 25
    5th Bde — 70, 86, 93
    6th Bde — 105
    7th Bde — 86, 93
    11th Bde — 82, 93
    13th Bde — 69 *et seq*
    15th Bde — 70, 72
    17th Bde — 69, 72
    128th Bde — 72
    138th Bde — 72 *et seq*
    139th Bde — 72
    167th Bde — 69, 73
    168th Bde — 73
    169th Bde — 69, 72 *et seq*
    1st Guards Bde — 73, *121*
    201st Guards Bde — 69, 72
    3rd Inf Bde — 15
    13th Inf Bde — 15
    17th Inf Bde — 15
    28th Inf Bde — 126

  Commonwealth
  Canadian
    I Corps — 31, 122
    5th Armoured Div — 122

    1st Inf Div — 15, 122
  Indian
    4th Div — 32, 59, 61, 78 *et seq*, 89 *et seq*, 98 *et seq*, *119*
    8th Inf Div — 34, 121
    5th Inf Bde — 107 *et seq*
    7th Inf Bde — 79 *et seq*
  New Zealand 79 *et seq*, *92*, 98 *et seq*
    Expeditionary Force — 33
    II Corps — 31 *et seq*, 78 *et seq*
    4th Armoured Bde — 100
    6th Inf Bde — *91*, 100, 104
  South African
    Engineer Corps — *145*
    Armoured Div — 122

  French
    Free French Forces — 32
    First French Army — 33, 78
    French North African Army — 32
    French Expeditionary Corps (CEF) — 25, 31 *et seq*, 53, 67 *et seq*, *67*, 79, 122, 126, 133 *et seq*, 151
    3rd Algerian Inf Div — 25, 32, 67, 78, 122
    2nd Moroccan Inf Div — 25, 32, 67, 122, 134
    4th Moroccan Mountain Div — 32, 122
    1st Motorised Inf Div — 32, 122, 134
    15th Motorised Inf Div — 32

  German
    Tenth Army — 14 *et seq*, 49 *et seq*, 70, 126, 135
    14th Army — 49 *et seq*, 70
    LI Mountain Corps — 52
    XIV Panzer Corps — 12, 15, 52, 113, 126
    LXXVI Panzer Corps — 14
    LXXXI Panzer Corps — 52
    I Paratroop Corps — 72
    XI Paratroop Corps — 15
    44th Inf Div — 53, 72, 80, 122
    71st Inf Div — 54, 72, 78, 80, 122
    94th Inf Div — 53, 68, 122
    305th Inf Div - 122
    5th Mountain Div — 53, 67, 80
    1st Paratroop Div — 14, 52, *53*, 81, 103, 122
    2nd Paratroop Div — 15
    3rd Panzer Gren Div — 15
    15th Panzer Gren Div — 12, 15, 51, 54, 67, 73, 122
    16th Panzer Div — 15
    26th Panzer Div — 14, 135
    29th Panzer Gren Div — 14, 53, 70, 72, 76
    90th Panzer Gren Div — 14, 52, 54, 70, 72, 80 et seq, 96, 103, 122

  Italian — 15, 34
    Tenth Army — 10

  Polish — 135 *et seq*
    II Corps — 31 *et seq*, 58, 121, *122*, 149, 151

    3rd Carpathian Div — 121, *137*, 139, 142
    5th Kresowa Inf Div — 121, 136, 139
    6 Lwow Bde — 136 *et seq*
    5 Wilno Bde — 136

  United States
    Fifth Army — 11 *et seq*, 30 *et seq*, 133
    Sixth Army Group — 30
    Seventh Army — 11 *et seq*
    II Air Support Command — 73
    II Corps — 25 *et seq*, 68, 73, 122, 126, 135
    VI Corps — 26, 31, 122
    82nd Airborne Div — 15
    1st Armoured Div — 25 *et seq*, 41, 100
    3rd Inf Div — 26
    34th Inf Div — 25, 31, 52, 68, 73 *et seq*, 149
    36th Inf Div — 15, 25, 31, 73 *et seq*, *74*, 122, 148, 153
    44th Inf Div — 76
    85th Inf Div — 122, 135
    88th Inf Div — 27, 122, 135
    179th Inf Div — 98
    10th Mountain Div — 36
    13th Field Artillery Bde — 33
    1st Special Service Force — 36

Artillery
  Howitzer M2A1 — *38*
  Mörser 18 — 51
  StuG 40 assault gun — *122*
  194mm railway gun — *34*
Astor, Nancy — 46
Auchinleck, Gen — 31
'Avalanche', Operation — 15, *16*

Baade, Gen Ernst-Günther — 52, 54, 81
Badoglio, Marshal — 15
'Battleaxe', Operation — 11
Baxter, Pvt J. C. — 133
'Baytown', Operation — 15
Beckett, Maj — 115
Birch, Maj — 116
Boardman, Jonathan — *156*
Bombs
  FX 1400 — 16
Bond, Harold L. — 74, 153
Bradley, Col — 12
Brosset, Brig-Gen Charles — 32
Buckeridge, Col John — 82 *et seq*
Bucknall, Gen — 70
Butler, Brig Gen Frederick — 78

Cannon, Maj Gen John K. 100
Casablanca Conference — 6, 11, 13
Castel Gandolfo — 88
Casualties — 47, 74, *91, 141*
Cemeteries — 148 *et seq*
Chronology — 8 *et seq*
Churchill, Winston S. — 10, 13, 17
Clark, Lt-Col Brian D. H. — 33, 155
Clark, Lt Gen Mark Wayne — 15, 25, *26, 29*, 30, 88, 121, 134
Clarke, John — 156

Commonwealth War Graves Com. — 148, *154, 155 et seq*

Conrath, Gen Paul — 54
Corsica — 14
Creagh, Maj-Gen Michael O'More — 26
Cunningham, Adm — 14

D-Day — 12, 16
'D-Day Dodgers' — 6, 46, 78
Daniell, Lt-Col A. P. de T. — 126 *et seq*
de Gaulle, Charles — 32
de Monsabert, Gen — 67
Devers, Lt Gen Jacob Loucks — 16, 30, 134
'Diadem', Operation — 120 *et seq*, 136
Diamare, Archbishop Gregorio — 23, *23*, 97
'Dickens', Operation — 100 *et seq*
Dietrich, Dr — 97
Dimoline, Brig — 90
Dody, Gen — 67
Drinkall, Cpt Micky — 109 *et seq*

Eaker, Gen Ira C. — 89
Egger, *Oblt* — 103
Eisenhower, General Dwight D. — 6, 12 *et seq*, 27, 46, 88
Elba — 33
El Alamein — 11
Etna Line — 12
Etterlin, Gen von Senger und — 48, 52, 97, *99*, 126

Feurstein, Gen Valentin — 52
Foltin, Maj — 103
Foulkes, Ken — 156 *et seq*
Fowler-Esson, Col — 131
Frederick, Col Robert — 36
Freyberg, Gen Bernard Cyril 33 *et seq*, 89 *et seq*, 118
Fries, Gen Walter — 53
Furness, Lt Jim — 102, *116*, 117 *et seq*

Gawlina, Chaplain Mon — 149
Glennie, Lt-Col — 93
Göring, Hermann — 51
Gothic Line — 48
Goums — 32, *33*, 66, 122, 134
Gruenther, Maj Gen 90
Guillaume, Brig-Gen Augustine — 32
Gurkhas (See also under Regiments) — 34, *34, 85*, 94, 108, 112 *et seq*
Gustav Line — 6, 17, 23 *et seq*, 48 *et seq*, *49*, 55, 57 *et seq*, 76, 79 *et seq*, 88, 97, 131, 134
Guzzoni, Gen Alfredo — 12

Hand grenades — *55*
   No. 36 Mills — 115, *136*
Hawkins, Corp Bill — 108, *108*, 115
Heidrich, Gen Richard — 52, *53*, 81, 113
Heilman, *Ob* — 103
Hitler Line — 48, *50*, 121 *et seq*, 135
Hitler, Adolf — 49
Hodgson, Lt-Col — *121*
'Honker', Operation — 126, 129
Hopkins, Neal — 105 *et seq*
Hotel Continental — 111 *et seq*
Hube, Gen Hans-Valentin — 12, 48
Huggan, Col Tom — 148
'Husky', Operation — 11

Jamrowski, *Oblt* Siegfried - 105
Jodl, Gen — 57

Juin, Gen Alphonse Pierre — *29,* 32, 53, 77

Keightley, Maj-Gen Charles F. — 31, *121, 122*
Kesselring, Field Marshal Albert — 15, *15,* 33, 48, *51, 53,* 55, 70, 135
Keyes, Gen Geoffrey — 12, 26, 31
Kharakhbahadur, Jemadar — 112
Kippenberger, Maj-Gen Howard — 79, 100
Kirakowski, Maj Zdistaw — 139
Kirkman, Gen Sir Sidney Chevalier — 31, 131
Klein, Herr Jupp — 155 *et seq*
Knight, Maj George — 126, 130 *et seq*
Knowles, David — 155
Kratzert, Maj Rudolf — 78

Lambertini, Federico — 148
Ledwidge, Rifleman John — 45
Lee, Maj Markham — 94
Leese, Lt-Gen Sir Oliver — 16, *30,* 31, 139, *143*
Lovett, Brig — 80
Lucas, Maj Gen John P. — 31

Machine guns
   Bren gun — 40, *45 ,* 138
   MG 42 — *4,* 51, *56, 71,* 149
   MG 44 — 51
   Thompson — *4*
   Vickers — 40, *96*
Mackensen, Gen Eberhard von — 52
Mahrattas — *34*
Maps — 10, 21, 22, 62, 84, 101, 109, 120, 133
Mareth Line — 11
Marshall, Col Carley L. — 76
Marshall, Gen — 134
McCreery, Lt-Gen Sir Richard — 31, 72, 75
Memorials and museums — 152 *et seq*
Mines
   Teller — *4*
Monte Cassino monastery — 6, 20, *24,* 89, *139, 143*
   Moving of treasures — 20 *et seq,* 54, 88
   Restoration — 148 *et seq*
Monte Cassino Veterans Assn — 156
Monte Trocchio — *46,* 68, *68,* 148
Montgomery, Lt-Gen Bernard Law — 11 *et seq,* 13, 16, 46
Mortars *71, 128*
   Granatwerfer 34 — *127*
   Nebelwerfer — 51, 61, 73, 105
   3in — *41*
   4.2in Chemical — *37, 72*
Mussolini — 14, 26

Normandy — 16

OKW — 57, 70
Orders of Battle
   Allied 63 *et seq,* 80 *et seq,* 102 *et seq,* 123 *et seq*
   German 65, 82, 103

Parkinson, Maj-Gen G. P. — 100, 104 *et seq*
Patton, Gen George — 11 *et seq*
Pope Pius XII — 88
Pullinger, Sgt-Maj — 133
Punjabis (See also under Regiments) — 34

RAF Association — 156
Rappke, Gen Wilhelm — 54
Rajputanas (See also under Regiments) — 34
Raymond, Lt-Col Robert — 88

Regiments, units etc
British
   Royal Tank Rgt — 148
   Yorks and Lancaster Rgt — *156*
   5th Btn The Buffs — 107
   69th African Artillery Rgt — 134
   16th Durham Lt Inf — 72, *132*
   1st/4th Essex — *83,* 108 *et seq, 108*
   1st/2nd Gurkhas — 82, 93 *et seq*
   1st/9th Gurkha Rifles — 93 *et seq,* 109 *et seq*
   2nd and 1st/4th Hampshires — 72, 131, *132*
   2nd Inniskillings — 69
   6th Inniskillings — *130, 131*
   1st Royal Irish Fus — 33
   17th/21st Lancers — 130 *et seq*
   2nd/5th Leicesters — 72
   2nd London Irish Rifles 44 *et seq, 130, 131*
   2nd Northamptonshires — 69
   7th Oxford and Bucks Lt Inf — 69
   4th/16th Punjabis — 82
   2nd/6th Queen's — *70*
   1st/6th Rajputana Rifles — 108 *et seq*
   4th/6th Rajputana Rifles — 93 *et seq,* 114
   194th Rec Btn — 69
   8th Royal Fusiliers — 69
   9th Royal Fusiliers — 69
   2nd Royal Scots Fusiliers — 69
   1st Royal Sussex — 82, *86,* 93
   6th Royal West Kents — 116
   6th Seaforth Highlanders — 69
   3rd Welsh Guards — *121*
   2nd Wiltshires — 69

Commonwealth
India
   17th Mule Co. — *43*
New Zealand
   17th Armoured Rgt — 115
   19th Armoured Rgt — 104
   28th (Maori) Inf Btn — *90,* 95
   22nd Motor Inf Btn — *18*
   24th Btn — *91,* 115
   25th Btn — 104, 107, 115

German
   211th Gren Rgt — 78
   85th Mountain Regt — 67
   100th Mountain Regt — 67, 141
   115th Panzer Gren Regt — 67
   361st Panzer Gren Rgt — 81
   1st Paratroop Rgt — 81
   3rd Paratroop Rgt — 78, 81, 103 *et seq,* 141
   4th Paratroop Rgt — 103
   211th Regt — 81, 96
   Paratroop Machine-Gun Btn — 81

Polish
   3rd Podolski Lancers — 142
   Poznan Lancers — 141

United States
   175th Art Rgt — 77
   132nd Field Art Rgt — *74*
   133rd Inf Rgt — 76 *et seq*
   141st Inf Rgt — 75, 78
   142nd Inf Rgt — 75
   168th Inf Rgt — 68, *68,* 77, 79
   74th Medium Rgt, RA — 38
   135th RCT — 78

141st RCT — 73, 78
142nd RCT — 77 *et seq*
143rd RCT — 73
1st Btn, 133rd — 76
3rd Btn, 133rd — 76
1st Btn, 168th — 77
3rd Btn, 168th — 77
100th Btn, 133rd — 76
760th Btn, 168th — 77
2nd Chemical Weapons Btn — *37, 72*
756th Tank Btn, 133rd — *76 et seq*

Reinhard Line — 55
Reynolds, Maj — *91*
Rifles
   Lee Enfield No. 4 Mk 1 (T) — 114
Ringel, Gen Julius — 53
Rodt, Gen Eberhard — 54
Rommel — 6, 10, 48
Roosevelt, President — 88
Royal British Legion — 155
Ryder, Maj Gen Charles W. — 31, *76 et seq*

Sacameno, Augustino — 156 *et seq*
Salerno — 14 *et seq, 16* , 55
Sardinia — 14
Schlegel, *Ob* Julius — 23, *23*
Schmidt, Maj — 81
Schultz, *Ob* — 81
Sevez, Maj-Gen François — 32
Sheehy, Cpt Jak — 78

'Shingle', Operation — *25,* 75
Ships
   Royal Navy
      HMS *Warspite* — 16
   US Navy
      LST. 77 — 25
      LST.375 — 16
Showers, Lt-Col — 94
Sicily — 6, 11 *et seq* 48
Skorzeny, Otto — 26
'Slapstick', Operation — 15
Steinmetz, Gen Bernhard — 53, 68
Steinmüller, Sgt-Maj — 113
Storie-Pugh, Piers — 155
Straits of Messina — 12, 15
Student, Gen Kurt — 15
Suez Canal — 10

Tanks and self-propelled guns
   Cromwell — 44
   M5 Stuart — *69, 134*
   M10 Wolverine Tank Destroyer — *79*
   Panther — *50*
   PzKpfw III — *121*
   Sherman — *25, 42,* 44, *77,* 114, 131, 148 *et seq, 155*
   Sturmgeschütz 40 Ausf F — *59*
Taranto — 15
Tassigny, Gen de Latre de — 32
Tedder, Air Marshal — 14
Thapa, Corp Bir Bahadur — 94

Thomas, Sir Derek — 155
Tobruk — 10 *et seq*
Todt, Organisation (OT) — 56 *et seq*
'Torch', Operation — 11, 30, 32
Trident Conference — 6, 13
Truscott, Maj Gen Lucian K. — 26, 29 *et seq,* 135
Tuker, Maj-Gen Francis — 32, 59, 89 *et seq,* 98

Victoria Cross — 131
   Richard Wakeford, Lt (Temp Cpt) — *132,* 133
Vietinghoff, Gen Heinrich von — 15, 51, *52,* 88, 126

Wakefield, Maj — 116
Wakeford, Cpt Richard — 131 *et seq, 132*
Walker, Maj Gen Fred L. — 31, 74
Ward, Maj-Gen A. D. — 131
Ward, Col Robert L. — 78
Warlimont, Gen — 57
Weatherley, Cpt — 116
Westphal, Gen Siegfried — *15,* 57, 126
Wilson, Gen Sir Henry Maitland 'Jumbo' — 16, *17,* 27, 89
Winter Line — 17, 36, 48, 51, 57
Woods, Maj Desmond — 44

Young, Lt-Col — 96

Above: A striking view of the monastery and the beginning of the Polish Cemetery. *(Commonwealth War Graves Commission — Col 1428)*